Page 1 ¶ 1 - glaring factual
error – a dismaying beginning.

150

NOW HEAR THIS!

No one who spent any time in the US Navy during World War II will be puzzled by the title of this book, but for others an explanation is indicated.

From boot camp to naval station to ship, "Now hear this!" followed the sailor. The first sound booming into the ears of the bewildered civilian as he came aboard the training station was a string of commands. New and perplexing orders bellowed from the bull horn every sixty seconds. At the end of his first five minutes the frightened boot was sure of only one thing —when the Navy said, "Now hear this!" it meant, "Dammit, LISTEN!"

The authors are using this salty Navy phrase to call attention to brief combat histories of some of the fighting ships of World War II.

Now Hear This!

HISTORIES OF U.S. SHIPS IN WORLD WAR II

By

JOHN J. MOTLEY

Lieutenant (j.g.) U. S. Naval Reserve

AND

PHILIP R. KELLY

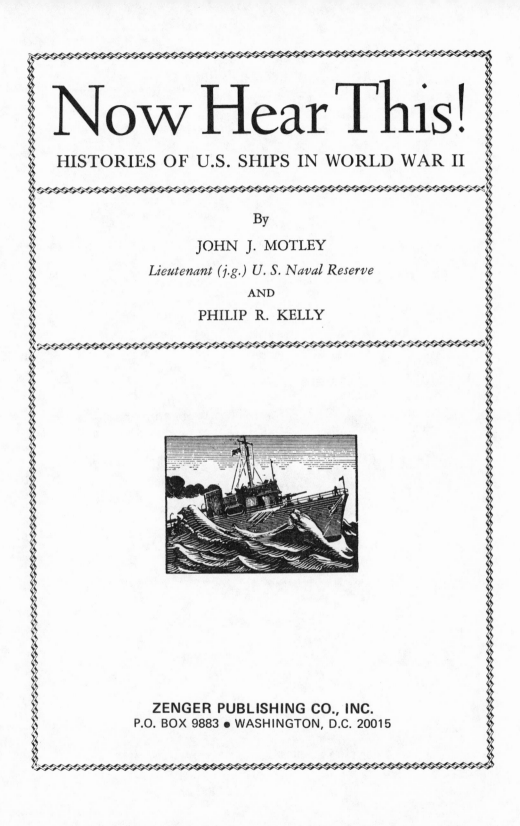

ZENGER PUBLISHING CO., INC.

P.O. BOX 9883 ● WASHINGTON, D.C. 20015

Library of Congress Cataloging in Publication Data

Motley, John J   1913-
    Now hear this!

    Reprint of the 1st ed. published in 1947 by Infantry
Journal Press, Washington.
    Includes index.
    1. World War, 1939-1945--Naval operations, American.
2. Warships--United States--History. I. Kelly,
Philip R., joint author. II. Title.
D773.M65 1979   940.54'59'73   79-18703
ISBN 0-89201-057-6

CONTENTS

CONTENTS

FOREWORD

In fury, scope and intensity, World War II climaxed anything the world has ever witnessed in the history of naval warfare. For the first time, our naval ships prowled every open sea in search of the enemy. This war had everything . . . from old-fashioned hand-to-hand combat between men aboard individual ships to great battles between massed fleets. This book records the end of an era, for there will never be another war in the classic pattern. The advent of the atomic bomb, the proximity-fuzed missile, rockets, radar and mass air assaults mark the end of naval warfare as we have known it in the past. One thing is indisputable. The old order had a fitting finale.

During the war, security prohibited reporting of the complete achievements of any one ship. A vessel might pop up in the news for a day or two, then disappear from public notice for months. Yet in those months, ships like the *Enterprise*, the *Boise*, the *Dace* or *Pringle* were often in scores of engagements, under constant air or sea attack. As a result it was impossible for the average civilian (and many servicemen) to realize the pace of the ceaseless combat operations.

The purpose of this book is to let the public know "what went on out there," to give some glimpse, however fleeting, of the relentless striking force that was the United States Navy in World War II. The fighting records of such giant-killers as the destroyer *Sterett* will demonstrate, we hope, that the war at sea was not an occasional flurry of excitement, but a gruelling, knock-down fight all the way. And this was true, not only for a few highly publicized ships, but for hundreds of others as well.

The authors realize that these ships' histories are inadequate in conveying the full battle stories of even the small Fleet units. For always, behind the casual phrase, death threatened. "Our destroyers engaged in screening operations off Leyte," the communiqué might say calmly. But to the men of the *Mahan* or the *Cooper,* engaged in these operations, there was more to it than that. No words can ever describe the horror and excitement, the terror and beauty of war at sea. The story of any one ship and the men aboard her is worthy of a book alone. So, completely told, are the events of any action, any day, any hour. Ostensibly about the Navy's fighting ships, this book is also, inevitably, about the men who fought—and died—aboard them.

In NOW HEAR THIS! we have tried to pull together in narrative form the chronological actions of representative ships of every major type. For our sources we have relied entirely on the files of the Navy Department's Office of Public Information and the Aviation History

Section of the Bureau of Aeronautics. However, the opinions or assertions contained in this book are those of the authors, and are not to be considered as official or as reflecting the views of the Navy Department or of the Naval Service at large. The histories are as accurate and complete as these sources allowed, during the spring of 1947 when this book was written.

The ships mentioned in Now Hear This! are not chosen or arranged according to any rule of thumb. It was not our intention to present only outstanding ships, but to select a representative grouping. Some ships which we might have included were omitted because of inadequate records, for the Navy is still compiling histories of its one hundred thousand ships in World War II.

In selecting the ships we have leaned heavily on the Navy's own estimates of its leading vessels—the 250-odd Fleet units awarded the Presidential Unit Citation or the Navy Unit Commendation, highest U. S. ship awards. But we have also gone farther, talking with division, squadron and task group commanders. Their opinions, as well as our own after digesting hundreds of individual ship histories, are also represented.

There is no doubt that some worthy ships have been omitted. The authors expect to receive a modest amount of angry letters inquiring, "Why the hell did you guys write about a ferryboat like the *Blank,* but never mention the USS *Fearnaught?*" For every sailor worth his salt felt that in some way, however peculiar, his ship was the best damn wagon in the Fleet.

It probably was.

Philip R. Kelly
John J. Motley

INTRODUCTION

In every war, except conflicts between contiguous land-locked nations, control of the waterways is a vital stake. The nation that controls the seas inevitably wins.

That was true in the Graeco-Persian wars, in the Punic War, in the Napoleonic wars and in every war this country has fought. Yet everyone of those wars was fought with different ships, different weapons, different tactics. Sea power was the constant factor throughout; its application varied radically from one contest to another. The Roman trireme, the 100-gun British man-o'-war, the carriers and submarines of the United States Pacific Fleet, all were instruments of the sea power which this war saw exercised not only on the surface of the ocean, but under it and over it.

There was never a war fought at sea like the last one. There will never be another war fought like the last one. Our hope and effort must be that there will never be another war. But if war cannot be prevented, then the struggle for domination of the water-routes between this nation and its opponents will mark its beginning and determine its ending, whatever the instruments of sea power future technichologists may devise.

Even a war such as the fiction-writers conjure, in which radio-guided, atom-smashing robots will be hurled through thousands of miles of space, would be a struggle for sea power. At the end, the nation whose fleet can convoy an army of occupation to the opponent's shores and keep it supplied, will be the victor. Without that, a mutual belaboring with buzz bombs could end only in stalemate.

We do not know what the warships of the future will look like. They may be true submarines, able to bombard inland cities with guided missiles while safely submerged at sea. We are too close to a revolutionarily new era in propellants and projectiles to make any safe prediction. Another war would also see the air as a more crowded field of action than the last. But, whatever the instruments, control of the routes overseas must be the dominating effort. Whether capitulation comes after a paralyzing air blow or from infantrymen storming the last shattered redoubt, the seas will have to be crossed in safe control. In the last war, the airplane that bombed Hiroshima and the soldiers who smashed through France and Germany to Berlin were both ultimate extensions of applied sea power.

Thus the story of combat ships is the narrowest interpretation of sea power, but it is also the *sine qua non* of a history of the war. A nation's war machine must be a balanced one, to deliver the maximum of power at the optimum targets. No one can say that this area or this branch of the military won the war. All the branches and arms are mutually interdependent. A fleet without an amphibious force to transport and supply and blast a beachhead, could not have won the war any more than an Army without a fleet to carry it to the enemy.

Japan, with a lively understanding of sea power at the outset of the war, sought to keep America's armies landlocked by crippling the fleet at Pearl Harbor. Japan's error was in discounting our recuperative powers and will to fight, to take the offensive with an outnumbered fleet under the additional handicap of great distances from base.

Germany put its dependence on unsupported air power and the submarines, both of which might have worked more effectively had Hitler's general staff conceived the significance of sea-air power. Even our great and stout-hearted ally, Great Britain, might have fared better at the war's onset if she had not experimented before 1939 with a severance of air power from sea power.

The two great oceans had to be conquered before the enemy lands on their far shores could be subjugated. Any book which helps to provide an understanding of the composition and the functions of the United States Navy is important. The beacon of victory which illuminates our nation today rests on a tripod of air power, land power and sea power, each sturdy limb essential to the stability of the other two. Each is a power unto itself, but capable of fully using its potentialities only so far as it draws strength from the other two, and contributes of itself to them.

CHESTER W. NIMITZ

PREFACE

In a war which at its height saw millions of men, hundreds of thousands of airplanes and thousands of ships locked in struggle the world around, individual ship exploits were lost to view save as public relations officers isolated and enlarged them for the benefit of public morale.

Thus it is that fleets and task forces, "Torpedo 8" and "The Black Cats," won collective acclaim where in other wars at sea the USS *Oregon*, USS *Kearsarge*, Admiral Dewey, Admiral Porter, John Paul Jones, individually symbolized the success of American sea power.

But to the men who served aboard a fighting ship, that vessel will forever be an object of fierce pride and abiding love. "Happy ship" or "taut ship," the good old *Texas* or the mighty *Missouri* will mean something to them as precious, as indefinable, as personal, as home and family. That is what makes old Navy men the greatest sentimentalists in the world, and causes them always to pity their colleagues in khaki who can never love a fort, a tank or a field piece as the Navy man identifies himself with a destroyer, a cruiser—yes, or a sea-going tug, homeliest craft of all.

The authors of this book have caught that spirit of ship-to-man relationship and present it well, miraculously well considering the economy of word they have had to employ. Lieutenant Motley, who served with distinction on the escort carrier *Guadalcanal*, was for some time after VJ-day associated with me in the Navy Department, where my respect for his ability developed into a cordial friendship. His collaborator, Phil Kelly, saw the Navy from another and perhaps more objective point of view, as a writer who remembers well the North Atlantic in winter, particularly as it appeared from the cruiser *Savannah*. Both are former newspapermen and together they form an admirable team.

The book will provide a pleasant nostalgia for all who served afloat, but its greater service will be to translate for all others the significance of the Navy, ship by ship, to the nation in its years of deadliest peril.

WALTER KARIG
Captain, USNR

ACKNOWLEDGMENTS

The authors acknowledge with thanks the assistance and guidance of Capt. Walter Karig of the Navy, Col. Arthur Symons of the *Infantry Journal* who edited the manuscript, Lt. Comdr. Leonard Hall and Lt. (jg) John Strohmeyer of the Ship Section and Kitty Clark Brouilette of the Magazine and Book Section of Navy Public Information, William D. Gorman and Sydney Blatt. Fleet Admiral Chester W. Nimitz took time out from his busy job of running the world's biggest Navy to write the introduction, for which we are more than grateful. Our wives, Sarah and Kay, rendered invaluable help in typing the manuscript. The story of the cruiser *Richmond* was taken from a letter of Capt. John H. Leppert of that ship to Mayor W. C. Herbert of Richmond, Va.

NOW HEAR THIS!

BATTLESHIPS

"The primary purpose of a battleship is to carry destruction to the enemy," says a Navy Department release. Early in the war there were many who believed this concept obsolete, arguing that the increased use of carrier or land-based planes spelled the end of the big ships. This gloomy prediction seemed justified after the sinking of Britain's *Prince of Wales* and *Repulse* early in 1942. But ships like the *South Dakota* and *Washington,* operating in a tightly-knit carrier-destroyer unit, soon proved that the heavily armored battleship, with its formidable array of 148 antiaircraft guns, was still a vital part of the fleet. Radar, carrier-plane coverage and the proximity fuze (which causes shells to explode automatically upon nearing a target) all played important roles in this comeback.

US battlewagons in World War II ran the gamut—from the dowager *Arkansas* to mammoths of the *South Dakota, North Carolina* and *Iowa* classes. Thirty years of naval development lay between. The 562-foot *Arkansas,* for example, packed twelve 12-inch guns and could push her 26,000 tons along at about 20 knots. The 880-foot *Iowa* had a standard tonnage of 45,000 tons, carried nine 16-inch guns and drove along at better than 30 knots! And these were only the more obvious differences dividing the old and new.

A battleship is born, not from a blueprint, but from discussions among the experts in the Navy's Bureau of Ships. After painstaking tests of model hulls, the ideas around which she is to be shaped are ready for conversion to the blueprint stage. More than 30,000 plans are drawn before the $100,000,000 ship becomes a reality.

Although the modern battlewagon usually carries about 2,700 men in wartime, her ten generators could supply electricity for a city of 20,000. In her intricate skein of nerves and arteries she packs 900 electric motors, 2,000 telephones, 442,000 feet of piping and 1,220,000 feet of wiring. Her main pumps can send 4,800 gallons of water per minute coursing through the endless fire mains, and her 1,000 watertight spaces are all protected by automatic sprinkler systems. Her anchors weigh 15 tons apiece and the 2,000 feet of chain attached add another 121 tons to her impressive bulk.

The installation of her turrets is a primary engineering feat, only slightly less complicated than her launching. A finished turret, with its three 16-inch guns, weighs over 1,800 long tons . . . and there are three of them. Installed about one month after launching, the turrets are first assembled, then divided into sections, disassembled, and towed alongside the fitting-out pier on a barge. Special gauges insure an accuracy of 1/64-inch centering in this delicate operation.

Of the 17 battleships in service in 1941, the *Arizona* and *Oklahoma* were lost at Pearl Harbor. There were 23 in service in October, 1945.

The *South Dakota*

Try to get most Navy men to agree on the outstanding ship of the war and you're apt to launch a new battle. But an official Navy report has this to say of the mighty "Sodak" . . . "Certainly no other battleship has a comparable record. What a ship goes through cannot be expressed in figures, but on paper her career looks something like this:

"Major operations, 15; major surface battles, 4; invasions, 7; major air strikes, 50; bombardments, 9; Japanese large surface vessels sunk, 3; Japanese aircraft shot down, 64; miles steamed from commissioning to Tokyo, 246,970!"

First of her class, the 35,000-ton monster was commissioned at Philadelphia Navy Yard on March 20, 1942. Named by President Roosevelt, she started her war cruise under Rear Adm. (then Captain) Thomas L. Gatch on August 16, 1942. Little was heard of her until October 26, when as "Battleship X" she startled the world by slaughtering the Jap attackers in her first battle at Santa Cruz Islands. In that fracas, Battleship X was in support of the carrier *Enterprise's* group—sent to strengthen our South Pacific forces. Eighty-four Jap planes poured out of the sky to tackle the group, directing the greatest air attack ever unleashed on a battleship. Fresh from easy kills over the famous British battleships, *Prince of Wales* and *Repulse,* the Japs came in confidently. Then the *South Dakota* took over. Maneuvering at better than 27 knots, she unleashed a curtain of steel so murderous that the commander of American planes signaled his men away. He yelled: "Stay away from that big bastard. She's shooting down the sky." When the smoke had cleared, the Sodak had shot down 34 Jap planes. More than that, she had disproved the then popular idea that the battleship was obsolete in the face of modern airpower. But she had not escaped unscathed. A 500-pound bomb smacked one turret, wounded Captain Gatch.

Yet three weeks later the *South Dakota* turned up in action again, this time in the night battle off Savo Island, turning point in the Guadalcanal campaign. In company with the battleship *Washington* and the carrier *Enterprise,* the Sodak slammed into the dangerously narrow straits off Guadalcanal and started what has been termed the most furious seafight of the war. Quickly ranging in, she set two cruisers afire with her first salvos. After sinking one of these, fire was directed to another light cruiser astern. On the fourth salvo this ship broke in two. Another group of Jap warships popped up, and three caught the Sodak with searchlights, concentrating their fire on her. Retaliating with heavy fire from her secondary batteries, she knocked out the searchlights, and slammed several salvos into another Jap ship, which also broke in two. The rest retreated. Again the Sodak had suffered damage. Thirty men had been killed, 60 wounded. And the 42 large enemy shells which hit her had inflicted grave damage. Back she came to New York for repairs.

In February 1943 she left the Navy Yard and in June joined the British Fleet in the North Atlantic, Arctic Ocean and North Sea off Norway, Spitsbergen, Iceland, Greenland and Bear Island. She was then under the command of Capt. Lyndex D. McCormick. Then in November 1943 she turned up again in the Pacific under the command of Capt. Allan E. Smith. As part of a carrier group assigned to the Gilbert Islands assaults, she began a marauding career which carried her into the heart of the Pacific campaigns.

After the Gilberts came the bombardment of Nauru, then the Marshall Islands landings and occupation. In January 1944 she unleashed her tremendous fire power on Roi and Namur. Then followed air strikes on Truk, Guam, Saipan and Tinian. The Sodak was on the prowl and the Japs were far from happy. More air strikes this time in March on Palau, Yap and Woleai. At this point Capt. Ralph S. Riggs took over. In April she turned up for the invasions of Hollandia and New Guinea and in May, for the bombardment of Ponape. In June Saipan felt the fury of her guns. Relentlessly, the attack pressed on. In the first battle of the Philippine Sea, the *South Dakota* again felt the sting of Jap raiders when another 500-pound bomb caught her. But the next day (June 20, 1944) she was in on the air strike against the Jap fleet, and on the very next day, on strikes at Pagan.

Back to Puget Sound Navy Yard in July and August for an overhaul, she rejoined the fleet in time for strikes on Okinawa, Luzon and Formosa in October 1944. And in December with a fast carrier task force of the Third Fleet, the Sodak plunged into the Second Battle of the Philippine Sea. One month later the same group supported the Luzon landings and occupation. The Sodak was there, too! In February she was with the Fifth Fleet, supporting the Iwo Jima landings and occupation; in March, the same role at Okinawa.

The *South Dakota* boasts of a number of "firsts," proudest of which occurred July 14, 1945. For on that date, under the command of Commodore C. B. Momsen, she blasted the Jap homeland, bombarding the town of Kamaishi in the first attack of its kind since 1863. Similar attacks on other Jap cities followed with sledgehammer effect. And now the Rising Sun was setting fast. On August 15 Japan capitulated. On August 29, the mighty Sodak dropped anchor in Tokyo Bay. The long fight was over. Few ships of any nation would ever equal her record.

The *Texas*

Pearl Harbor brought a whole new life to many US ships, but the *Texas* (BB 35) simply took war's outbreak in stride. To begin, the *Texas,* commissioned March 12, 1914, was a veteran of the First World War, serving as a unit of the Sixth Battle Squadron against the Germans in 1918. After the Armistice was signed she led a comparatively sedate career, but in April, 1941 she steamed into Norfolk Navy Yard to prepare for war.

May, June and July she was on neutrality patrol across the stormy North Atlantic, with her crews ready for instant action—six months before the United States was brought into the war.

On December 7, 1941 she was in Portland, Maine, and from January until October, 1942 she convoyed ships to Europe, Africa and the Canal Zone.

In November, 1942 she covered the landings in the Mehdia-Port Lyautey area, pumping 14-inch shells into enemy roads and ammunition dumps. During 1943 she resumed her convoy escort duties, steaming to Casablanca, Morocco, Gibraltar, Scotland and Ireland. Then in June, 1944 she was in on the big show, hurling hundreds of shells into selected targets during pre-invasion bombardments of Normandy.

The *Texas* was finally tagged by the enemy on June 25, 1944 during a three-hour duel with German guns at Cherbourg. She was straddled 30 times and suffered two direct hits. One shell wiped out the navigation bridge, killing 1 and wounding 14, but the other hit luckily proved a dud, causing no damage except a hole in the side. After repairs she took part in the invasion of Southern France in July. From there she returned to New York in September, 1944, joining the Fleet at Ulithi in time to participate in the Iwo Jima operations. One of the crew's most exciting moments came when those topside witnessed the famous flag-raising on Mount Suribachi.

It was in the Okinawa invasion that the *Texas* really unleased her shootin' irons, firing four complete shiploads of ammunition: more than two thousand 14-inch and two thousand six hundred 5-inch shells. And her crew made some kind of record by remaining at battle stations for days, sleeping at their posts beside the guns.

The *New York*

The venerable *New York* (BB 34), commissioned in April, 1914 was one of the three old US battleships to weather the war undamaged. After playing an important part in World War I, she wasted no time in getting into World War II, escorting troops to Iceland in July, 1941 when that island was occupied as a defense base.

Then followed a cruise in the North Atlantic and three months off Newfoundland, protecting our new bases there. On December 7 the *New York* was being overhauled at Norfolk, Virginia. Two months later she was on convoy duty again in the wintry North Atlantic. During the summer of 1942, she made two runs to Scotland at the height of the U-boat menace. Both cruises were punctuated by numerous scrapes with subs, but the *New York's* convoys escaped.

In the landings at North Africa, in November, 1942 the *New York,* along with the *Philadelphia,* neutralized the strongest coastal defense unit in the region. From there she went on to Casablanca and was in Safi Harbor when six ships were torpedoed on November 11-12. After returning to New York, she made two convoy trips to Casablanca. Then from June, 1943 to August, 1944 she served as a training ship along the East Coast.

In January, 1945 the *New York* proceeded to Ulithi to join the assault on Iwo Jima. Forced to leave the task force when she lost part of her port screw, the *New York* recovered in time to begin the pre-invasion bombardment of Iwo Jima on February 16. During this bombardment she scored a direct hit on a large Jap ammunition dump which went up like a 4th-of-July display.

After a stay at Manus for repairs, the *New York* arrived at Okinawa on March 27, where she remained in action for 76 consecutive days. Though repeatedly subjected to all kinds of enemy attack, the *New York* was the only capital ship to stay on the job without relief. One Kamikaze made an unsuccessful suicide run through a hail of antiaircraft fire but crashed harmlessly into the sea. The *New York* poured more than five million pounds of shells into targets on Okinawa.

After Okinawa had been declared secured, the *New York* proceeded to Pearl Harbor on June 12, 1945 where she was completely regunned.

The *Pennsylvania*

The *Pennsylvania* (BB 38) had to wait for her second war to get into the fighting. After sitting out World War I without seeing any real action, the "Pennsy" took part in the fire and smoke of World War II from Pearl Harbor to Okinawa, got shot up a few times, and lost a lot of good men.

The *Pennsylvania* was commissioned in June, 1916 and was named Fleet flagship in October. She remained flagship of the Fleet until September, 1945, 29 years later.

On December 7, 1941 the Pennsy was in drydock at Pearl with her propellers removed. Jap planes made repeated attempts to torpedo the drydock caisson so that a wall of water could sweep in on the battleship, but they failed. Even though the *Pennsylvania* was not in fighting trim, her crews manned light guns and fought back. The ship was severely strafed and bombed; 24 of the men were killed, many others wounded.

In two weeks the Pennsy was underway for San Francisco and repairs, and although she was able to be at sea by January 12, 1942, the Navy decided to modernize the old battlewagon. It wasn't until April, 1943 that she returned to a combat theater, arriving in the Aleutians for the bombardment of Attu, with the *Idaho* and *Nevada*. The *Pennsylvania's* fire support of our infantry weakened enemy resistance on the west arm of Holtz Bay and permitted troops to occupy the area. Twice the Pennsy escaped torpedo attacks, the destroyer *Edwards* later sinking the sub which launched the tin fish. The battleship left the Aleutians in May for Puget Sound Navy Yard and more modernization, but was back for the landing of assault troops at Kiska in August.

The first big US attack on Japanese positions in the Central Pacific—the Gilbert Islands campaign—found the *Pennsylvania* carrying the 5th Amphibious Force Commander, Rear Adm. Richmond Kelly Turner. On November 20 the task force moved in on Makin and Butaritari with the Pennsy and other battleships and cruisers smashing at the enemy on shore. (The tropical heat was so intense that men fainted in the magazines.) During the Gilberts engagement the Japs attacked the task force viciously by air and by sea; the escort carrier *Liscome Bay* was torpedoed with a heavy loss of life. In January, 1944, after a trip back to Pearl, the *Pennsylvania* took part in another major operation, this time the Marshall Islands. It was in the dark before dawn on the 30th that the battlewagon's big guns thundered at Kwajalein and a sailor standing topside shouted, "Reveille, you slant-eyed so-and so's!" Scout planes from the Pennsy did outstanding work in reporting ranges and spotting targets. On the third day of the battle the ship entered Kwajalein lagoon to anchor.

In mid-February the *Pennsylvania* and *Tennessee* bombarded Eniwetok and Engebi and covered landing teams. Parry Island was taken under fire next. When the Marshalls operation was over the Pennsy turned southward to the New Hebrides and then to Australia for replenishment. In June the campaign in the Marianas began, the *Pennsylvania* blasting Saipan on the 14th, Tinian on the 15th, Guam on the 16th; twice the AA gunners took enemy planes under fire. The Pennsy was ordered back to Saipan, then Eniwetok until July 9, when she returned to Guam for the bombardment preceding the invasion. Troops went in on the 21st, backed up by the ship's fire support, which continued until August 3. The *Pennsylvania* put out of action 15 planes, 85 guns, numerous mortars and much field artillery.

Peleliu in the Palau Islands, in the western Carolines, was next, and the Pennsy threw in her shells there and at Angaur, from September 12 until the 17th, when she had to leave for the Admiralty Islands to undergo temporary repairs. By October 18 she was with the Bombardment and Fire Support Group smashing at Leyte. She pounded the beaches until the 24th, when the Battle of Surigao Strait began shaping up. The Japs lost 2 battleships and 3 destroyers at Surigao, but without the *Pennsylvania* opening fire. Enemy aircraft felt the Pennsy's sting, however; she shot down ten Jap planes in Leyte Gulf before she left on November 25. After bombarding Lingayen in the January, 1945 invasion, she had to return to the States for repairs to a troublesome bearing.

The *Pennsylvania* did not see the battle areas again, except for pot shots at Wake on the return westward, until August 12, three days before hostilities ended. On that day she entered Buckner Bay, Okinawa, and that night took an aerial torpedo from a Jap plane which almost sent her down. Twenty men were killed and 10 injured. The Pennsy was attacked again on the 13th; on the 18th, after the shooting stopped, she was towed to Guam. On October 24, 1945, she made Puget Sound, limping and thoroughly war-weary.

The *Tennessee*

The first *Tennessee* was a captured Confederate side-wheel steamer, the second was a similarly-converted Confederate ram, the third was a steam sloop and the fourth an armored cruiser. But the fifth fightin' *Tennessee* (BB 43) was a battleship, commissioned June 3, 1920 at the New York Navy Yard, and one of the eight battlewagons the Japs caught at Pearl Harbor. The first indication of war for the *Tennessee* crew was war itself. Five Jap planes fell to her guns, but others planted hits on turrets 2 and 3. After steaming under her own power to Bremerton she was patched up and came out for the start of the second round, rough and ready. The second round took her to join Task Force One, where she protected the Hawaiian Islands until September, 1942.

After a complete refurnishing at Puget Sound Navy Yard, the *Tennessee* put to sea again in May, 1943 for a two-month patrol in the Aleutians, climaxed by the bombardment of Kiska. Her history in the last two years of the war was largely written by the thunder of her guns on Jap pillboxes, land installations and ships across the Pacific. After bloody Tarawa, the *Tennessee* polished off a sub on November 22 before going to the Marshalls, with Secretary of the Navy Forrestal aboard, for the drumming of Roi and Namur, Eniwetok and Engebi. After that she ranged in on Parry Island, and anchoring only nine hundred yards off shore, gave that hapless chunk of earth the old carpet-beater treatment, with everything from 40mm to 14-inch in the barrage.

When General MacArthur wanted a bombardment of Kavieng, New Ireland, on March 20, the *Tennessee* was one of the ships picked for the job. After that performance, she turned eastward to prepare for the largest amphibious operation up to that time—Saipan. Closing in on June 15, the *Tennessee* nosed into narrow Saipan Channel, between Saipan and Tinian. Suddenly three carefully camouflaged 6-inch guns on Tinian cut loose. The first two salvos bracketed the *Tennessee,* and one shell from the third pierced a 5-inch mount, killing eight and wounding many others. But the *Tennessee's* revenge was quick and final, for even before the fourth enemy salvo could be fired, the ship's 5-inchers silenced the Jap battery in one furious blast.

After more pre-invasion work at Guam and Tinian, she headed for the Palaus, arriving there in time to bombard Angaur Island on September 15, 1944. She then moved in on the Philippines, steaming through a typhoon and uncharted minefields to enter Leyte Gulf on October 20. In the fierce battle that followed, the *Tennessee* threw plenty of steel at the waves of Jap planes sweeping in relentlessly. And on October 25, 1944 she moved in on the epic battle of Surigao Strait.

As the Jap fleet threaded through the Strait early that morning the *Tennessee* waited, in company with five other battleships, and cruisers, destroyers, submarines and PT boats. The *Tennessee* spotted the Japs when they were twenty miles away. But the order came: "Wait!" The Japs came on. Finally, at twenty thousand yards, the *Tennessee* opened fire and in the following thirteen minutes she slammed over thirteen salvos, with only one known miss. When the furious fire subsided Leyte Gulf was secure and the Japs had lost two battleships, two cruisers and four destroyers. A few days later the *Tennessee* steamed back to the States for a badly-needed overhauling and leave for all hands.

On January 27, 1945 she was ready again and on February 16,

Iwo Jima felt the impact of *Tennessee* shells as she fired day and night at the stubborn island. Then came Okinawa, and seven straight days of intensive bombardment. When it ended, the *Tennessee* received this message: "Commanding Officer Sixth Marines himself saw *Tennessee* fire and expresses his appreciation for . . . outstanding support. Well done!" And from the Army's controlling units: "*Tennessee* is best ship we ever worked with!"

Then, suddenly on April 12, disaster struck, when seven Kamikazes bored in at once. Six were shot down but the seventh crashed into the starboard side, killing 26 and injuring 103. Despite this the *Tennessee* was patched up immediately, staying in action until May 3, when she returned to Ulithi for repairs. Three weeks later she was back at Okinawa, smacking the Japs tied up in the last gasps of that campaign. When Vice Admiral Oldendorf, leader during the Surigao Strait victory, became commander of all forces in the Ryukyus, the *Tennessee* continued to serve as his flagship. She was at Okinawa preparing for further operations when the war ended.

When the *Tennessee* received her Navy Unit Commendation in April, 1945 it read: "For outstanding heroism in action . . . throughout thirteen major operations." It had been quite a war.

The *Maryland*

The Japs thought they had "The Fighting Mary" (BB 46) out of the war 24 hours after it started. But this venerable battlewagon came back to absorb more punishment while dishing out enough hell to the Nips to make them regret their aim at Pearl Harbor. From July 21, 1921 (when she was commissioned at Newport News), to December 7, 1941, the *Maryland* had led a quiet life. But from Pearl Harbor on she led a life hardly in keeping with a lady of her years. After Pearl Harbor the Japs gave her three more blows—one a torpedo and two from Kamikaze. But the Mary, far from getting weaker, came back stronger after each shock.

After repairs, the *Maryland* returned to sea in June, 1942, standing by for possible action at Midway. From here, where nothing eventful happened to her, she went on to Pearl Harbor, then to the Fijis where she stayed till February, 1943, leaving then for the New Hebrides. After a hot and dull six months there, she returned to Pearl Harbor to be refitted with clusters of 40mm antiaircraft guns. From then on the Fighting Mary was in the thick of things, starting as Admiral Harry Hill's flagship in the invasion of Betio Island, Tarawa, in November, 1943. During this 13-day action she plugged shore batteries unmercifully, while two of her observation planes were damaged by enemy fire.

Her next action was on January 31, 1944 when she smacked down more shore batteries in the bloody invasion of Kwajalein, blasting blockhouses on Roi Island at point-blank range.

Saipan followed, on June 14, but after punching the Japs again, the Mary took a counter-blow on June 22, when a torpedo plane sneaked in and planted a fish in her bow, killing two men. Ship-repair parties miraculously nullified the gaping wound and she limped back to Pearl Harbor, rejoining the fleet on September 12 at Peleliu for another pre-invasion bombardment.

With the Japanese now claiming that she had been sunk three times, the *Maryland* confounded their claims by turning up in Leyte Gulf on October 17. After shore bombardments, she joined Task Force 77 in the now famous battle of Surigao Strait, thumping the hapless Japs with armor-piercing shot from her 16-inchers. Following this victory, the Mary patrolled off Leyte, undergoing one of the worst air assaults of the Pacific war before taking a Kamikaze hit between turrets 1 and 2 at sunset on November 29. Penetrating the main and armored decks, the bomb exploded, killing 31 enlisted men and seriously injuring 30 others. Back went the *Maryland* to Pearl again for repairs.

In March, 1945, the *Maryland* was bound for Ulithi, and on March 25 she was plastering enemy positions on Okinawa, largest amphibious operation of World War II. The caliber of her gunnery showed plainly here when she destroyed an enemy gun position with six four-gun salvos. (The skipper of the cruiser *Minneapolis* sent: "Nice going!") From April 1, Easter Sunday, until April 7, the *Maryland's* crew underwent terrific strain from heat, continued action and enemy plane activity. At 6:49 P. M. a Jap suicide plane crashed into the top of turret No. 3 killing 10, with 6 missing and 27 injured. Manning the 20mm antiaircraft battery, these men had refused to budge as the plane bored in. The 500-pound bomb did not enter the turret, but its blast damaged supporting stanchions. Nevertheless, the *Maryland* stayed on the line for seven more days before heading for Guam, and later the Bremerton Navy Yard, where she arrived on VE-day.

Early in August, just as the rejuvenated *Maryland* left Bremerton, the war ended . . . but the Fighting Mary wasn't quite finished, for she joined the Magic Carpet operation, part of a vast fleet of warships rushing the service men home. She lost some good men . . . Luis Zamorra Cedillo, James Ginn, Jack Stephen Lucas, Laten Francis Riley and others. She fought her war.

The *Washington*

Placed in commission on May 15, 1941, the *Washington* was the second battleship commissioned by the Navy since December 1923. After ten months of shakedown operations, the *Washington* (BB 56) reported for active war duty in March, 1942, operating as a unit of the British Home Fleet out of Scapa Flow. From then until August, 1942 the ship was constantly in waters swarming with Nazi submarines as she convoyed ships headed for Murmansk.

This duty was followed by an overhaul at New York, then on September 14 the *Washington* joined our South Pacific forces; the only fast battleship operating in that area.

From the end of October to the beginning of May, 1943 she supported our operations around the Solomon Islands. The *Washington* arrived at a crucial time in these operations, soon after the Japs had administered severe punishment to our small cruiser and destroyer forces. On the night of November 14-15 the *Washington,* along with the *South Dakota* and destroyers *Benham, Walke, Preston,* and *Gwin,* fell into a trap the Japs had baited for smaller game. Steaming confidently along in the hope of engaging our battered cruiser and destroyer forces, the Japs suddenly found that they had a bear by the tail as the *Washington* (then the flagship of Vice Adm. Willis Lee) and the *South Dakota* opened up with their 16-inch guns. The Third Battle of Savo Island, as this action was called, marked the turning point in the fierce series of naval battles and helped win the vital Guadalcanal campaign.

Eye witnesses to the slaughter that followed described the Navy gunnery as "uncanny." Said one observer, "It was beautiful. One minute I saw two Jap ships sitting there, then three blobs of red fire came soaring over from our ships. The next time I looked the Japs were gone." In the course of this action the *Washington* sank the first Jap battleship destroyed by surface action during the war. Not content with this she also sank or assisted in sinking several enemy cruisers and destroyers.

After a brief overhaul at Pearl Harbor the *Washington* was back in action on August 7, supporting operations in the Northern Solomons. That over she headed for the Fiji Islands where our forces were gathering for the invasion of the Gilberts. Following the successful occupation and capture of the Gilberts, the *Washington* joined five other fast battleships in bombarding the island of Nauru.

Steaming out of Funa Futi on January 24, 1944 the ship joined Task Unit 58.1.3 in a pre-invasion bombardment of the Kwajalein chain in the Marshall Islands. In two intense sessions, the *Washington* sank an enemy tanker and put several gun batteries out of action.

After a trip to Puget Sound Navy Yard, the battleship returned to the Marshalls on May 30, joining Task Force 58 for the invasion of Saipan. On June 19-21 she participated in the famous Marianas "turkey shoot," in which our planes and ships shot down hundreds of enemy pilots. And from August 30 to October 5 she was in on the operations leading to the capture of Peleliu and Angaur. During October the ship participated in the first carrier force raids on Okinawa and at Formosa in the Battle of Cape Engaño.

November 5 to February 17, 1945 the *Washington* operated as a unit of the fast carrier force striking at Luzon, Camranh Bay, Saigon, Hong Kong, Canton, Hainan, Nansei Shoto and Tokyo. Then February 19-22 the battleship stood in close to Iwo Jima, throwing 790 rounds from her 16-inch guns into enemy installations. From February 23 to March 16 she was engaged in operations connected with the Iwo Jima landings, including a carrier raid on Tokyo on February 25.

She struck at Kyushu, then went on to bombard Okinawa during March and April in support of our amphibious landings there. Following this she returned to the west coast for overhauling and was there when the war ended.

The *Washington's* longest course was made during the Okinawa campaign when she was underway for a period of 79 consecutive days, undergoing 33 air attacks during this period.

In November, 1945, she became part of the "Magic Carpet" fleet bringing troops back from Europe.

The *North Carolina*

When the *North Carolina* (BB 55) was commissioned at New York Navy Yard in April, 1941, she was the first US battleship to join the fleet since the *West Virginia* in 1921. Naturally the question whether naval designers and builders had lost their touch during the 19-year shipbuilding holiday was bound to be asked.

The *North Carolina,* first battleship to take a Jap submarine torpedo and continue at full speed, soon erased such doubts. And during the Guadalcanal fighting the "Show Boat," with all her antiaircraft batteries firing, presented such an awesome sight that the carrier *Enterprise* messaged: "Are you afire?" The *North Carolina* wasn't, but it is reasonable to assume that the Japs were burnt up.

Under the command of Capt. George H. Fort, the *North Carolina* went into action early in the summer of 1942, supporting the landings on Guadalcanal and Tulagi. And right then and there the Japs began to report the Show Boat sunk, a practice they apparently never tired of, for by the end of the war she had been "sunk" at least six different times—according to enemy broadcasts.

As the newest battleship to arrive in the Pacific war area, the *North Carolina,* with her bristling array of antiaircraft weapons, was the first battleship to be part of a carrier task force. The most formidable naval striking power the world has ever seen was built around such groups as this, and by her breath-taking performance the *North Carolina* led the way. In her first enemy action off Guadalcanal on August 24, 1942 she downed at least six attacking Jap planes.

Near the end of 1942 Capt. Wilder D. Baker took over as the Show Boat continued to patrol and support carrier raids. Early in 1943 Capt. Frank P. Thomas took command and directed her activities against the New Georgia group in July. Then in November she struck against Makin and Tarawa in the Gilbert Islands, bombarding the Jap phosphate mines on Nauru Island in December. In January, 1944 she accompanied strikes at Kavieng, New Ireland, and later in the month became the first battleship to open fire on pre-war Jap territory as she bombarded Roi and Namur in the Kwajalein group. Here she sank an enemy supply ship and pounded enemy installations with her nine 16-inch guns.

At Truk, in February, with Task Force 58, the *North Carolina* helped inflict great losses when 2 Jap cruisers, 3 destroyers and numerous other ships were sent down. After the Truk strike, Guam, Saipan and Tinian were hit, and in the latter engagement the *North Carolina* gunners destroyed 14 enemy planes. Blows against Palau, Yap and Woleai continued through March, and in April the Show Boat covered the New Guinea landings at Humboldt Bay. In June, Saipan and Tinian again were targets; the *North Carolina* brought down two attacking planes. On November 11, after she returned from an overhaul in the States, the big battlewagon's task unit wiped out a nine-ship Jap convoy west of Leyte. During the invasion which followed, the *North Carolina* operated as a support unit for the carriers, and repelled many air attacks.

In January, 1945 the Show Boat revisited Kwajalein with bombardment runs, and in February was part of a task force which smashed at the Honshu coast. The force made a quick turn south and the *North Carolina* was soon shelling Iwo Jima before the landings there, switching next to the Okinawa campaign in March and April.

Off Okinawa on April 7, a 5-inch enemy shell killed 3 and wounded 44 of her men—but in retaliation she shot down 24 Jap planes in 15 engagements. Because of her duties with the carrier group, the *North Carolina* was subjected to scores of aerial attacks and had so many narrow escapes that she became known as one of the luckiest ships in the Fleet. When the war ended she was anchored in Tokyo Bay, one of two major ships to come all the way through from the first action at Guadalcanal.

The *Indiana*

When the Pacific "fleet" totalled but three battleships, the *Indiana* was there, and when US troops made their first landings on the Japanese home islands, the *Indiana* was still there. In between, with but two brief exceptions, she was there no matter what went on in the Pacific. Although her battle stars read like a history of the Pacific War, she was never harmed by enemy action and never lost a man through enemy action! The *Indiana*—"Mighty Item"—took part in operations against Guadalcanal, Rennell Island, New Georgia, Marcus Island, Gilbert Islands, Marshall Islands, Truk, Ponape, Marianas, Palau, Iwo Jima, Okinawa and the bombardments of the Japanese home islands, and did it unscathed by retaliatory fire, dive-bombings or torpedoings.

Some of her escapes were miraculous. In the Marianas campaign, with a torpedo only yards from the Mighty Item's plates, even Capt. Thomas J. Keliher, Jr. announced, "Looks like it's got us." Then gunners opened fire on the torpedo itself in a last-chance stab . . . and miraculously, it worked. The torpedo exploded before it hit the ship.

Again, a Kamikaze plane was shot down so close that the splash drenched the ship. Another plane was shot apart, and its debris was strewn over the *Indiana's* decks. But with effective guns and gunners, the *Indiana* came through it all, at one time piling up a perfect average by splashing 15 Japanese planes out of a flight of fifteen.

The *Indiana,* from the start, wasn't a showboat. She was a battleship—with the accent on the first two syllables. Commissioned April 30, 1942, she reported for duty with the Pacific Fleet on November 28. There were only two other new battlewagons with the fleet at the time, the *Washington* and *South Dakota*. With two carriers, the *Saratoga* and *Enterprise,* they were all the heavy naval might that stood between the Japanese and the fighting on Guadalcanal. With the addition of the *Massachusetts* and *Alabama* from the Atlantic, and the *North Carolina* from Pearl Harbor, the famous Task Force 58 was formed. The defensive war finished, the *Indiana* and her sisters went on the prowl.

The Mighty Item received her baptism of fire off Tarawa. She was near Makin Island when Jap torpedo bombers from the Marshalls caught her silhouetted against the Western sun. A beacon of fire in the sea marked the *Indiana's* first kill seconds later.

Nauru, rich little British-owned phosphate island stolen by the Japs in the early stages of the war, was the next to feel the might of the Mighty Item. Then in January, 1944 her guns pounded at Kwajalein. Toward evening, a Jap shore battery opened up against the ship and was promptly ground to dust by the 5-inch batteries.

Disaster struck the following night. In the pitch blackness the bow of the *Washington* slammed into the starboard plates of the *Indiana* in a crash which could be heard for miles. With two hundred feet of her armor-plating gone and a 20-foot hole in her side, the *Indiana* limped back to Pearl. She was out of Pearl for the Hollandia campaign, raided Truk and bombarded Ponape. In June she was one of the first ships to open up on Saipan, despite a hail of bombs and torpedoes from Jap shore-based planes. Bombs crashed all around the Mighty Item and though her sister ships (*South Dakota* and *San Francisco*) were hit, the *Indiana* again came out unscratched.

Then for 64 consecutive days the *Indiana* and Task Force 58 stayed at sea. Three Jap carriers were hit during this period. After a brief rest for the men and replenishment of supplies, the *Indiana* turned south from Eniwetok as part of Admiral Halsey's Third Fleet, covering the Palau landings. But after two years of high speed operation the *Indiana's* power plant faltered, and she was ordered home to the States.

Through all this the *Indiana* had fought as part of a team. For her there had been no individual glory. She had bombarded shores, protected carriers and shot down attacking planes. She had rescued so many fliers that the task seemed almost routine. Still, nobody wrote headlines about the *Indiana,* dubbed "Old Anonymous" by the correspondents.

Protecting carriers for a raid on Tokyo was her next assignment after the overhaul at Bremerton. Then came strikes at Iwo, Chichi and Haha Jima, a return engagement on Tokyo and several smashes at Okinawa. Suddenly intelligence reported the Jap fleet, or what was left of it, heading southward. The *Indiana's* task force went after it and in a long-range plane battle on April 7, planes from the group sank the powerful battleship *Yamato,* a cruiser and three destroyers. At the same time, three Kamikaze planes made a simultaneous attack on the Mighty Item, but all three were beaten off.

During the next two months the Mighty Item supported the Okinawa ground operations, surviving more frantic Kamikaze smashes.

But June 5, 1945 was a day of harrowing experiences, for on that day the *Indiana* and her sister ships were caught in a typhoon. Buffeted by enormous waves the *Indiana* lost steering control, with one engine knocked out. But the Mighty Item sailed on, and to prove the typhoon hadn't pulled her fangs, took a healthy bite at Kyushu and Minami Daito.

Then in a rousing finale she steamed up to the home islands of Japan and blasted the Japanese steel mills of Kamaishi, in company with the *South Dakota* and *Massachusetts*. After that there were air strikes on Tokyo and Hokkaido, smashes at Kyushu and southern Honshu, a midnight bombardment of Hamamatsu and a return trip to Kamaishi to prove to the Japs that salvage operations there were futile.

On September 5 the Mighty Item marked finis to a great war-time career by dropping her hook in Tokyo Bay—234,888 fighting miles behind her.

The *Alabama*

The *Alabama* (BB 60) was no glamor girl, but as a highly respected 25,000-ton *South Dakota*-class battlewagon, she did all right. Commissioned August 16, 1942, she was under the command of Capt. George B. Wilson when she joined the British Home Fleet in May, 1943 at Scapa Flow. Her first war tour involved operations to lure the German battleship *Tirpitz* from its Norway lair, and Murmansk convoy runs.

In September, 1943, the *Alabama* joined the Pacific Fleet at Efate, New Hebrides, for the Gilberts campaign. On December 8, 1943 she participated in the bombardment of Nauru. After a four-day period at Pearl Harbor she rejoined the Fleet for the Marshalls operation, and the bombardment of Roi and Namur on January 30, 1944 in direct support of landings there.

After a short stay at Majuro, the *Alabama* joined in the first Truk raid in February, then moved on for the first strikes at Saipan, Tinian and Guam. In March she participated in strikes on Palau and Woleai.

Subsequent operations included Hollandia, the bombardment of Ponape and the Marianas, strikes in the Palau-Yap-Ulithi area, the Philippines, Okinawa, Formosa, Leyte landings, Battle of Cape Engaño, Visayan engagement, and the seizure of Mindoro.

During the Marianas operation, the *Alabama* was credited with giving the warning on June 19 of the approach of large forces of enemy aircraft. This early alert enabled carrier planes to stage the "turkey shoot" of that day.

In December, 1944 the *Alabama* was ordered to Puget Sound Navy Yard, after actively operating for 23 months without major overhaul.

In May, 1945 she rejoined the Fleet, acting with fast carrier groups supporting the Okinawa ground operations by strikes against Kyushu and targets on Okinawa. On June 5, 1945 the *Alabama* was among the ships damaged by a typhoon whose wind intensities reached 90 to 120 knots.   Her last war action took her on the "Tokyo Plains-Northern Honshu-Hokkaido" strikes and the night bombardment of the Hitachi-Mito area on July 17.   Sixty-seven days after sortie from Leyte, the *Alabama* anchored in Tokyo Bay.

(In addition to her faithful performance against the enemy, the *Alabama* won the mythical fleet baseball championship, under the able guidance of Chief Petty Officer Bob Feller, better known for his work with Cleveland Indians.)

The *Iowa*

Only God and the Japanese Navy know what went through the strange Nipponese mind when the *Iowa* (BB 61) turned up in the Pacific . . . 45,000 tons of destruction, 887 feet long, and over 108 feet of beam, this behemoth mounts nine 16-inch guns, bristles with anti-aircraft batteries, and has speed to burn.   First of her class, this super-dreadnaught was just too much for the punch-drunk Japs.

After her commissioning at New York Navy Yard on February 22, 1943 the speedy *Iowa* was placed on the "Tirpitz Watch" off New-foundland, patrolling to neutralize the threat of the Nazi battleship-raider.   This ended in November, 1943 when the *Iowa* was chosen to carry President Roosevelt to North Africa for his historic conference with Churchill and Stalin.

The *Iowa* left for the Pacific on January 2, 1944, joining Task Force 58 for the Marshall Islands air strikes preceding the battles for Kwajalein and Eniwetok.   On February 16 she swept with other ships around Truk, and on February 22 was part of Vice Admiral Mitscher's carrier blow at Tinian.   The *Iowa* received her only damage of the war on March 18, sustaining hits from two 4.7 shells from a Jap shore battery.   Damage was negligible however, with casualties confined to one man.

Still with Task Force 58, the *Iowa* jammed furious action into the next months with strikes and bombardments on Palau, Woleai, Hol-landia, Aitape, Wakde and Truk again.   April 29 found the *Iowa* splashing five Jap planes off Truk and two days later she served as Adm. O. M. Hustvedt's flagship in bombarding Ponape.   Next came the Marianas campaign, culminating in the invasion of Saipan, Tinian and Guam.   And on June 19 she was present at the First Battle of the Philippine Sea, sometimes called the Marianas "turkey shoot," where the *Iowa* got two more planes.

September found her with the Third Fleet, in support of the fast carrier attacks on the middle Philippine Islands, then, following more strikes on the Palaus, Luzon and Visayas, the *Iowa* retired to Ulithi where she commenced serving as press ship for the Fleet in October Now came more air strikes with the *Iowa* in support . . . the Ryukyus, Formosa and Luzon (for the invasion of Leyte). Finally, in December she developed shaft trouble and returned to San Francisco for repairs. These completed, on March 19, 1945 she rejoined Task Force 58 for the tea party off Okinawa. Her tremendous fire power and speed brought her safely through the Kamikaze ordeal, and during July and August she participated in air attacks on the Jap homeland, later bombarding Muroran, Hokkaido, Hitachi and Honshu.

Rejoining the carriers, she was busy with more devastating air strikes and bombardments until the end of the war. On August 27, 1945, three years to the day of her launching, she dropped anchor thirty miles off Tokyo. Her log read 190,313 miles.

The *New Jersey*

When the battleship *New Jersey* (BB 62) put to sea in January, 1944 she packed the most deadly gunnery punch ever seen aboard ship. Displacing over 53,000 tons, this giant carried nine 16-inch guns, twenty 5-inch guns, eighty 40mm guns and fifty-seven 20mm guns. Along with her sister ships the *Iowa, Wisconsin* and *Missouri,* she was one of the most powerful battleships in the world; four engines kicked her along at 33 knots.

The *New Jersey* slipped into the Pacific war ring by supporting air strikes in the Marshall Islands in January, 1944. On February 9, 1944 she became the flagship of Adm. Raymond Spruance, Commander of the Fifth Fleet. With Admiral Spruance directing, the *New Jersey* acted as a hub of the huge wheel of fighting ships which rolled over Jap island bases.

After more air strikes against Truk in February, the *New Jersey* went on to pound the Japanese on Mili Atoll in the Marshalls, then supported air strikes against Palau, Woleai, Aitape and Hollandia.

When Admiral Spruance transferred to the *Indianapolis* on April 7, the *New Jersey* carried on with Capt. Carl Holden in command. She bombarded Saipan and Tinian and covered the landings operations that followed. Then on June 19 she turned up in the middle of the famous Marianas "turkey shoot" in which the Japs lost 402 planes. On January 25 she supported air strikes against Guam and Rota and later supported the Guam landings. After more air strikes against Palau, she returned to Pearl Harbor for a routine checkup.

Admiral Halsey broke his flag on August 24, 1944 as the *New Jersey* became flagship of the Third Fleet. Then under heavy attack from enemy aircraft, she supported air strikes in the Philippines through December, 1944, fighting off constant Jap suicide attacks.

Fleet Admiral Chester Nimitz came aboard on December 24 as the *New Jersey* celebrated 103,000 fighting miles during the year. After renewing attacks against Formosa in January, she supported air strikes against Camranh, Saigon and Jap shipping off French Indo-China. On January 22 Admiral Badger, commander of Battleship Division Seven, broke his flag. And now the *New Jersey* moved in for the kill, with the Japs hanging on the ropes. In February she supported large-scale air strikes against Tokyo and Yokohama, then cruised off Iwo Jima in support of landing operations there. On March 24 she bombarded Okinawa and struck at southern Kyushu and Amami Oshima. Until April 16 she stood by for the Okinawa invasion, pumping 16-inch shells into Jap offenses. On April 27 she headed back to Puget Sound Navy Yard where she remained until July 3.

Steaming back to the Pacific, the *New Jersey's* last action in World War II was the bombardment of Wake Island on August 8. Later in August she again became Admiral Spruance's flagship. When the *New Jersey* anchored in Tokyo Bay on September 17, 1945 she held 11 battle stars and had had no crew members killed or wounded during the entire war. She is credited with 20 Jap planes, 1 cruiser and an oiler.

The *Arkansas*

Old Lady of the Fleet, the *Arkansas* (BB 33) for all her 33 years, proved herself a potent dreadnaught during five major engagements in both European and Pacific theaters. The oldest US battleship—commissioned in 1912—could look back on a distinguished career that stretched from carrying President Taft for his inspection of the Panama Canal, to the bombardment of Iwo Jima.

The old dowager came through both World Wars without a scratch or a single casualty, but she had many a narrow escape. In this respect, the ship was carrying on a tradition established by her distinguished predecessor, the CSS *Arkansas*. This Confederate ironclad dashed through Admiral Farragut's fleet on the Mississippi, driving a Federal battleship ashore, disabling a ram, burning one vessel, damaging several others, and escaping without injury.

Although the present *Arkansas* encountered Kamikaze attacks in the Pacific and bit into the teeth of a typhoon in the East China Sea, perhaps her closest brush with disaster came in the Atlantic, when she got her first taste of action in World War II.

Early in the morning of June 6, 1944 the *Arkansas,* under the command of Capt. Frederick G. Richards, steamed toward the Baie de la Seine area off the French coast. Her job was to support the Allied landings in Normandy, and she dropped anchor off Port en Bessin. Just before dawn she was sighted by a German coastal battery which took her under fire. When the Arky opened up her main batteries and 5-inch guns, the Nazis were soon silenced. After that the Arky settled down to her job: blowing up everything within sight on the French coast. Throughout the day's spirited firing, many a "target destroyed" signal was relayed from the *Arkansas'* bridge.

Just before midnight the crew heard the whine of four German Junkers 88s coming in low. Two of the raiders made straight for the Arky. A 250-pound bomb struck the water only 35 yards off the starboard beam, but the Nazi planes, caught in the fire of the *Arkansas'* antiaircraft units, crashed in flames.

Next day the *Arkansas* resumed shore bombardment and remained in uninterrupted duty off various parts of the French coast for 20 days. During this period a junior officer and two enlisted men operating a powerful transmitter in cooperation with other neighboring ships were able to "jam" between 30 to 40 radio-controlled bombs launched at Allied ships. The Arky concluded her assignment in this sector by participating in the bombardment of Cherbourg in support of Allied attacks which led to the capture of this port on the following day.

After a brief respite in Portland Harbor, England, the *Arkansas* got underway for the Mediterranean as part of a bombardment group under the command of Rear Adm. M. L. Deyo. Here her guns helped to cover the beaches of southern France with a curtain of fire while US Army troops moved inland.

Back home once more for an overhaul in the Boston Navy Yard, the *Arkansas* soon got orders to proceed through the Panama Canal to join the Pacific Fleet. She showed up in the forward area as the fleet assembled in preparation for the landing of Marines on Iwo Jima. On February 16, 1945 the Arky moved within seventeen hundred yards of Iwo's western beach and while transports loaded with Marine assault troops waited behind her, she worked over pin-point targets. Her main battery gave Mount Suribachi, the dead volcano at the island's southern tip, three weeks of hell. It was a banner day for the Arky when her lookouts reported the first American flag being raised on Suribachi's crest.

It was during her next assignment, her last engagement in World War II, that the *Arkansas* met the Japs' most dangerous weapon—the Kamikaze or "Divine Wind" planes. She stood up under the heaviest Jap air raid of the war, when hundreds of these Jap suicide planes were launched in a last, desperate, and futile attempt to break up the steel ring of naval forces closed in on Okinawa.

By the time she put in at Seattle, the Arky had steamed close to 150,000 miles and fired some 18,000 rounds of ammunition. Although the *Arkansas* had long since lost her 1913 title of "the world's most powerful battleship," her record in World War II was one that many a newer, faster ship might have been proud to hold.

The *Missouri*

The "Big Mo," beautiful, fast and bristling with guns, was a great ship to have on your side. She didn't get into the fight with the Japs until Iwo Jima in February, 1945, but after that she was on her way; she was in at the kill and afterwards served as coffin for the Japs as they signed the surrender papers.

The *Missouri* (BB 63) reported to Commander Fifth Fleet on January 26, 1945, then departed Ulithi anchorage on February 10, and as part of Task Force 58 participated in the first Fast Carrier Task Force strikes against Tokyo on February 16-17, 1945.

On the evening of February 19, off Iwo Jima, several groups of unidentified aircraft were discovered closing in on the formation. The ship opened fire and a Jap "Helen" burst into flames and crashed—a successful conclusion to the ship's first enemy action.

After strikes against Iwo Jima, Tokyo and Okinawa, the *Missouri* remained at Ulithi until March 13. As part of Task Force 58 the ship participated in the March 18-19 air attacks against Kyushu and Inland Sea area. On March 18 an enemy plane succeeded in dropping a bomb on the *Enterprise* off the *Missouri's* port bow.

On April 11, 1945, Task Force 58 was engaged in sweeps against southern Kyushu airfields. During the morning one enemy raid was broken up by the Combat Air Patrol but at 1:30 several groups of unidentified planes were reported approaching the formation. By 1:40 reports were that 13 enemy planes had been splashed and 3 others were approaching the formation at high speed.

At 2:30 the Mo opened fire on a low flying "Zeke" and although many hits were observed, the pilot succeeded in crashing the side of the *Missouri* immediately below the main deck at frame 169 on the starboard side. Parts of the plane were scattered along the starboard side of the ship and the pilot's body landed aboard, one wing of the plane was thrown forward and lodged near a 5-inch mount, starting a fire. The *Missouri* sustained only superficial damage, with some men injured.

On April 16 Task Force 58 was again conducting raids on Okinawa

Shima and the Japanese airfields on southern Kyushu. Shortly after 1:30 P. M. the ship opened fire on a low flying "Zeke" which crashed close aboard the *Intrepid*. Two minutes later fire was opened on a second which when hit attempted to crash the *Missouri*. The wing tip struck the ship's aircraft crane and the Jap crashed a short distance astern, exploding violently. Debris was thrown aboard but only minor material damage was sustained.

A third plane was fired upon while diving, burst into flames and crashed close aboard off the starboard bow. At 3:16 the *Missouri* fired upon two more planes. One crashed forward of the *Intrepid* and the other close aboard a destroyer. Two minutes later a third plane was fired on and disappeared over the horizon.

On May 6 the *Missouri* proceeded to Ulithi anchorage, and on May 17 Adm. William F. Halsey, Commander Third Fleet, hoisted his flag aboard the *Missouri* at Guam.

The Mighty Mo and destroyers *McNair* and *Wedderburn* formed Task Group 30.1 off Okinawa, arriving there May 26. She bombarded targets on Okinawa on May 28, then joined Task Force 38. In June reports of a typhoon were received and the force withdrew from the path of the typhoon. On June 8 the force returned to strike southern Kyushu airfields and on June 9-10, air strikes were made against the islands of Kaito Shoto.

The *Missouri* returned to slug the Japs on July 13, ending up with operations against Honshu, Hokkaido, Kyushu and Tokyo. On September 2 the formal document of the Japanese surrender was executed aboard the *Missouri* in Tokyo Bay.

CARRIERS

World War II was a naval struggle of many types of ships, and while it might be useless to attempt a final determination of which type was of most value in the victory, it is certain that aircraft carriers, because of their varied roles and great achievements, would be a factor in any such final determination.

The carrier is simply a floating airfield. It allows a mobile naval unit to carry with it air power for attack on enemy bases and fleets, and air power for defense against attack by planes from enemy bases and fleets. It was the extension of air power by means of sea-going units that enabled the United States to make effective its amphibious operations in the Pacific, and to finally drive the German U-boat fleet from the Atlantic.

The naval war in the Pacific, and to a large extent in the Atlantic, was a carrier war. It is true that carriers could not be used alone, because they were too vulnerable to surface and submarine attack, but neither could battleships be used alone, for the reason of their great susceptibility to air attack. When the hard-hitting task forces in the Pacific and the anti-submarine task groups in the Atlantic finally emerged from the trial-and-error of the conflict, it was the carrier that was the backbone of both those naval units. It was the carriers in the Pacific that delivered the heaviest offensive naval blows, that supported the numerous amphibious landings, and that softened up, by early aerial strikes, those enemy bastions which could not be otherwise reached. And it was the carriers in the Atlantic which dealt the knockout punch to the German submarine fleet.

When the war began the Navy had eight aircraft carriers, one an escort carrier. One hundred forty-nine carriers of all classes were built in United States shipyards during the war, 38 of which were turned over to the British. One hundred fourteen carriers saw service with the US fleet during the war, and 11 of those were sunk and 30 damaged.

The Navy had many classes of carriers, from the 33,000-ton 909-foot *Saratoga* to the 6,730-ton, 498-foot *Casablanca.* The *Midway* class, 45,000 tons and 986 feet long, did not get into action. The large operating flattops carried 80 bombing, torpedo and fighter planes, the lighter ships carried 45 planes, and the escort carriers had a compliment of 21. Speed ranged from 16 knots to 34, crews from 800 to 2,500, and main batteries from 1 5-inch gun to 12 5-inchers.

The US began the war with two ex-battle cruisers converted to carriers, the *Lexington* and *Saratoga;* three 20,000-ton carriers, *Yorktown, Enterprise* and *Hornet;* two 15,000-tonners, *Ranger* and *Wasp,* and one 8,000-ton escort carrier, the *Long Island,* a converted motorship. During 1942, 4 fleet oilers were fitted with flight decks and became escort carriers of the *Sangamon* class; in 1942 and 1943, 12 vessels originally destined as C3 cargo ships were completed as escort carriers of the *Bogue* class; 50 escort carriers of the *Casablanca* class were commissioned in 1943 and 1944; 9 *Independence* class light carriers went into service in 1943; 21 *Essex* class 27,000-ton carriers were commissioned between 1942 and the end of the war, and 10 *Commencement Bay* 12,000-ton escort carriers were commissioned after hostilities ceased, and others in various stages of construction at the war's end were cancelled.

The *Enterprise*

Admiral Halsey called her "The Galloping Ghost of the Oahu Coast." To her men and the Fleet she was the "Big E." The Japs' name for her has never been discovered, but "Sudden Death!" would have fitted her to perfection.   She is the only capital ship to receive both the Presidential Unit Citation and the Navy Unit Commendation, highest awards vessels can get.   What the Navy and the nation thought of the indestructible carrier was revealed by President Truman's approval of Navy Secretary Forrestal's suggestion that the famous carrier be preserved "As a visible symbol of American valor and tenacity in war and of our will to fight all enemies who assail us."

Said Secretary Forrestal's letter:

"This ship was the heart of the Fleet when the war was going badly for us.   The names of more than a score of battles are in her record of service and she has survived many attacks.   She made our first attack on Japanese territory at the Marshalls and Gilberts in February of 1942, she flew the flag of Admiral (then Rear Admiral) Spruance in the Battle of Midway, one of the decisive battles of history, and after the *Hornet* was lost in the battle of the Santa Cruz Islands the *Enterprise* was our only carrier in the Pacific.   Her crew proudly proclaimed that it was *Enterprise* against Japan and steamed into the battle of Guadalcanal.   Her squadrons shot down nearly a thousand of the enemy's planes and sank 74 of his ships.

"The men who have fought her love this ship.   It would grieve me to put my name to the documents which would consign her to be broken up for scrap."

The carrier *Enterprise* (CV 6) was the seventh US naval vessel to bear that name.   Commissioned on September 30, 1937, at Newport News, the *Enterprise* displaced almost twenty thousand tons with a length of 825 feet and breadth of 109 feet.

On November 28, 1941 she left Pearl Harbor, flagship of a task force carrying Marine Corps planes and equipment to Wake Island. The *Enterprise* launched the 12 Marine planes she was carrying about 175 miles north of Wake Island on December 2, 1941 and the force retired toward Pearl Harbor.

At dawn on December 7, some two hundred miles from the island of Oahu, the Big E sent some of her planes ahead to land.   Shortly afterwards one of these pilots was heard to explain over the radio, "Please don't shoot, this is an American plane."   Then another pilot radioed, "Pearl Harbor is being attacked by enemy planes," followed by message from Fleet headquarters, "Pearl Harbor is being attacked by enemy planes.   This is no drill."   The war was on.

The *Enterprise* immediately launched her aircraft to seek the Japanese, but the search was unsuccessful.   On December 21 the Big E headed a task force to rescue the Marines on Wake Island, but a message that the garrison had fallen stopped that attempt.

On February 1, 1942 the *Enterprise,* with protecting cruisers and destroyers, sent her planes buzzing down on Kwajalein, Roi, Wotje and Taroa Islands with ensuing heavy damage to enemy shipping and installations. On February 24 the *Enterprise* force struck at Wake and Marcus Islands. These were the first major retaliatory blows by the US Navy in World War II, and their success did much to shape the Navy's entire war strategy built around the first carrier task force.

In April, 1942 the Big E left Pearl Harbor to join the *Hornet* task force as planes from that ship carried out the now-famous bombing of Tokyo. On April 30 she raced south with the *Yorktown* and *Lexington* in an unsuccessful effort to join in the battle of the Coral Sea—the only major engagement that the *Enterprise* missed in the entire Pacific war!

On June 2 the Big E was part of the US fleet that held back the Japs in the decisive Battle of Midway, turning point in the tide of Japanese aggression. The *Yorktown* was lost in this battle, but planes from the Big E sent two carriers to the bottom, damaged four other ships and shot down nine enemy planes. She also exacted revenge for the loss of the *Yorktown* by attacking the Jap carrier responsible, leaving it a mass of flames.

Late in July the *Enterprise* moved in on the occupation of Guadalcanal, giving invaluable air support to the hard-hit invasion forces there. On August 23 it was apparent that the Japs had concentrated forces in the Rabaul area in an effort to force a showdown. That night a US force built around the *Saratoga* and *Enterprise* set out, meeting the enemy on the afternoon of the 24th. Seventy-five enemy bombers and torpedo planes singled out the Big E in one of the most furious air attacks in history. Damaged and blazing from three heavy bomb hits, the carrier pulled through, shooting down 44 enemy planes, sinking one enemy vessel and damaging another.

Back at Pearl Harbor for an overhaul on September 10, the Galloping Ghost moved out again to seek the Jap fleet. On October 26 she was with the *Hornet* and supporting vessels when report came that two large Jap aircraft carriers had been spotted about two hundred miles off Santa Cruz Island. As planes from the American ships flew to attack the enemy, they ran into heavy flights of Japanese. At the same time they encountered another Jap force of battleships, cruisers and destroyers. The *Enterprise's* planes flew through a terrific screen of enemy antiaircraft fire and Zero fighters to plant hits on a heavy cruiser and two carriers, and joined with planes from the *Hornet* in scoring hits on a battleship, two light cruisers and two heavy cruisers.

Meanwhile the *Hornet* and the *Enterprise* were having their own troubles. The *Hornet,* bombed and torpedoed repeatedly, lay dead in the water. The *Enterprise,* hard hit by three bombs, was able to continue the battle without interruption. The *Enterprise's* score for this action was 63 planes destroyed and three ships damaged.

After repairs at Noumea the Big E headed back for Guadalcanal in time for the battle of November 15. The Big E's planes consistently attacked Jap combat ships and transports while the carrier herself completely escaped enemy attention.

After a month at Espíritu Santo the Big E got underway again to Guadalcanal late in January, 1943 to offer cover to the damaged cruiser *Chicago.* At dusk on January 30 the *Chicago,* then being towed by the cruiser *Louisville,* was attacked by 12 enemy torpedo planes. Fighters from the *Enterprise* shot down 11 but the 12th swooped in to sink the damaged cruiser with an aerial tin fish.

On May 27, 1943 the *Enterprise* received a Presidential Unit Citation which said:

"For consistently outstanding performance and distinguished achievement during repeated action against enemy Japanese forces in the Pacific war area, December 7, 1941 to November 15, 1942. Participating in nearly every major carrier engagement in the first year of the war, the *Enterprise* and her air group, exclusive of far-flung destruction of hostile shore installations throughout the battle area, did sink or damage on her own a total of 25 Japanese vessels and shot down a total of 185 Japanese aircraft. Her aggressive spirit and superb combat efficiency are fitting tribute to the officers and men who so gallantly established her as an ahead bulwark in defense of the American nation."

(The *Enterprise* was the first aircraft carrier to win the Presidential Unit Citation.)

In July, 1943 the battered carrier arrived at Puget Sound Navy Yard for an overhaul, leaving there on October 31 to join Task Force 50 in raids on the Gilbert Islands late in November. During this campaign planes from the *Enterprise* developed the art of night combat fighting by radar under the leadership of Com. Edward H. (Butch) O'Hare.

On December 4, 1943 the Galloping Ghost participated in the Kwajalein raid, coming back on January 29, 1944 to cover the raids on this atoll in the Marshalls.

On February 17 she was with Task Force 58 when it raided the Jap fortress of Truk, where her planes sent ten ships to the bottom and damaged 28 more, destroying 75 planes. On the way back to base her planes took a crack at Jaluit, damaging another enemy ship. In March the Big E's marauding eagles soared in to strike Palau, Yap and Woleai, sinking three more ships and damaging twenty while destroying another 29 enemy planes. One week later she sortied along the coast of New Guinea to support the capture of the Hollandia area late in April. She wound up the month by again raiding Truk, damaging five more Jap ships and destroying 23 planes.

On June 11 the Big E launched her planes against Saipan and for the next month the carrier was in on the operations leading to the capture of this enemy base.

The Jap fleet, which had stayed well away from our advancing forces, decided to strike at our invasion of the Marianas. Admiral Spruance sent a fast carrier and battleship group west to meet this threat and on June 19 the battle of the Philippine Sea began. The incredible result of this action saw 402 enemy planes destroyed against 17 American planes lost. The enemy retreated in confusion and it was the *Enterprise* search planes that located the Jap fleet just when it seemed as if it might escape. In the ensuing air attacks the Japs lost two carriers, two destroyers, and one tanker, while three carriers, one battleship, three cruisers, one destroyer and three tankers were badly damaged. After this debacle for the enemy the Big E returned to Pearl Harbor.

On August 28 to October 24 the carrier was in on strikes on the Volcano and Bonin Islands; Yap and Ulithi, Okinawa, Formosa and Luzon. During the occupation of Leyte the Jap fleet made another attempt to strike back at US sea power and another battle of the Philippine Sea developed, later designated as the battle for Leyte Gulf. These engagements involved the battle for Surigao Strait, the battle off Samar, and the battle off Cape Engaño. The *Enterprise* had the distinction of being the only carrier in action against all three Jap fleets thrown into this operation.

On the first morning *Enterprise* planes damaged two battleships and a heavy cruiser in the Sulu Sea. In the afternoon her bombers blasted the battleship *Musashi,* and the next day the Big E took part in an all-day battle against the Jap carrier force, assisting in the sinking of 4 enemy carriers, 2 cruisers, and several destroyers, and damaging 2 more battleships.

From November 5, 1944 to the end of the war the Big E roamed the waters off the Japs' homelands as her planes struck at Yap, Luzon, French Indo-China, Hong Kong, Canton, Formosa, Okinawa, Kyushu, Amami Gunto, Daito Gunto, and Shikoku.

In December, 1944 she took aboard Night Air Group 90, first unit of this type aboard a large carrier. On March 19 five planes from this group flew at night over the Inland Sea, damaging a carrier, a battleship, a destroyer, and three merchant vessels, shooting down a Jap flying boat and scoring bomb hits on an aircraft factory.

Meanwhile the Jap Kamikaze pilots were making life increasingly more difficult for the crew of the Big E. Late in March one dive bomber dropped a bomb on her forward elevator. AMM Karl J. Smith described the attack:

"All at once this Jap bomber came out of the clouds and made his run over the ship. He dropped a single bomb and started strafing at the same time.

"When I saw the bomb coming down I took off . . . down the flight deck, up over a cat-walk and down a ladder. That bomb hit about five feet from where I had been standing and rolled along the same path that I had taken along the flight deck. I couldn't have been more surprised or scared if it had followed me down the ladder, too.

"The only reason that I am able to tell the story is because that bomb was a dud. That Jap was so low over our deck that the bomb was still falling in a flat position when it hit. It never did get the detonating head pointing down."

When the dud bomb came to rest it was quickly thrown overboard by SFs Pedro Sandoval and Robert G. Terreberry, and Sea. James A. Vest.

Two days later off Kyushu the Big E wasn't quite so lucky when four Kamikaze pilots singled her out. All were shot down, but three jarred the ship badly with near misses.

One of the near misses was described by Cox. Leslie P. Nancolas who was awarded the Purple Heart for injuries received in this action. Nancolas was serving in an antiaircraft battery and said, "That plane looked so low when it passed over us that I think I could have reached up and touched it. At the last second the pilot flipped the plane over on its back. That twist caused it to plunge into the sea instead of onto the flight deck.

"When she hit the sea," Nancolas recalled, "the explosion was so terrific that we were all knocked off our feet. Ammunition was scattered all over our gun position. The whole place was a mess but not nearly as bad as it would have been if she had hit the flight deck."

An antiaircraft shell from another US ship exploded over the *Enterprise* during this action, causing serious fires, and it was necessary for the carrier to retire to Ulithi for repairs.

Back in action on April 11 the Big E was attacked by four suicide planes. One hit, leaving his engine imbedded in the side of the ship, and the other three crashed close aboard. The *Enterprise* was again forced to retire.

Despite this damaging blow the Big E was in combat three weeks later, steaming to within sixty miles of Kyushu on May 12 as flagship of Task Force 58. The enemy attacked in force on May 14 sending in thirty raids. *Enterprise* fighter planes knocked down four of the attackers but a single Zeke got through. Just as it appeared certain that the Kamikaze would overshoot, the pilot flipped the Zeke over on its back and dived it straight into the forward part of the flight deck. His bomb exploded under the forward elevator, throwing it four hundred feet in the air and killing 14 men and wounding 34. Fires broke out immediately but damage control parties brought the flames under control within 17 minutes and extinguished them in 30 minutes.

TM Charles M. Fronzuto, Jr., offered his own idea on how the Jap pilot selected his target.

"The plane was headed right for us," said Fronzuto, who was at his battle station on the ship's island structure, "then it suddenly changed its course and hit the ship near the forward elevator, which was knocked a thousand feet into the air. The Jap pilot must have changed his course when he saw the look of terror on my face."

AO Roger M. Van Frank started running as he saw the Jap plane coming directly towards him on the flight deck.

"The explosion tossed me into the air against the cat-walk and then the deck buckled and I landed on top of some other men," he related. "By that time the gunners were fighting their way out of the flaming antiaircraft battery and they used us for carpets. That suicide plane went through the deck not twenty feet behind me and it darn near scared me to death. How I missed getting killed I'll never know."

Again despite terrific damage the Big E stayed in line as the force underwent 21 more raids. Then on May 16 she withdrew from action for the last time, proceeding to Bremerton via Pearl Harbor for repairs that held her there until the end of the war.

The final record of the *Enterprise* in the Pacific war was 911 Japanese planes shot down by the ship's guns and planes, 74 enemy ships sunk by her pilots, another 192 ships damaged or probably sunk, and vast damage to enemy shore installations. The enemy damaged the ship 16 times with hits and near misses, and claimed her sunk on six different occasions. Actually the ship had never been inoperative. While accumulating 18 of a possible 22 combat stars for carriers in the Pacific area, the *Enterprise* had steamed more than 275,000 miles in pursuit of the foe and had recorded some 45,000 plane landings.

On July 1, 1946 she was awarded the Navy Unit Commendation:

For outstanding heroism in action against enemy Japanese forces in the air, ashore and afloat in the Pacific War Area from November 19, 1943 to May 14, 1945. Operating continuously in the most forward areas the USS *Enterprise* and her air groups struck crushing blows toward annihilating Japanese fighting power; they provided air cover for our amphibious forces, they fiercely countered the enemy's aerial attacks and destroyed his planes; and they inflicted terrific losses on the Japanese in Fleet and merchant marine units sunk or damaged. Daring and dependable in combat the *Enterprise* with her gallant officers and men rendered loyal service in achieving the ultimate defeat of the Japanese Empire.

The *Saratoga*

There was wailing and gnashing of teeth when the Navy announced that the "Sara," its oldest aircraft carrier (CV-3) would be sacrificed on the altar of the atomic age in the Bikini Atoll test "Operation Crossroads." The bitter lament came from the thousands upon thousands of Navy men who had sailed on her since she was first commissioned back in 1927 at Camden, New Jersey.

The Sara can remember both World Wars, for she was being born in 1917. Designed as a battle cruiser, work on her was delayed when war came. Half completed in 1922, she was converted into an aircraft carrier, along with her sister ship *Lexington.*

The Sara had been 15 years in the fleet when Pearl Harbor came, but she stood up to the enemy as vigorously and belligerently as any new ship off the ways. She was in the thick of the fighting almost to the very end, ran with the Fast Carrier Task Forces like no "old lady" ever should, roamed more of the Pacific against the enemy than any of our other carriers, and survived damage three times to fight again. Seven times the Japs announced the sinking of the *Saratoga.*

The Sara was at San Diego on December 7, 1941. The next day she sailed for Pearl with a full load of planes, breaking her speed record on the run. For several weeks she scurried from California to Hawaii as a plane ferry to bolster the island garrisons, but on January 11, 1942, 500 miles southwest of Pearl, she took a torpedo in the port side. Three firerooms flooded, but despite the damage the Sara increased speed to escape and return to Puget Sound for repairs.

By May the *Saratoga* was back in service. Her first job was to train more than two hundred new pilots for carrier duty, then ferry these pilots and a large number of new aircraft to the battle zone. Arriving at Pearl just as the Battle of Midway began, she refueled hastily and with her decks swarming with pilots and planes, shoved off for Midway, hoping to get in her first licks of revenge for her earlier torpedoing. But she just missed it.

When our first big Pacific land offensive came at Guadalcanal in August, the *Saratoga* was there under Capt. Dewitt C. Ramsey to launch her fighters, dive bombers and torpedo planes to provide air bombardment and cover for the Marines. Here for the first time *Saratoga* pilots and crewmen were able to strike back at the enemy, as they demolished shore positions and strafed Jap personnel. After the Marines were ashore the Sara remained to guard supply lines and supply air cover for the small carriers.

On August 24 the *Saratoga* steamed into the Battle of the Eastern Solomons, until then an engagement second only to Midway in the size of the forces involved. Air Group 3, flying from the Sara, found the Japanese carrier *Ryujo* and sank it. On other sorties her airmen sank a destroyer and crippled two cruisers, while others of her fighters shot many Jap planes down in flames.

On August 31 she took her second tin fish when she was hit by a sub off the Solomon Islands, the torpedo exploding on the starboard side and flooding the compartments. Power failed and the *Saratoga* was taken in tow until temporary repairs could be made. Then she went back to Pearl again for overhaul. Planes from her air group continued to operate from Guadalcanal to defend the small Marine beachhead.

She returned to the combat zones in late 1942 with a new skipper, Capt. C. F. Bogan, and until early 1943 was the only American carrier left in the South Pacific to fight off the enemy naval air. On November 1, 1943, as part of a task force, with Capt. Henry M. Mullinix in command, the *Saratoga* steamed north to send her air group against Buka; later she provided air support for the landings on Bougainville.

In the wake of this successful action the Sara raced northeast toward Rabaul where as part of a task force she delivered a smashing blow on a large concentration of Japanese warships and transports in Simpson Harbor—a force assembled to break up the Bougainville invasion. Having caught the enemy napping, the *Saratoga's* aircraft destroyed 20 planes, probably destroyed 24 more, and severely damaged five heavy and two light cruisers. Several destroyers were strafed, two were damaged by torpedoes and one cargo ship was sunk. As a result of this raid, the Jap threat to US supply lines was removed, the Navy said.

Six days later the Sara's task group joined another one and both wheeled back for a second attack on Simpson Harbor. With her Hellcats providing a fighter umbrella, her dive bombers and torpedo planes struck savagely against more Jap ships trying to form. *Saratoga* bombers scored three hits on one destroyer, two on another and one on a cruiser. One sloop was strafed and one Zero shot down.

When the action was over, 76 Jap planes had been downed by the combined forces. Then the *Saratoga* and her forces cruised to the approaches to Truk, hoping to lure the Jap fleet into an engagement, but the enemy refused to come out. Captain Mullinix went to the *Liscome Bay,* new escort carrier, and Capt. John H. Cassady took over.

The Sara set a record on November 19 with nine strikes at the Gilberts to neutralize the Japanese forces there. From the 23d to the 27th she supported the Marine landings on Tarawa. When the Tarawa airfield was secure she sent her planes ashore to help defend the island and set sail for Pearl where she picked up survivors of the *Liscome Bay* and carried them to the States. Captain Mullinix was among those missing in action.

But there wasn't much rest for the Sara. By January, 1944 she was back in the Marshalls, striking at Wotje, Maloelap and Tarawa in 453 sorties in the first three days of that invasion. Jap airfields, hangars, radio stations and fuel dumps were turned into rubble in that great pounding. She then sailed to the westward to give direct support to the Eniwetok landings, setting another record of 25 strikes in 16 days. In March the *Saratoga* embarked on a 27-day cruise covering 9,000 miles, to join the British Far Eastern Fleet in the Indian Ocean. There, in a task force under tactical command of Admiral Sir James Somerville of the Royal Navy, she joined HMS *Illustrious* in two heavy raids on the Jap bases at Soerabaja and Sebang in the Netherlands East Indies, destroying naval and shore installations and valuable oil supplies.

Early in 1945 the giant Sara, still the largest carrier in the fleet despite the *Essex*-class dreadnaughts, returned to battle. Under the command now of Capt. L. A. Moebus, she was one of more than a dozen flattops in Vice Admiral Mitscher's Task Force 58 which blasted the Tokyo area. Admiral Mitscher, then a lieutenant commander, had made the first flight from the *Saratoga's* deck on January 11, 1928. Fighting their way through storm and overcast, planes from the Sara swept clean the airfields at Mammamatoo and Mikatagahera, then turned south for the big show at Iwo Jima.

Some of her luck ran out at Iwo, where she was smashed and battered by seven direct hits two days after the landings, which the *Saratoga* had been supporting. Her first moment of pain came at 5:00 P. M. on February 21 as she was cruising northeast of Iwo with a fast carrier task group. As she was into the wind launching planes, ten Jap bombers bent on suicide missions closed in. Antiaircraft fire and the *Saratoga's* pilots shot down four of the attackers, but four others crashed on her decks, spreading death and destruction. Another Jap, shot down alongside, caromed off the water and exploded, tearing a large hole in her side. A bomb from one of the other planes blew another hole in the side below the waterline, rupturing fuel lines, as the ship took a six-degree list.

Fires broke out and burning planes and fuel scattered over great areas. The forward part of the flight deck was in shreds. One Kamikaze had crashed through the side into the hangar deck, where he exploded. Cranes, catapults and guns were smashed, and the wreckage fell into the gun galleries, starting more fires. The hangar deck could not be entered, so heroic bluejackets went over the side to fight the flames. With the ship underway the firefighters finally managed to bring the blaze under control. Lt. Archie M. Buckley, catapult officer, was killed when he remained at his post to save his men and the pilots of two aircraft.

AerM Jack Brady left his bunk in the sick bay to go to the aid of his wounded mates as a medical corpsman.

"It was just like a nightmare," Brady said. "Men were brought in burned black from head to foot. Others had their arms and legs torn off. We worked straight through until dawn the next day without a chance to catch our breath. It took several days more to clear out all the dead."

The trouble wasn't over. An hour and a half after the first attack, with darkness setting in, more Jap planes appeared. A bomb from one of them hit the crippled Sara and a few minutes later the suicide plane itself crashed on the port side. *Saratoga* pilots were in the air, circling the ship, with gas running low. Despite more severe damage from the second attack, the old lady of the fleet was able to take them aboard. Her casualties from the attacks were 123 killed and 192 wounded.

Photographs of her damage were flown to the Puget Sound Navy Yard, and when the *Saratoga* arrived all plans and equipment for her repair were ready. She was refitted for sea in record time, less than two months, despite the fact she was one of the most extensively damaged ships ever to enter the yard.

"She received more varied types of damage all at once than any ship we've seen since Pearl Harbor," it was said at the repair yard.

Overshadowed in size by the super-carriers *Midway, Franklin D. Roosevelt,* and *Tarawa,* the Sara will never be overshadowed in the memory of those thousands of crewmen and pilots who sailed her and fought her through more than eighty thousand plane landings.

The *Yorktown*

At Newport News, Virginia, in April, 1936, Mrs. Franklin D. Roosevelt smashed the traditional bottle of champagne over the prow of a new aircraft carrier as it slid into the James River. It was the *Yorktown* (CV 5). Seven years later at Newport News Mrs. Roosevelt again sponsored a carrier named *Yorktown* (CV 10), built to replace the one sunk by the Japs at Midway in 1942.

The first *Yorktown* fought the war in the Pacific in the "bow and arrow" days when the United States Fleet was just a thin line of ships strung from Pearl Harbor to Australia. Before she succumbed she brought to the attention of the Japanese Imperial Navy the realization of what kind of war it had started. And when the second *Yorktown* got into action she persistently proved to the Japs they couldn't finish that kind of war.

The earlier *Yorktown* was a sister ship of the *Enterprise*, 20,000 tons and 761 feet long, carrying a 75-plane air group. She was in the Atlantic when Pearl Harbor was attacked, but shifted quickly to the Pacific, where her first mission was to spearhead, with the *Enterprise,* the strikes at the Gilbert and Marshall islands in February 1942. At the Marshalls the *Yorktown* pilots took off in soupy weather, flew to their targets by instruments, and had to descend to 1000 feet to drop bombs. Despite the bad visibility they sunk several small ships, plastered shore installations, and shot down a four-engine bomber. At Makin they damaged a seaplane tender and destroyed two four-engine bombers sitting on the water.

Salamaua and Lae in New Guinea were next on March 10. Enemy troops had landed at those points three days earlier, and the *Yorktown* and *Lexington* were ordered to break up their land and sea concentrations. Fliers from the two carriers were eminently successful, and the score was 1 heavy cruiser sunk, 4 cruisers damaged, 1 destroyer damaged, 2 transports sunk, and 3 vessels burned and beached. On May 4 the *Yorktown* hit Tulagi harbor where the Japanese were gathering for the occupation of the Solomons. Seventeen small vessels were sunk in three attacks, and cruisers, destroyers and transports were damaged. The *Yorktown* lost three fighter planes.

The Battle of the Coral Sea was developing, in which the *Lexington* was lost and the *Yorktown* damaged. Garbled information from a *Yorktown* scout plane that a carrier had been sighted caused the attack groups to be launched. The Jap force that had been spotted was a cruiser and destroyer group, but after the *Yorktown* planes were airborne an Army pilot picked up the Jap carrier force, and the *Yorktown* and the *Lexington* fliers headed for the enemy flattop, the *Shoso,* which was sent to the bottom in five minutes. *Yorktown* torpedo planes hit and sank a cruiser in the same action. Next day, May 8, a carrier and cruiser force was attacked by the *Yorktown,* and one of the carriers severely damaged. One *Yorktown* pilot who was unable to return to the ship because his fuel was gone, radioed: "Good-bye boys. Remember I got a hit on that flattop." Jap planes counterattacked and while the battle was raging the *Yorktown's* radar antenna was knocked out. A daring radio electrician climbed the mast to repair it. A few minutes later the *Yorktown* was hit by an enemy bomb which lifted her out of the water and opened her seams. When the carrier put into Pearl for repairs it was completing a 101-day battle cruise.

The Battle of Midway, June 4-5-6, was the last for the *Yorktown,* which was the carrier unit of Task Force 17. The *Hornet* and *Enterprise* were in Task Force 16. The two forces joined up on the 3d, and the enemy carriers were sighted on June 4. Attacking *Hornet* torpedo planes were shot down by Jap fighters, and then the *Yorktown* and *Enterprise* fliers went in, also suffering heavy losses but hitting the carriers. Bombers from the *Yorktown* hit a third carrier, a cruiser and a battleship, but 36 Jap carrier planes attacked the *Yorktown* and scored three bomb hits. *Yorktown* planes still in the air had to land on the *Enterprise* or in the water. Temporary repairs were made and the *Yorktown* prepared to launch aircraft when a wave of enemy torpedo planes came over and hurled two aerial tin fish into the damaged carrier. The *Yorktown* was taken in tow and the destroyer *Hammann* went alongside to put on board a salvage party. A lurking Japanese submarine fired two torpedoes at the *Yorktown* and one at the destroyer, and both vessels went down. But the enemy fleet was in retirement, licking its wounds over the sinking of the carriers *Kaga, Akagi,* and *Doryu,* in which the *Yorktown* had played a major part.

The second *Yorktown* was an *Essex*-class carrier, famed as "The Fighting Lady." That famous documentary war film of naval aviation used the *Yorktown* as its "heroine," a role which needed no Hollywood embellishment for the ship. Her air groups flew more than 8,000 sorties over enemy targets, shot down 311 Jap planes, sunk an estimated 221,000 tons of shipping.

The *Yorktown* began under Captain "Jocko" Clark with a strike at Marcus in August, 1943, pounding that small island with 55 tons of bombs in a raid in which eighty per cent of shore installations was destroyed. A month later at Wake she struck again, raising the bomb total to 89 tons. Her fighter pilots shot down 17 Japs and destroyed 16 on the ground. Eight more were damaged. In the invasion of the

Gilberts in November her planes supported the landings with bombing and strafing, and also neutralized enemy bases in the Marshalls.

Next for The Fighting Lady was Kwajalein, where her fighters splashed five of the enemy and shot up 44 planes on the ground. Four ships were sunk by bombing and strafing, 18 set afire and 8 damaged. Eleven direct hits and 22 near misses were scored on 10 Jap cargo vessels. During this action four Jap torpedo planes came racing in on the *Yorktown's* port side just off the water. All were shot down by the ship's antiaircraft gunners, the fourth being splashed just as it was about to hit the bridge.

Capt. R. E. Jennings relieved Captain Clark on February 10, and then the *Yorktown* moved against Truk on February 16 and 17, followed by assignment to Task Force 58 in operations against Saipan and Tinian late in the month. After a short rest and some gunnery practice, the big carrier smashed at the Japs on Palau and Woleai on March 30, causing heavy damage to shore installations. Fighting for the *Yorktown* then shifted to New Guinea, where she supported Army landings in the Hollandia area. Her pilots flew 73 sorties on D-day, April 21, sinking 12 barges and 4 landing craft in addition to strafing enemy troops. Back to Truk The Fighting Lady sailed, showing up there on April 29 for further strikes against the beleaguered Nipponese.

Orders called for regrouping at the Marshalls and Pearl Harbor, and it was June 11 before the *Yorktown* was again in the fray, this time supporting the landings on Saipan. In the action on June 20 the *Yorktown's* strike group flew three hundred miles to attack an enemy fleet composed of 2 heavy cruisers, 3 battleships, 3 carriers, 18 destroyers and several oilers, and tankers cruising in four sections. *Yorktown* planes hit the largest carrier with three 1000-pound bombs and six 250-pound bombs, dropped four 500-pounders on the other two carriers, and smashed a cruiser. The Jap fleet threw up heavy AA fire and enemy fighter pilots were much in evidence. Eighteen *Yorktown* planes were lost, but only seven men failed to return.

From June 30 until July 21 the *Yorktown* was a unit in the support group at the occupation of the Marianas, and from there she steamed to the Carolines for strikes against Yap and Ulithi. In August she was ordered to the States for overhaul, putting in at Puget Sound on the 17th, but was back at Pearl Harbor on October 18 with Capt. T. S. Combs in command, standing out on the 24th for Ulithi.

The war had moved up to the Philippines, and on November 11 the *Yorktown's* planes struck at shipping in Manila Bay, then ran fighter sweeps over Southern Luzon and Mindoro Strait. The smashes in the Philippines continued until mid-December. The turn of the year found

The Fighting Lady launching air attacks against the harassed enemy at Formosa, French Indo-China, and Nansei Shoto. In February she hurled her planes at the Bonins and at Japanese air strength in the Tokyo Bay area, and in March made strikes on Kyushu, Shikoku and Honshu. On the 18th Jap bombers attacked the *Yorktown,* scoring a hit on the signal bridge which killed 3 men and wounded 18. As April began the carrier was furnishing air support for the landings on Okinawa, and on the 7th, when an enemy fleet was discovered southwest of Kyushu, *Yorktown* bomber and torpedo planes sank a battleship and light cruiser, and seriously damaged two destroyers. The battleship was hit with five tin fish, five 500-pound bombs, and eight 1000-pounders, causing her to break in two.

A new skipper took over on April 23, when Capt. W. F. Boone relieved Captain Combs, and the *Yorktown* operated in the Okinawa area until the end of May. In June she was at Leyte for upkeep, and from early July until the end of the war she ranged the coast of Japan from Kyushu to Hokkaido, striking constantly at shipping and shore targets.

On September 16, 1945, The Fighting Lady wound up her combat career as part of the triumphant fleet which steamed into Tokyo Bay for the surrender of Japan.

The *Hornet*

The offensive sting of the United States Navy has seldom been delivered more sharply than by the different eight warships named USS *Hornet* in the history of our sea power. In World War II, planes from two aircraft carriers named *Hornet* buzzed angrily and destructively about the ears of the Japs.

Three weeks after Pearl Harbor the seventh *Hornet* (CV-8), just commissioned in October, 1941 sailed from Norfolk on her shakedown cruise. But there were great ideas brewing and to the mystification of the *Hornet's* green crew, her shakedown was cut short. Returning hastily to Norfolk, the spanking new flattop took aboard two Army B-25s. Scuttlebutt hung heavy in the air. What were Army medium bombers doing on the flight deck of a Navy carrier? The *Hornet* shoved off again, as men watched incredulously, and the B-25s were launched, flying back to base. The long weeks of training given the Army pilots under General Jimmy Doolittle and Lt. Comdr. Henry L. Miller had paid off.

But now that Army bombers could take off from a Navy carrier, how was that fact to be applied to war? Again the rumors flew as the *Hornet* went through the Panama Canal, stopped to pick up 16 B-25s, and stood into the Pacific. Not until the *Hornet's* skipper, Capt. Marc Mitscher, opened his sealed orders did he know that it was "Destination Tokyo" in one of the most daring operations of this or any other war.

The *Hornet's* task force, with the carrier *Enterprise* and cruisers *Northampton, Salt Lake City, Vincennes,* and *Nashville;* destroyers *Balch, Benham, Ellet, Fanning, Grayson, Gwin, Meredith,* and *Monssen,* and the oilers *Cimarron* and *Sabine,* with Vice Admiral William Halsey in charge, steamed boldly through enemy waters. The plan was to approach within four hundred miles of Japan and get the planes off Sunday night, April 19, so that they would be over Tokyo at dawn, giving the *Hornet* a cloak of darkness in which to escape. But on the morning of the 18th, as the group entered a storm area, a Japanese gunboat was sighted. Guns spat and the *Enterprise's* planes roared into action. The gunboat went down. Had the Japs been warned?

Hasty conferences resulted in a decision to launch the bombers at once, and the *Hornet* turned into the teeth of a raging gale, eight hundred miles from Japan. The big flattop pitched and tossed. While the entire crew held its breath, General Doolittle got away first, and then the other 15 raiders made it, too. The *Hornet* swung and sped away, and next day the Japs and the world knew that America had begun to carry the war to the enemy. (President Roosevelt said that the planes had come from "Shangri-La," and it was nine months before the word was passed that the *Hornet* was the airfield for the first US raid on Tokyo.)

The cruise of the *Hornet* continued as she swept the waters searching for Japanese units. She was not to find them, however, and late in May she put into Pearl to take on fuel and provisions. Almost immediately she was ordered west for the Battle of Midway. The *Hornet's* planes made five separate attacks during this decisive victory, scoring more than 14 direct hits and 2 near misses on Japanese warships, heavily strafing a destroyer, and shooting down 3 Zeros and 2 dive bombers. In addition, the *Hornet* took aboard the famous Fighting Squadron 3 when the carrier *Yorktown* was put out of action.

The *Hornet's* air group—squadrons Scouting 8, Torpedo 8, Bombing 8, and Fighting 8—first roared into action at Midway on the morning of June 4, when, searching for a Jap force of four carriers 150 miles away, Torpedo Squadron 8 became separated from its escorting fighters and scout bombers and was attacked by an overwhelming flight of Zeros. Despite hopeless odds, the *Hornet's* planes bored in, but there were just too many Zeros, and every plane of Torpedo 8 was shot down with only one man, Ens. G. H. Gay, surviving.

The *Hornet's* second attack was launched at 6:00 P. M. the same day when a large force of Dauntless dive bombers from Scouting 8 scored three direct hits on a Jap battleship, two more on a heavy cruiser. The third assault came the next day when another group of dive bombers, searching for Jap carriers, blasted a light cruiser. Early on June 6 the *Hornet* sent off its heaviest charge, a wave of dive bombers and fighters. The bombers smashed an enemy group of a battleship, a heavy cruiser and three destroyers. Lt. Comdr. William J. (Gus) Widhelm, leader of Scouting 8, scored two 1000-pound bomb hits on the battleship and won the Navy Cross in this action. Another pilot hit the same ship with a 500-pound bomb. The cruiser was set afire by two 1000-pound hits, a destroyer crippled with a 500-pounder. Four of the *Hornet's* fighters strafed another destroyer with machine guns, causing heavy loss of Jap life. The fifth *Hornet* attack was made that same afternoon by dive bombers which found a Jap force of two cruisers and two destroyers more than 100 miles away. The bombers swooped in, hitting one of the cruisers six times and leaving it completely gutted with the crew abandoning ship. Only one destroyer escaped damaged as the *Hornet's* stings helped turn the tide of war at Midway.

The *Hornet's* next big battle was Santa Cruz, thousands of miles south of Midway, east of the Solomons. But between Midway and Santa Cruz, the *Hornet* struck at the Buin-Faisi area, scoring hits on a tanker, a light cruiser and two cargo ships. Just to keep things moving she shot down several planes, bombed the Kahili airfield, and raided Rekata Bay, downing 12 seaplanes, and burning transports, landing barges, fuel dumps and antiaircraft installations. On September 6 the big carrier almost met her end when a torpedo from a submarine flashed toward her hull. Only an inspired move by the pilot of an Avenger, who managed to hit the torpedo with a depth charge, saved her.

The climax of the *Hornet's* career came on October 26, 1942 in the Battle of Santa Cruz. The enemy force gathered for this action was one of the greatest sea concentrations in history. The Japs had assembled 2 cruisers, 7 destroyers and 2 carriers in one group with 2 battleships, 2 cruisers, 7 destroyers and 2 carriers in another.

Scouting Eight of the *Hornet* found the Jap ships of both forces but by-passed the battleships and cruisers to go after the carriers. Zeros attacked for thirty minutes, but Scouting Eight pressed relentlessly towards the enemy flattops. Leader Widhelm was shot down, but the gunners of his squadron sent 15 Zeros along with him. Then the rest of Scouting Eight closed in on a big Jap carrier. From a rubber life raft Widhelm and his rear gunner, ARM George D. Stokely, saw their mates smash the carrier with seven 1000-pound bombs, setting it aflame and leaving it dead in the water. (Widhelm and Stokely were rescued three days later.)

Meanwhile the *Hornet* had fallen under Japanese fire and was fighting desperately. Attack after attack of Jap bombers and torpedo planes hurtled against the carrier, fire after fire breaking out on her hangar and flight decks. Finally her firefighting apparatus was destroyed and the next raging inferno had to be extinguished with a bucket brigade! She was then taken in tow but the Japs, determined to finish this ship with the bulldog will, sent over more bombers and torpedo planes.

Finally, after ten hours of attack the order to sink the *Hornet* was given to prevent her from falling into enemy hands. With all but 129 of her 2,900 men rescued, destroyers sent shells and torpedoes into her sides, and as dusk fell over the South Pacific that night of October 26, the seventh USS *Hornet* slipped beneath the surface.

The eighth *Hornet* (CV-12) was an even greater scourge to the enemy than its predecessor. Commissioned on November 29, 1943, in 14 months of action she cut a twisting, 150,000-mile path of destruction through the Pacific, leaving 1,270,000 tons of enemy shipping sunk or damaged and 1,410 ruined enemy planes in her wake. And the Japs never touched her.

Here are some of the things this *Hornet* did: Struck the first blow for the liberation of the Philippines; hit Tokyo in the first full-scale carrier attack; first hit the *Yamamoto,* 45,000-ton pride of the Jap fleet, now on the bottom of the China Sea; destroyed 668 planes on the ground; sank a carrier, a cruiser, ten destroyers, and 42 cargo ships; spent a total of 52 days under air attack without being hit by a single bullet.

Under Capt. Miles R. Browning the *Hornet* joined Task Force 58 in March, 1944 as the flagship of Adm. J. J. (Jocko) Clark. Shortly afterwards she supported landings at Hollandia, and made stabs at Truk, Satawan and Ponape. Late in May Capt. William D. Sample took command and the *Hornet* went into the Marianas operation, a two-month deal which took the ship through the Guam invasion, the Battle of the Philippine Sea, and strikes at the Bonins, Eniwetok, the Volcanos, Yap and Ulithi. During this time the *Hornet's* planes flew more than three thousand sorties, shooting down 233 planes. On June 24, the second visit to the Bonins, a record 67 planes were knocked out of the sky. When the task force was attacked by more than 500 planes during a single day of the Battle of the Philippine Sea, the *Hornet's* planes accounted for 52 of them. And during the battle *Hornet* fliers bagged the biggest prize, a *Shokaku*-class carrier sunk.

In September, with Capt. Austin K. Doyle as skipper, the *Hornet* steamed up the coast of Luzon and launched the first attack on enemy shipping, installations and airfields in and around Manila Bay, after having struck at Davao, Cebu, Mindanao and Negros. In October the *Hornet* slammed in at Okinawa, sinking three ships, damaging ten others, and destroying 27 planes. Then she appeared off Formosa where she experienced the heaviest air attacks of her career.

On October 20, when US troops landed in Leyte Gulf, the *Hornet* was there in support. Four days later came the great sea battle of Leyte Gulf when the *Hornet* and other fleet units beat off the Japs in one of the greatest naval fights of all time. The *Hornet's* plan-of-the-day for October 26, last day of the Battle for Leyte Gulf, read:

"Today will be a Field Day! Air department dust off all overheads, removing any snoopers which may be adrift and sweep out all corners of the Philippines, sending to incinerator or throwing over the side (first punching hole in bottom) any Nip cans, APs or AKs still on topside. Gunnery Department assist as necessary. Engineering, continue to pour on the coal. Medicos, stand by with heat-rash lotion. Damage Control, observe holiday routine."

During the months until February, 1945 the *Hornet* ranged through the Philippines, supporting landings, attacking airfields and turning back Jap convoys. In February the *Hornet* moved to keep a date made for her 34 months earlier by another *Hornet*. In the pre-dawn hours of February 16 her planes were launched and joined wave after wave of aircraft from other carriers for the first full-scale aerial attack on Tokyo. For two days she steamed two hundred miles from Honshu while her planes shuttled back and forth through the heavy overcast to carry bombs to Jap cities. Also in February she supported the Iwo Jima landings, then back to Tokyo for another raid, hitting Okinawa again later. The Japs were seeing plenty of the *Hornet.* On March 19 she cruised forty miles from Japan while her planes raided the enemy at Kure and Kobe.

On April 6 and 7, while supporting the invasion of Okinawa, more than five hundred Jap planes swept down on the task force. When the smoke cleared 152 of the attacking craft were in the sea, the *Hornet* credited with more than 50. Early on April 7 the task force raced north at top speed to intercept a heavy Jap concentration, including the big battlewagon *Yamamoto.* The *Hornet's* planes were first to arrive, scoring four torpedo hits and three bomb hits on the dreadnaught, which was sunk. Then they slammed bombs into two cruisers and four destroyers. For the rest of the month the *Hornet* ranged the length of the Ryukyu chain and the home islands of Kyushu, downing rocket bombs and suicide pilots. On April 16 alone 54 Jap planes felt the *Hornet's* sting.

Finally, on April 17 the *Hornet,* her flyers and crew tired and weary, set course for base. For forty days she had been in continuous action. She had launched attacks on 32 of those days, had been under fire 105 times. Her flyers had made more than 4,000 sorties while the ship's gunners had fired more rounds in forty days than they had during all of the previous year. But on May 13 she was "up and at 'em" again, this time destroying a huge new Jap aircraft factory on Kyushu.

The *Hornet* had come through the terrible days of battle without a scratch, but she was not to remain undamaged. She had come through the typhoon in the Philippines but on June 5, 1945 she was caught in the 120-knot typhoon off Okinawa. Bounced around like a chip, a mountainous wave smashed down on her bow, folding the forward part of the flight deck along her sides. Unable to launch planes, the *Hornet* was useless, and back to the States she went for repairs. The elements had done something the Japs couldn't—stopped the *Hornet's* buzzing.

The *Essex*

The *Essex*-class carriers were the scourge of the Japanese during the war, and the first ship of that line (CV-9) was perhaps the most awesome ship of the class the enemy encountered. The *Essex* has a two-year record of battle action, 17 months of it in continuous operation. She fought in 68 engagements, from the Marcus Island strike in August, 1943 to the last-day-of-the-war strike at Tokyo on August 15, 1945.

The *Essex* created several records, with her feat of operating combat aircraft for 79 consecutive days in support of the Okinawa campaign, the most outstanding. She had aboard the Navy's leading flying ace, Comdr. David McCampbell, who shot down 34 Jap planes. She was the first carrier to load bombs at sea and the first of her class to carry a Marine squadron into action. Her Air Groups, 4, 9, 15 and 83, were among the greatest in the war.

The *Essex* was launched in August, 1942, 15 months after her keel was laid, and got into action a year later. She is the fourth Navy ship to bear the name. Sailing her out of Norfolk in December, 1942, Capt. D. B. Duncan told his crew:

"It is my intention and expectation that between us we shall make the name of *Essex* carry fear and destruction to our enemies, win the praises of our friends, and be an everlasting credit to our country and our flag."

The *Essex* (CV-9) did just that.

Her antiaircraft guns shot down 33 attacking planes and her air groups destroyed 1,531 Japanese aircraft and received credit for "probably" destroying 800 more. *Essex* airmen sent 25 warships and 86 other ships to the bottom while hitting and damaging 308 other vessels.

The *Essex* struck at Marcus and Wake in August and October, 1943, and at Wake, Lieutenant (One Slug) McWhorter got his first Jap. "One Slug" had been with the squadron in Africa and had a reputation of hitting the enemy pilot between the eyes with his first bullet. *Essex* fighters shot down 4 Japs and destroyed 8 planes on the ground.

The first major offensive came on November 11, at Rabaul. With other carriers, the *Essex* sent its bombers and fighters over the base in a driving rain. The bombers sank a destroyer and damaged nine cruisers in the harbor, while the fighters tangled with 50 Zeros and brought down 14. The *Essex* refueled her planes and launched them again, just in time to mix it with a furious Jap attack of 126 aircraft—80 dive bombers and torpedo planes, half a dozen large bombers, and 40 Zeros. As they struck for the *Essex,* the fliers from the *Essex* struck at them. The Japs lost 41 planes to *Essex* airmen, bringing the day's total to 55, a new Pacific record. Lt. (j.g.) Albert E. Martin shot down four and Lt. (j.g.) Eugene A. Valencia got three. The most sensational victory belonged to Lt. (j.g.) George M. Blair. With guns jammed, he got into position on the tail of a Jap torpedo plane. Zooming over the Jap at 12 feet, he released his "belly" fuel tank, sent it crashing into his foe, whose plane went flaming into the sea. Five of the Jap planes attacking the *Essex* were shot down by dive bombers and torpedo planes. Two of them were credited to Gordon K. Jenkins, Aviation Machinist's Mate, second class.

On November 18 the *Essex* took part in the invasion of the Gilberts, bagging three planes. She then raided the Marshalls, damaging a cruiser and shooting down seven planes at Kwajalein on December 4. Lieutenant Blair again scored an unusual success when he got on top of a Jap plane and forced it into the water after his ammunition ran out.

The coming of 1944 brought new and bigger exploits for the *Essex.* She was at the invasion of the Marshalls, the attack on Truk, and the raids on Saipan and Tinian. At Truk Lt. (j.g.) Louis Menard, who had downed a German plane in Africa, shot down four Zeros.

Next big action was the "Marianas turkey shoot" in June, officially the Battle of the Philippine Sea. The carrier task force shot Japs out of the sky like pigeons, the *Essex* boys raising their record to 67 with Commander McCampbell alone getting nine. From then until April, 1945 she smashed at Guam and Palau, Luzon, Manila and Formosa, capping these actions with support in the occupation of Iwo Jima and Okinawa. She was hit by a suicide plane once off Luzon.

While the *Essex* steamed off Okinawa for 79 consecutive days without dropping anchor, Air Group 83 shot 220 planes out of the sky, destroyed another 87 on the ground, sank 17 ships and damaged 57. The group raised the *Essex* one-day total of planes shot down to seventy. As her planes slashed at the enemy, the *Essex* had to beat off 357 Japanese raids during the 79 days. During one 51-hour period there were 44 night raids and 42 day raids. When she returned to Leyte Gulf in June she had completed the longest combat cruise ever made by a carrier, 33,865 miles. From July until the end of the war the *Essex* operated against the Japanese homeland—Tokyo, Kure and Hokkaido. Lt. William H. Harris, Jr., one of the pilots from Air Group 83, was posthumously awarded nine citations, including the Navy Cross and Distinguished Flying Cross, for missions from the *Essex* during this period.

Besides Captain Duncan, other skippers of the *Essex* were Capts. Ralph W. Ofstie, C. W. Wieber and Roscoe L. Bowman.

The last enemy plane to be shot down by an *Essex* pilot went to Lt. T. H. Reidy. Already credited with five kills, he splashed another Jap early on August 15, 1945. Then preparing to bomb a target in the Tokyo area, he heard over the radio that the war had ended.

One commentary on the saga of the *Essex* is a story her crew like to tell. A civilian came aboard when all the shooting was over and studied the scoreboard on the bridge, where more than 1,500 planes and almost 500 ships had been chalked up.

"Is that the record of Task Force 58?" he asked.

The *Bunker Hill*

Until November 11, 1943, Rabaul, New Guinea, was one of Japan's most formidable bastions in the Bismarck area of the Pacific. On that day a Navy task force which included the aircraft carrier USS *Bunker Hill* (CV 17) smashed at Rabaul harbor, where the Japs had a large concentration of cruisers and destroyers. In the Navy's own words, after the *Bunker Hill's* force struck, Rabaul "withered away to virtual unimportance."

For the *Essex*-class "BH" the strike at Rabaul was the first action after being commissioned at Quincy, Massachusetts, on May 25, 1943. Commanded by Capt. John J. Ballantine, the fast, sleek carrier sailed out of peaceful Quincy for the turmoil of the South Pacific. When she limped back to the States in mid-1945 she was marked "as the most extensively damaged ship ever to enter the Puget Sound Navy

Yard." In the meantime she had paid the Japs a hundredfold for her scars.

From the time she went into combat until Jap planes and bombs put her out of action at Okinawa almost two years after commissioning, the *Bunker Hill* participated in every major carrier strike, supported every major amphibious landing. Her groups flying from her deck shot down 475 Jap planes, 169 of them in less than sixty days. On two days at Okinawa her fighters brought down 33 and 34 planes.

The BH saw 58 consecutive days of action from Iwo Jima through Tokyo, the Inland Sea, Kyushu and Okinawa. In the latter engagement her AA gunners accounted for 14 enemy aircraft, and during the February, 1945 raid on Tokyo, *Bunker Hill* planes dropped more bombs on Tokyo than any other carrier. In March at Kure Harbor BH pilots blasted three Jap carriers and a cruiser, and three weeks later off Kyushu they administered the finishing blow against the 45,000-ton *Yamamoto* with nine torpedo hits, and sent a destroyer to the bottom. None of that includes the havoc she wreaked at Tarawa, the Gilberts, Nauru Island, New Ireland and the Marshalls. Yes, the Japs had a stake in putting the *Bunker Hill* in drydock.

In that first action at Rabaul the *Bunker Hill's* airmen shot down 76 enemy planes, in addition to inflicting heavy damage and severe casualties on the Japanese fleet. The BH lost 9 planes and 8 men in the engagement.

A week after the first attack the *Bunker Hill* raked Bitutu at Tarawa, setting fire to a fuel dump, sinking a cargo ship, strafing a freighter, silencing antiaircraft guns and bombing two buildings. For 13 days following the BH ranged the Gilbert Islands from Tarawa to Makin, bringing 13 more enemy planes crashing into the sea, smashing at shipping, buildings, dumps and gun positions. From the Gilberts she turned southwest, and on December 8 she stood off Nauru Island to knock down three more Jap pilots, tear up the airfield and scatter death and destruction.

Christmas Day, 1943 found the *Bunker Hill* beginning a series of operations off Kavieng, New Ireland. In the first action her air group sank two cargo vessels, crippled 2 torpedo boats and destroyed 3 enemy planes. On New Year's Day she again lashed out at Japanese warships, scoring effectively but failing to send any to the bottom. Nine more enemy planes were chalked up on the bridge scoreboard, with ten more being added to the "probable" column. On January 5 she put a Japanese destroyer out of action and shot 2 more planes out of the sky. With the Japs now somewhat subdued at New Ireland, the

Bunker Hill sailed northeast to the Marshalls, and from January 29, 1944 until February 2, she pounded Kwajalein and Eniwetok.

Adm. Marc Mitscher, forming Task Force 58, made the *Bunker Hill* his flagship, and in quick succession she wheeled west and struck at Truk in the Carolines, then north, to Guam and Tinian in the Marianas, southwest to Palau, and east again to the Carolines on April 1. On April 21 she moved into Hollandia in support of the invasion of New Guinea, hitting again at Truk a week later, and supporting the Saipan landings in June and the Guam invasion in July. In late summer, 1944 she slashed at the Japanese in the Volcano and Bonin islands and then set the stage for final victory with strikes at the Philippines and Okinawa, following up in early 1945 with blows directly at the heart of Japan. (The complete list of her engagements alone would cover over two pages.) Her skippers during this period were Capt. Thomas P. Jeter and Capt. Marshall R. Greer.

The climax of the *Bunker Hill's* career came at the end of 58 days of continuous action on the morning of May 11, 1945.

The *Bunker Hill's* planes were supporting Marine and Army ground troops on Okinawa that fateful day when a Jap "Zeke" fighter sneaked in fast and low on the starboard quarter. The Zeke dropped a 500-pound delayed action bomb, then dived into the 34 planes parked forward on the flight deck. The plane itself started fires among the fueled and armed planes before the Jap skidded over the side into the water, while the bomb tore through the flight deck and out the side of the ship, exploding in the air before it hit the water. Seconds later a "Judy" single-engine divebomber whipped in on the stricken craft from astern. *Bunker Hill* gunners caught the Judy with a 5-inch shell and 40mm AA fire, but the Jap suicide pilot kept coming in, dropping another 500-pounder which penetrated the after flight deck and exploded in the gallery deck immediately below. Scores of the crew were blown into the water. The plane crashed on the flight deck at the base of the island structure. A third Kamikaze attacked but was shot down before it closed in.

With fires and exploding ammunition sweeping the flight deck where pilots and crewmen had been caught in their planes, the men of the *Bunker Hill* rushed to save their flaming ship. The hangar deck below was a furnace of burning gasoline and smoke rose hundreds of feet above the ship. Fire fighters battled the flames while the rest of the crew rescued the wounded and stood by to ward off further attacks. Men died below decks keeping the boilers going and pressure in the fire mains. Comdr. H. J. Dyson, executive officer, who had been wounded by an exploding bomb, continued to lead the fire-fighting parties.

ACMM Clifford Jacobs was in a locker just off the *Bunker Hill's* flight deck when the first plane struck. The second blast knocked him flat, but he got up to pull some men free who were trapped in a ship-fitter's shop, then went to work with the fire hose. Tales of heroism were common. MM3c Marcel L. Levesque not only volunteered to carry breathing masks into the smoking bowels of the ship, but gave up his own mask to another man. A musician, Charles R. Barner, left his disabled gun, and in utter disregard of his own safety, entered the ammunition storage spaces to fight off advancing flames. Std M 1c Herbert J. Crawford fought the smoke and flames for five hours without rest, and was one of those whose refusal to quit saved the *Bunker Hill* from going down.

The planes aboard the *Bunker Hill* at the time of the attack were destroyed. Marine fighter planes had been launched earlier for a rocket attack against Okinawa, and the Kamikazes struck just as the Marines were returning. The fighters made a run for the third Jap suicide pilot, but the *Bunker Hill* gunners were quicker. Meanwhile, the planes circled the blazing ship, unable to land and eventually a neighboring carrier took them aboard. In that flight were Lieut. Ralph Glendinning, Capt. James E. Swett and Lieut. Fred Briggs, who, with Glendinning, had just downed a Jap twin-engine torpedo bomber; Capt. William R. Snider, and Lieut. Dewey J. Wambsgans.

The long fight to keep the *Bunker Hill* afloat continued for six hours. The cruiser *Wilkes-Barre* came alongside, playing her fire hose on the burning flattop and taking off the men who had been trapped on the hangar deck. The destroyers *Stembel, Charles S. Sperry,* and *English* came to the rescue in the face of the constantly exploding bombs and shells. The *Wilkes-Barre* evacuated the seriously wounded and the destroyers took hundreds from the sea, but many went down.

One sharply dramatic incident marked the long struggle for the *Bunker Hill's* survival. As the ship listed dangerously, with tons of water playing upon thousands of gallons of flaming gasoline and oil and forcing the fire fighters back against the bulkhead on the hangar deck, Capt. George A. Seitz gave the order to his navigator, Comdr. Charles J. Odend'hal:

"Tell the *Wilkes-Barre* to make ready for a turn. Order the destroyers to stand clear."

To his helmsman Commander Odend'hal said, "Come right carefully. Not over two and a half degrees rudder."

Slowly the blazing *Bunker Hill* turned. Gradually, then with a roar, tons of water, burning gasoline and oil on the hangar deck sloshed away from the fire fighters and poured over the edges of the deck into the sea, dumping the core of the roaring inferno. Men with lips too burned to cheer rushed forward with their hose. Fresh air whipped across the deck, forcing the heavy smoke and fumes away. Men lying on the blistered decks below knew as they breathed the fresh air that the ship had a new life. They felt, some of them said later, that the *Bunker Hill* would live. And it did.

Captain Seitz recommended 280 of the crew for awards from Navy Crosses to Commendation Ribbons.

"Their devotion to duty," he said, "saved the *Bunker Hill*."

The *Hancock*

In the words of Capt. Robert F. Hickey, skipper of this *Essex*-class carrier (CV-19), "records are made to be broken." The *Hancock* lived up to its commanding officer's slogan.

This ship's planes and guns (a) scored the largest single day's bag of enemy planes, 72 in the air and 19 on the ground, (b) sank 9 enemy warships in one day, and (c) made 600 sorties against objectives on Okinawa.

Admiral Halsey, Third Fleet commander, said the *Hancock* was the "damnedest" ship he had ever seen in action. "She starts firing first and quits last," was Halsey's tribute.

The *Hancock* scoreboard, when it was all over, showed 733 Jap planes rubbed out, 17 warships and 31 merchant vessels sent to the bottom. It cost the *Hancock* 221 killed or missing and 76 wounded.

The *Hancock,* commissioned on April 15, 1944, won the Navy Unit Commendation for her campaigns. She was in almost continuous combat operation for ten months, through the actions off Formosa, Philippines, Ryukyus, China Sea, Japan, Bonins, Okinawa and Wake.

On April 7, 1945 when the *Hancock* was south of Kyushu carrying the war to the enemy, she was hit first by a bomb and then by the plane which had released it. The Jap came out of a cloud on the starboard bow about three thousand feet over the carrier, cut across, banked, and dived from dead ahead. The bomb went through the forward section of the flight deck, the attacking plane crashing into aircraft on the after end of the deck. Casualties were heavy, with severe damage to matériel.

Despite terrific fires, the *Hancock* was able to resume landing planes aboard after five hours.

But for CAMM Dennie P. Vermillion, eight more *Hancock* crewmen would have been added to the casualty list. Chief Vermillion plunged through billowing smoke and exploding ammunition to lead eight men trapped in a hangar-deck compartment to safety. He was commended for gallantry in action, his second citation.

On one occasion the ship was the target of four Kamikaze attacks, but the accuracy of Marine gun crews spelled curtains for the suicide planes. "The Marines were literally shooting them off their gun barrels," said Captain Hickey.

Among other *Hancock* jobs were: helping escort the burning carrier *Franklin* to safety; pre-invasion blows on Okinawa, and the tactical air support of the Army and Marine troops fighting there. The *Hancock* wound up the war in Tokyo Bay and then went into the "Magic Carpet" fleet transporting soldiers and sailors back home.

The *Princeton*

The *Princeton* (CVL-23) was the only light carrier the US lost during the war. The *Princeton* was the second ship of the light carrier (*Independence*) class and after she went down in the Battle for Leyte Gulf another *Princeton* (CV-37) was named for her. The latter ship, a 27,000-ton *Essex*-class carrier, was commissioned late in 1945 and did not get into combat.

The *Princeton* (CVL-23) was the fourth ship in the Navy to be named for the Battle of Princeton, which followed George Washington's crossing of the Delaware River. She was built on a hull originally designed as a light, fast 10,000-ton cruiser, and was first launched as the *Tallahassee*. Converted to a carrier, she was commissioned at the Philadelphia Navy Yard in February, 1943. Her first skipper was Capt. George R. Henderson.

Up to the Marianas operation in the summer of 1944 the *Princeton* took part in more engagements than any other carrier in her class, and was known to her crew as the "Peerless P". Moreover, it was from her flight deck that the famed F6F Hellcat Navy fighters made their debut in the Baker Island landings on September 1, 1943. From that time on the Hellcat was a familiar sight in the Pacific battle zones.

In the *Princeton's* first action at Baker Island her Hellcats shot down the first Japanese "Emily" reconnaissance plane to show up in the Pacific. In the following 12 days, while providing air cover, they sent more "Emilys" down in flames and furnished the fleet with its first photographs of this 4-engine bomber.

The *Princeton* was engaged in nine major engagements between Baker Island and her sinking. On September 18, 1943 she struck at Makin and Tarawa with her bombers and torpedo planes, as her fighters formed an air umbrella over the task force. In this strike her fliers were credited with downing one "Betty," a twin-engine Jap bomber.

When US troops were landing in Empress Augusta Bay in November, the *Princeton* flew four strikes against airfields on Buka and Buin in the northern Solomons to prevent Jap planes from operating against the men going ashore. So effective was the bombardment and strafing of the planes from the *Princeton* and other ships that not a single enemy aircraft was able to get into the sky. The *Princeton* then raced for Rabaul where the Japanese had assembled a powerful force of cruisers and destroyers to hurl against the Americans on Bougainville. With shore-based Navy and Marine Corps planes swarming overhead as fighter cover, the *Princeton* sent her torpedo bombers in against the Jap warships, blasting two enemy cruisers and one destroyer. Her fighters shot down ten enemy pilots in the face of strong opposition and withering AA fire. Six days later the *Princeton* smashed again at Rabaul in a great drive that put that base out of operation.

From Rabaul, the *Princeton* steamed north to take part in the Gilbert Islands operation, containing Japanese air power on Nauru as other forces supported the Tarawa and Makin landings. In an all-day fighter attack on November 19, planes from the *Princeton* shot down two Japs in the air and damaged many on the ground. The engagement continued for 19 days during which the *Princeton* flew nine strikes.

The Peerless P was due for a short rest, but resumed the offensive in the drive against the Marshalls on January 29, 1944, starting off with a three-day strafing attack on Wotje and Taroa. Support of the occupation of Kwajalein and Majuro followed until February 8, and a few days later the *Princeton's* air group helped inaugurate the softening up of Eniwetok. Here her pilots flew 118 sorties, dropping 23 tons of bombs and expending 13,000 rounds of bullets in strafing ground troops and installations. Between February 16 and 29, when the strategically vital Eniwetok base was invaded and secured, *Princeton* airmen again were in the forefront, with 458 sorties. Two of the *Princeton's* most devastating blows at the enemy were struck in the next thirty days. In April, Palau and Woleai were attacked. Then the carrier pilots drove at Hollandia and Truk, accounting for 30 Jap planes in the air and 4 on the ground in 548 sorties that used up 31,000 rounds of ammunition.

There was another brief rest and the *Princeton* went back into action, this time in the capture and occupation of Saipan early in June; the Battle of the Philippine Sea, and then the invasion of Guam and Tinian. In quick succession followed the Western Carolines operation and the strikes against the Philippines, all setting the stage for the Leyte Gulf show in October.

On the 10th of that month the *Princeton* was with Admiral Halsey in the Third Fleet attack on Okinawa, heading for northern Luzon and Formosa for strikes there until the 19th. The Leyte landings began on October 20.

Capt. William H. Buracker was then skipper of the *Princeton,* and his job that morning of the 24th was to effect the fighter sweep over Manila and run air searches to the west of the Philippines.

The *Princeton's* dawn patrol was in the air when a group of 90 to 100 Jap planes was reported winging in from Manila. *Princeton* fighters and others from the task group intercepted the force about 40 miles from the carrier, completely disrupted the attack and shot down most of the planes. About 9:30 A. M., as the *Princeton* prepared to launch her attack group of torpedo planes, a Japanese dive bomber came screaming out of the clouds overhead, diving straight for the ship. The guns took him under fire and the *Princeton* started to swing hard, but there wasn't much time. The Jap swooped in and released the bomb, which hit between the elevators and penetrated the hangar deck, exploding below. A fueled torpedo plane on the hangar deck was set afire, the flames quickly spreading to other planes. Torpedoes began exploding and blazing gasoline spread everywhere. Some of the crew had to jump off the stern before all hands were ordered topside. Two cruisers, the *Birmingham* and the *Reno,* and the destroyers *Morrison, Irwin, Cassin Young* and *Gatling* came to the aid of the burning carrier, taking off personnel and picking up men in the water. With the flames almost under control, Jap planes returned and the rescue ships were forced to disperse.

With water no longer pouring from the hoses of the other vessels, flames blazed anew on the *Princeton.* Finally the *Birmingham* returned when, without warning, a magazine on the carrier blew up, tearing away the *Princeton's* stern and raining destruction on the crew of the *Birmingham.* On the cruiser 237 were killed, 4 missing and 426 wounded. Practically all left aboard the *Princeton* were injured. With all chances for saving her gone, the crew abandoned ship, and torpedoes from her own force were pumped into the *Princeton* until she sank. Her planes landed on the decks of other carriers.

Some of the men on the *Princeton* had fought aboard the *Lexington* and *Hornet* when those flattops went down. For CSM Edward L. Glover and RM James L. Ayers, this was the third carrier they had been forced to abandon. MMs M. D. Brown and Howard M. Boll, and WT Egbert A. Blanton had been aboard the *Hornet* when she met her death.

Henry R. Bellavance, Sea. 1c, dived from the flight deck and swam to the rescue of an injured shipmate. James A. Mollette, A Msmth., helped a wounded chief petty officer reach a floating plank and then inflated the injured man's life jacket. There were other deeds of heroism which went unrecorded.

There were 1,440 men saved from the *Princeton*. When four hundred of the survivors arrived at San Diego, one of them said he expressed the sentiments of all. He asked: "How can we get aboard another *Princeton?*"

The *Langley*

It took two World Wars to sink the old *Langley* (AV-3), the Navy's first aircraft carrier, built in 1911. The second *Langley* (CVL-27) ended the war with the Navy Unit Commendation flag flying from her foremast.

The original *Langley* started out as a collier, *Jupiter* by name. She was the first ship to pass through the Panama Canal from west to east in 1914, and was converted to an aircraft carrier in 1919 after duty in World War I. In 1937, when the Navy had acquired some newer carriers, the *Langley* was again converted, this time to an aircraft tender.

The tender *Langley* went down in a hail of Jap bombs off Java in February, 1942. Three times before official Tokyo reports had claimed the sinking of the *Langley,* but she was never hit until the day of her demise. Only 14 *Langley* men were lost when she sank, but hundreds of other perished when their rescue ship, the tanker *Pecos,* was sent down a few days later.

There were brave men on that old aircraft tender on which so many of the Navy's early airmen had served. BM J. J. Black and RM Claude J. Hinds were two who stuck to their posts until the *Langley* went down, and then were bombed off the *Pecos.* The skipper, Capt. R. P. McConnell, manned a machine gun to fight back at the Jap dive bombers. Sea. Roy T. McNabb, after being rescued by the *Pecos,* was commended for his action under fire when the *Pecos* was attacked.

The new *Langley,* a light aircraft carrier, was in the Pacific struggle from January, 1944 until the end of hostilities, getting hit once in the South China Sea in January, 1945. Her men won awards from the Legion of Merit to Commendation Ribbon, and Purple Heart badges were conspicuous on many a jumper. Some of the wounded were Marine Sgt. Edward P. Mason, Sea. Walter L. Jones, Cox. William H. Harris, SF Joseph N. Paonessa . . . the list is long.

The *Langley* was commissioned at Philadelphia on August 31, 1943 and sailed to Pearl under Capt. William M. Dillon. In January she hit Wotje, and in February supported the great amphibious assault on Eniwetok and Kwajalein. Then she was attached to Task Force 58 and hurled her planes at Palau and Woleai, proceeding to New Guinea for the seizure and occupation of Hollandia in April. Next it was Truk, followed by quick strikes on Saipan, Tinian, Guam and Rota.

Task Force 38 called the *Langley* in September, and there were raids on the Philippines and Formosa. In October the crippled Jap fleet, retiring from the disaster of Surigao Strait, felt the *Langley's* sting again. In January, 1945, it was the South China Sea and then she rejoined Task Force 58 for the Tokyo raids, the Iwo Jima landings, and the Okinawa campaign.

Langley pilots shot down 119 enemy planes, destroyed more than 100 on the ground, sank 7 Jap warships and 27 merchant vessels. Ship's gunners splashed five attacking aircraft. Her skippers after Captain Dillon were Capt. John F. Wegforth and Herbert E. Regan.

The *Cabot*

"It is with great joy, but deep regret, that I see one of my most effective units depart," blinkered Vice Adm. Marc A. Mitscher, Fast Carrier Task Force Commander, when the "homeward bound" pennant was hoisted on the light carrier (CVL-28) known in the fleet as the "Iron Woman."

The *Cabot* was a charter member of Task Force 58, and her nickname, the Iron Woman, was well earned. She displayed her endurance through 225,000 miles of the war at Kwajalein, Eniwetok, Truk, Palau, Hollandia, Saipan, Chichi Jima, Mindanao, Luzon, Formosa, Hong Kong, Saigon, Iwo Jima, Tokyo, Kyushu, and Shikoku. She fought without respite, and was away from the States longer than any other flattop in the Pacific.

The late Ernie Pyle sailed aboard her, called her "My Carrier" in his newspaper columns, and wrote with highest praise of the ship and her men.

In the battle for Leyte Gulf the *Cabot* scored both battleship and cruiser hits. And when the Fast Carrier Force steamed boldly into the China Sea fight, the Iron Woman had the honor of being first in, last out.

At the First Battle of the Philippine Sea (the "Marianas turkey shoot") she won: "You are tops in the league today" from the task group commander for the group's top score, 27 Jap planes splashed. Her bombers also hit an enemy carrier twice and a battleship once. When the fleet turned on the lights that night to bring in the airmen staggering back from the long flight, the *Cabot* took aboard her own planes and nine craft from other ships, more planes than a light carrier had ever before handled operationally.

Other honors are chalked on her island. The *Cabot's* fighter pilots knocked down 260 planes, ship's gunners accounted for eight. Thirty big Japanese ships went to the bottom because of her aerial marksmanship. In a clash with the dwindling units of the Imperial Fleet, *Cabot* fliers sent three torpedoes into the *Yamato,* last of the modern Jap battlewagons.

One of the most notable of the Iron Woman's accomplishments occurred in October, 1944 in the fighting off Formosa. The cruisers *Houston* and *Canberra* were hit and the *Cabot* was sent to escort them to safety, using her fighters to furnish air cover. During the course of this slow-moving escape, Jap planes twice swarmed in to attack the crippled ships. Seventy bombers were in each wave, but the *Cabot* beat off both assaults, as eight of her fighters shot down 31 Japs in one of the actions.

On November 18, 1944 the *Cabot* struck Luzon. On the 25th an enemy suicide plane dove on the carrier, was hit, smashed into the flight deck on the port side. Another, attacking from ahead, was shot down but fell close aboard on the port quarter and exploded under a gun mount. Thirty-six of the crew were killed, 14 seriously injured, as two gaping holes were torn in the flight deck and the hull was ripped wide open. The *Cabot* was forced to retire to Ulithi for repairs, but was back in a month for more strikes at the Philippines. At Manila she led her task group for the second time, with 28 Japs shot down into the sea.

The Iron Woman went right on from the Philippines, and was in on Formosa, Iwo Jima, Okinawa and the attacks on Japan before the war ended. She received the country's highest award, the Presidential Unit Citation.

The *Cabot* was commissioned at Camden, New Jersey in July, 1943 and put to sea under Capt. M. F. Schoeffel. Her succeeding skippers were Capts. Stanley J. Michael and Walton W. Smith.

The *San Jacinto*

The light carrier USS *San Jacinto* (CVL-30), commissioned December 15, 1943, took part in seven major operations, escaped being hit by Japanese suicide planes and bombers by a hair on six occasions, and was in action up to the very last minute of the Pacific war.

But one of her outstanding accomplishments, in a career that saw her battle feats surpass each other in quick succession, was the *San Jacinto's* sinking of her Japanese counterpart, the light carrier *Zuiho*.

The "San Jay" or "San Jacint" as the fleet knew her, sailed out of Camden, New Jersey, for Pearl Harbor under command of Capt.

William D. Anderson. When she left Pearl on May 3, 1944 for her first taste of action, her skipper was Capt. Harold M. Martin. On that cruise the San Jay started on the road to success when, in company with the cruiser *San Diego* and some destroyers, she made what was then the farthest penetration by surface craft into Japanese-held waters. That venture came after her air assault against Marcus and Wake.

Back to port for replenishment, the *San Jacinto* steamed up to the Marianas in June with Task Force 58. Her torpedo planes took part in a long-range air strike, blasting a Jap destroyer and scoring repeated hits on a *Riyatka*-class cruiser. In this action the San Jacint gunners bagged a Jap plane when the confused enemy pilot tried to land on the carrier's flight deck. Until July 6, when she left for Eniwetok, the San Jay covered our ships and shore installations in the area, fighting off and breaking up continuous enemy air raids.

Later in the month she popped up again in the Marianas, striking at Guam and Rota, then against Palau, Yap and Ulithi. A Jap destroyer, loaded with ammunition, exploded with a mighty roar and disappeared when bombs from *San Jacinto* planes found their mark. Back to Saipan she went to refuel, and then into battle once more, this time letting the Japs have it at the Bonin and Volcano Islands. The Palau campaign was next, with the San Jay now attached to the Second Carrier Task Force of Admiral Halsey's Third Fleet. The force struck again at the Bonins and Volcanos in a diversionary action, and then hit heavily at Ulithi and Yap, completely devastating shore installations at both places. At Peleliu and Angaur *San Jacinto* pilots softened up the beaches for the landings.

Early in October the carrier, now part of Task Force 38, launched an all-out attack on Okinawa, setting the towns of Naha and Yonabaru afire, and torpedoing two ships in Naha harbor. Jap planes attacked the *San Jacinto* in force but they shouldn't have; when it was over 24 enemy planes had been knocked down. The Okinawa operation was the *San Jacinto's* part in the plan to prevent the reinforcement of Japanese troops attempting to hold Leyte.

Capt. Michael H. Kernodle now arrived to take over from Captain Martin. The new skipper found himself in the thick of it off Luzon as swarms of Jap fighters and bombers sought the *San Jacinto* as a target. Net result: nine more enemy planes in the drink. The action continued for six days and then the ship was ordered to Ulithi for refitting. But the Japanese fleet was moving on the Philippines and Captain Kernodle received orders to run full speed for Leyte.

With her planes flying long range, the *San Jacinto* and other units joined action with the Japs off Cape Engaño at the northeastern tip of Luzon. Here it was that the Jap carrier *Zuiho* became the victim of the savage attacks of the San Jay planes. Struck first with two heavy bombs, the *Zuiho* started to smoke and burn. In a few minutes a TBF Avenger hit the burning ship with a torpedo, putting it out of control. Listing and unable to maneuver, the *Zuiho* became a target for two more aerial "tin fish" and sank to the bottom. In the same action another carrier and a cruiser were hit by *San Jacinto* torpedoes.

On October 29 the *San Jacinto* prepared to return for refueling, but this was the time the Japs picked to ferry planes into Cebu and Negros. She wheeled back to Samar and the next day had her first escape from Kamikazes, her accurate gunfire and expert seamanship helping her out. The *San Jacinto* had to refuel, but on November 13 was back in the Manila Bay area, sinking a large floating drydock, bombing Cavite, hitting a cargo vessel and setting a Jap DE on fire. She next supported the capture of Mindoro, struck at central Formosa, and then entered the South China Sea and blasted positions in French Indo-China. One Jap destroyer was hit and another damaged and driven ashore. Resuming attacks against Formosa, the *San Jacinto* escaped suicide planes for the third time when the *Ticonderoga,* a larger carrier, became the victim, and the *Langley,* another carrier, was hit by bombs. The fourth escape came after attacks on the Tokyo area and Iwo Jima, when, refuelling again, the carrier *Randolph* in the next berth was hit by a Kamikaze. The fifth escape, not from suicide planes but from Jap dive bombers, was on March 20 when the *Franklin* and the *Enterprise,* in company with the San Jay, got theirs: but the *San Jacinto,* after four days of incessant air attack, was unscathed.

A few days later near Okinawa the ship helped annihilate a convoy, sank 8 small craft, destroyed 16 planes on the ground, and sent to the bottom 6 cargo ships. On April 6 the Japs sent out five hundred suicide planes to stem the Okinawa invasion, and again the *San Jacinto* was unharmed as she fought back furiously. In May, June and July she took part in the great attacks on Japan, on one occasion damaging the battleship *Ise,* which was later sunk. In August, planes from the *San Jacinto* located a camouflaged enemy airfield, destroyed 78 planes and damaged 71 others. A few days later 69 more Jap planes were smashed on their airfields and 24 damaged.

The atomic bomb had been dropped and surrender was being talked on August 14. When there was no word from Japan on the 15th, the *San Jacinto* returned to strike the Tokyo area again and shot down seven enemy fighters before getting the word to cease fire. Capt. Hugh H. Goodwin assumed command of the ship on August 24.

The *Cowpens*

Not everyone knows United States history, and at first the fleet had a lot of fun with the name of this light carrier, making all the deadly puns that came easily for a ship named after that battle of the Revolution. But when the *Cowpens* (CVL-25) showed her stuff in campaign after campaign it boiled down, respectfully, to the "Mighty Moo." When it was all over, the Mighty Moo had the last laugh, because she won the Navy Unit Commendation.

The *Cowpens* operated in the Pacific from October, 1943 until the end of the war, taking part in three major actions within four months of her arrival in the battle zone. Her first engagement was in the raids of October 5 and 6 on Wake Island.

As part of a task group, the Mighty Moo struck at the Gilberts in December, her planes flying 150 sorties as air cover for the force, striking four times at enemy installations. In January and February, 1944 aircraft from the *Cowpens* dropped 38 tons of bombs and incendiaries on Kwajalein in support of landing forces, without losing a single plane. After that she saw action at Hollandia, Truk, Marianas, Philippines, Formosa and the China Sea.

In February, 1945 she was in on the Tokyo raids that neutralized the Jap air force while the Marines invaded Iwo Jima. The weather was bad, yet Mighty Moo pilots found the targets and unloaded their bombs. A few days later the same fliers were attacking the enemy on Iwo Jima, but in another week the ship was again steaming up the shores of Japan. In March the *Cowpens* was on her way back to the States, but by June she was back in the thick of it again, this time with Admiral "Bull" Halsey's Third Fleet in those great blows against the Empire itself. After the surrender the Mighty Moo was one of the carriers assigned to enter Japanese waters in the first stages of the naval occupation of Tokyo.

The *Cowpens* was commissioned at Philadelphia on May 28, 1943, and was commanded during the war by Capts. R. P. McConnell, H. W. Taylor, and George H. DeBaum.

Her citation:

For outstanding heroism in action against the enemy Japanese forces in the air, ashore and afloat in the Pacific War Area from October 5, 1943, to August 15, 1945. Operating continuously in the most forward areas, the USS *Cowpens* and her air groups struck crushing blows toward annihilating Japanese fighting power; they provided air cover for our amphibious forces; they fiercely countered the enemy's aerial attacks and destroyed his planes; and they inflicted terrific losses on the Japanese in Fleet and merchant marine units sunk or damaged. Daring and dependable in combat the *Cowpens* with her gallant officers and men rendered loyal service in achieving the ultimate defeat of the Japanese Empire.

The *Belleau Wood*

This ship, the third built of the light carrier class (CVL-24), named for the Marines' famous battle of the first World War, was in action in the Pacific for almost two years. During that time her air group shot down 208 Japs, destroyed 285 enemy planes on the ground, and the *Belleau Wood's* antiaircraft gunners accounted for 9 more. Japanese shipping to the tune of 107,000 tons was sunk and heavy blows were struck on shore installations from Tarawa to the home islands of the Empire.

The *Belleau Wood,* which saw plenty of action and had many close calls, was hit by a Kamikaze plane near Leyte Gulf on October 30, 1944 and was out of combat for three months. She returned to the battle zones in 1945 in time to take part in the Iwo Jima and Okinawa engagements, and was awarded the Presidential Unit Citation for her campaigns.

The *Belleau Wood* was commissioned at Philadelphia in March, 1942. She reached the Pacific in August, 1943 under command of Capt. Alfred M. Pride. Her first real action came in the raid on Tarawa in September. In December, after smashes at Wake and Makin, she barely escaped being sunk in the Marshalls as a "left hard rudder" from the bridge swung the ship ten yards out of the line of an aerial torpedo. Between the Marshalls and Saipan the ship took part in the occupation of Kwajalein and the raid on Truk, Capt. John Perry succeeding Captain Pride.

There was another close call off Saipan in February, 1944 when a "Betty," coming in low with a torpedo, exploded just off the port beam. *Belleau Wood* gunners shot down two other planes. Following the Haha and Chichi Jima strikes in June, one of the carrier's fighters crashed a barrier on landing, hit the bridge and burst into flames which threatened the safety of the ship before the blaze was brought under control. Next came the Marianas "turkey shoot" and then the *Belleau Wood's* planes sank a Japanese carrier of the Hayataka class. The fighting increased in intensity, marked by the occupation of Guam and Morotai, and strikes at Palau, the Philippines, Okinawa and Formosa.

On the second day of the strike against Formosa in October, 1944, *Belleau Wood* gunners brought down three Jap bombers about to attack the carrier *Franklin.* A little later a plane making a run on the *Enterprise* was brought down in flames by *Belleau Wood* sharpshooters. On the night of October 12, the ship withstood 47 separate air attacks without taking a hit.

But on the 30th, disaster struck. After a great job by *Belleau Wood* pilots in the Battle for Leyte Gulf, the ship retired sixty miles east to await orders. In midafternoon an enemy plane swooped in, bombed the *Franklin,* then pulled up to dive on the *Belleau Wood,* crashing into 11 armed and fueled fighter planes about to be launched. Fire and explosions broke out instantly; 92 were killed and many injured. Back to the States went the *Belleau Wood* for major repairs, and when the ship returned to the Pacific in January, 1945, Capt. William G. Tomlinson was in command.

In March, steaming three hundred miles east of Nansei Shoto after strikes there, *Belleau Wood* fighters shot down 10 enemy bombers and 11 fighters streaking in to attack the force. Six weeks later, 150 miles northeast of Okinawa, a single-engine Jap making a suicide dive on the ship was brought down by the starboard batteries. Its bomb exploded over the flight deck. Later the same day Air Group 30 from the *Belleau Wood* had a field day in a clash with a large formation of Jap planes attempting to raid Okinawa, splashing seven of the enemy.

In June the great 100-mile-an-hour typhoon was encountered, which the light carrier rode out with the loss of one man and eleven planes. After final strikes against the Japanese home islands in July and August, the *Belleau Wood* wound up her war service assisting in the occupation.

Air groups which flew from the *Belleau Wood* were 24, 21, 30 and 31.

The *Card*

The US Navy's answer to the German submarine in World War II was the escort aircraft carrier. The men who served aboard CVE-11 had their own angle on this. They felt that the Navy's best answer to the Atlantic U-boat threat was the *Card.*

The *Card* and her task group destroyed more Nazi subs than any team in naval history, and the *Card* was the first carrier to receive the Presidential Unit Citation for antisubmarine warfare.

The *Card,* like the *Bogue,* was converted into an escort aircraft carrier from a C-3 merchant ship hull. She was commissioned on the day the Allies launched the historic invasion of North Africa in November, 1942. Her first commanding officer was Capt. James B. Sykes.

It was in September, 1943 that the *Card* began to get into the fights that won her the Presidential Unit Citation. The Germans, alarmed by their growing losses, had installed heavier guns to blast back at our planes. The *Card* skipper, Capt. Arnold J. Isbell, still believed his gang could win by wading into a sub pack and fighting it out at close quarters.

One morning a *Card* torpedo-bomber pilot, Lieut. Asbury H. Sallenger, spotted two surfaced subs. The U-boats immediately let loose with heavy antiaircraft fire but the Avenger tore in. One submarine was damaged so severely that it could not submerge; the other was sunk with an accurate salvo of depth charges. Ten minutes later other *Card* fliers were over the damaged German craft, finishing her off with bombing and strafing attacks. Later in the day the *Borie* went after a U-boat which escaped, and the truth began to dawn on the *Card* group. They were smack in the midst of an enemy wolf-pack.

The next day Lieutenant Sallenger and fighter-pilot Ens. John F. Sprague failed to return from a dawn patrol. In the face of a mounting storm, the *Card* and her escorts began a search for the lost fliers. Seven hours later Sallenger and AMM James H. O'Hagan, his turret gunner, were sighted clinging to a life raft. Sprague was not around.

Here is Lieutenant Sallenger's story of what happened:

The weather was poor when we took off, with a solid overcast, rain squalls and poor visibility. Sprague was flying on my wing. All at once I spotted two U-boats, only 150 yards apart, moving slowly on almost parallel courses.

I signalled Sprague to attack and he made a beautiful strafing run, giving that sub a methodical going-over with his machine-guns. But as I followed him in, I got some AA in my fuselage, putting out my inter-plane communication and electrical systems and also damaging the vertical fin of my plane and the rudder. Everything happened suddenly, and the damage to my electrical system prevented the release of bombs on my first run.

I pulled up and out for a second attack, with my engine popping and cutting out. Meanwhile, Sprague was making another excellent strafing run on the other sub.

When I went in on my second run, I got hit again and the wing burst into flames. However, I made my "drop" and looked back to make sure my bombs exploded in the proper place. The explosions, which seemed to go off right under the sub, covered it with water.

My wing was now burning badly, so I dropped my remaining bombs and made a water landing. It put out the fire in the wing.

I got out of the plane and saw that O'Hagan and I got the life raft inflated. I didn't see or hear Sprague again.

After paddling their way through the stricken U-boat's oil slick "so new we could smell fresh oil," Lieutenant Sallenger and O'Hagan were picked up by the USS *Barry*.

(After seeing the torpedo plane go down, Sprague had apparently persisted in his strafing runs against the U-boat's heavy antiaircraft barrage.)

The same day two planes from the *Card,* working with the destroyer *Goff,* "probably sank" another sub, and the *Borie* dropped depth charges on another. The U-boats were coming thick and fast and the *Card's* skipper, assured of good hunting, stayed in the area. The next day brought another kill when a fighter and two Avengers caught a boat on the surface, completely off guard. The fighter cleared the deck of the sub with machine-gun fire and the Avengers dropped their bombs just as the sub started to dive. Rocked and split by the charges, the U-boat was unable to submerge and the crew abandoned the struggle.

On the night the destroyer *Borie* went down, taking with her two enemy subs, *Card* planes finished off another U-boat. The carrier was far to the north, tracking enemy undersea raiders through storms and icy waters. The little ship was pitching and tossing in the wind and waves, trying to land her planes aboard, when two surfaced subs were sighted 11 miles dead ahead. Two fighters raced to the spot where the torpedo planes hovered over the Jerries. One big U-boat crash-dived, but the other lashed out with bristling AA fire. The three planes bore down with machine guns and bombs, and the submarine was caught in two perfect straddles. The surface filled with oil and debris as the crippled sub slid under.

There is another incident *Card* men remember; the night Lieut. Roger C. Kuhn stood by to risk his life for his buddy, Lieut. Harry E. Fryatt. Fryatt's plane, hit by a 40mm shell from a Nazi sub, could get only one wheel down for a landing, forcing a crash-landing. Kuhn went forward to the forecastle deck and waited, flashlight in hand, ready to go over the side if Fryatt's plane went into the water. Fryatt's plane came in, missed the barriers, smashed into a parked plane, driving it over the bow and carrying Kuhn with it into the water. Kuhn was injured in the fall, almost drowned in the icy Atlantic before the *Barry* rescued him.

The *Card's* Presidential Unit Citation sums up the story of this outstanding Navy ship and her task group:

For outstanding performance during anti-submarine operations in mid-Atlantic from July 27, 1943. At a time when continual flow of supplies along the United States-North Africa convoy route was essential to the maintenance of our established military supremacy and to the accumulation of reserves, the *Card,* her embarked aircraft and her escorts pressed home a vigorous offensive which was largely responsible for the complete withdrawal of hostile U-boats from this vital supply area. Later, when submarines returned with deadlier weapons and augmented antiaircraft defenses, this heroic Task Unit, by striking damaging blows at the onset of renewed campaigns, wrested the initiative from the enemy before actual inception of projected large-scale attacks. Its distinctive fulfillment of difficult and hazardous missions contributed materially to victorious achievements by our land forces.

The *Fanshaw Bay*

Of the seven carriers of the Navy which have received the highest award a ship can get for combat—the Presidential Unit Citation—six were escort carriers. And of those six the USS *Fanshaw Bay* (CVE- 70) was dubbed by one naval writer, Lieut. Edward E. Glasser:

> The Fighting Fanny Bee,
> The mightiest and fightin'est CVE

Whether or not the *Fanshaw Bay* was "the mightiest and fightin'est CVE," record proved that she was really a fighting ship, and well deserved her nickname "The Fighting Fanny Bee."

The *Fanshaw Bay* won one Presidential Unit Citation and was recommended later for another high award, the Navy Unit Commendation, which was later raised to a recommendation for a second Presidential Unit Citation. The proposal of the Navy Unit Commendation was for "an unbroken career of combatant duty except when going or coming from repair due to battle damage and exposure, through the ship's entire career from 1 April 1944, after shakedowns, to 15 August 1945. During these years she was a front-line carrier in six successive campaigns—Saipan, Morotai, Leyte, Okinawa, East China Sea and occupation of Japanese homeland at Ominato, and was task force flagship in five of these."

The Commander Air Force, Pacific Fleet, said this:

"On the basis of a comparative study of the war records of all CVE-type carriers in the Pacific, and in consideration of her outstanding contribution to the defeat of Japan, Commander Air Force, Pacific Fleet, considers that the USS *Fanshaw Bay* thoroughly merits the award of a second Presidential Unit Citation in lieu of the Navy Unit Commendation."

June 1, 1944 found the Fanny Bee en route to Saipan for what was to be the first, and very nearly the last, major operation for the carrier. On June 15, with the *Fanshaw Bay* providing direct air support for the Marines crawling ashore, five Jap torpedo planes attacked at dusk. All but one were shot down by the combat air patrol. That one launched his flying tin fish at the ship, and as the carrier maneuvered successfully to avoid being hit, a pilot who had been catapulted from the flight deck sixty seconds before brought down the Jap plane. Two days later the *Fanshaw Bay* was in the midst of a terrifying attack by seventy enemy planes. Although the gunners threw up a heavy curtain of flak, one of the seventy attackers got through to plant a bomb on the Fanny Bee's after elevator. Fragments ripped through the thin decks and bulkheads, fires broke out, and the ship listed to port as water filled the after hold. All night long a bucket brigade of officers and men, waist deep in water, fought to save the ship, now down by the stern. Morning came and with the carrier almost on even keel, she began her limping journey back to Pearl. Fourteen men were dead and 22 wounded.

In September she was back at the invasion of Morotai as the carrier group flagship of Rear Adm. C. A. F. Sprague. The first plane to land on Morotai was from the *Fanshaw Bay*. With one pilot in the drink, other Fanny Bee planes covered PT boats which darted to within 100 yards of enemy shore guns to rescue him. On October 3 general quarters sounded a sudden Jap torpedo attack, and as the men tumbled from their bunks and rushed topside, torpedo wakes were already crossing astern. Again the ship outmaneuvered the attack, but one of the tin fish struck and sank the destroyer *Shelton*.

Late in October the *Fanshaw Bay* was on station outside Leyte Gulf, her planes striking at enemy airfields as the invasion troops went ashore. Eight Jap fighters came out of the sun headed for the carrier, but only three survived to fly away. The morning of October 25 dawned as an ordinary day, but before the sun set over Leyte Gulf the Fighting Fanny Bee was to be in on the making of history. Through the overcast one of the scouting planes spotted a huge Jap force headed for the helpless transports off Leyte. Almost immediately salvos from the enemy battlewagons sent geysers just astern of the *Fanshaw Bay*. Then ensued, for nearly three hours, one of the most amazing battles in sea warfare.

The major portion of the Japanese Navy—4 battleships, 10 cruisers and 12 destroyers—was pitted against the *Fanshaw Bay* and 5 other thin-skinned CVE's and their 7 gallant destroyers, plus some planes from task units to the south. Riddled and nearly shattered by enemy shellfire, the baby flattops staggered southward as their planes gave the Jap warships a merciless pounding, with the destroyers and DE's laying smokescreens, their guns blazing as they made repeated torpedo attacks. First the *Johnston*, then the *Samuel B. Roberts*, then the *Hoel* went down, all fighting to the last. The *Gambier Bay* took a hit in the forward engine room, fell behind and was demolished by enemy shell fire at point-blank range. But the other "jeep" carriers fought on, a lone 5-inch gun roaring from the fantail of each as enemy cruisers closed to thirteen thousand yards and Japanese destroyers sent in torpedo after torpedo. Despite overwhelming odds in their favor, the Japs broke off, apparently being unable to take the punishment. But in an hour enemy suicide planes were over the *Fanshaw Bay* and the other carriers. The *St. Lô* was struck squarely on the flight deck and sank. The Fanny Bee, fighting all the way, was hit six times by shells from Jap cruisers, but her casualties were light: 5 dead and 3 wounded.

The *Fanshaw Bay* and her sister ships headed toward Manus, encountering a surface submarine which was sunk with the help of destroyers from another task unit. Back to Pearl Harbor, then to the

States for repairs, the ship put to sea again with Capt. Murr E. Arnold as skipper. Admiral Sprague again hoisted his flag as Commander Carrier Division 26.

Beginning March 21, 1945, the *Fanshaw Bay* went through 69 days of continuous operation. Her planes flew 2,089 sorties, shot down five of the enemy, and smashed numerous ground installations. At the end of May she returned to Leyte, then in June engaged in strikes at Sakashima Gunto. She now joined a new operating unit of cruisers, battleships and carriers roaming the East China Sea in heavy support of the mine-sweeping operations off the coast of China and narrowly escaped both suicide planes and torpedoes on many occasions. In July the Fanny Bee led a new escort-carrier operation in the Kuriles and Sea of Okhotsk, and in September, after hostilities ceased, led another Navy force through the Tsugaru Strait for the occupation of Ominato in Japan. Shortly after, Capt. Marshall B. Gurney took command.

Here is how Lieut. R. B. Herbert, historian of the Fighting Fanny Bee, summed it up:

"Although the USS *Fanshaw Bay* will one day be stricken from the list of naval vessels, nevertheless her name and some of her exploits will live on forever with the men who sailed her, and in naval annals and traditions."

The *Bogue*

According to the citation which accompanied an award from the President of the United States: "The gallantry and superb teamwork of the officers and men who fought the embarked planes and who manned the USS *Bogue* and her escort vessels were largely instrumental in forcing the complete withdrawal of enemy submarines from supply routes essential to the maintenance of our established military supremacy."

Escort aircraft "Carrier B" was one of the first of the "baby flattops" to carry the war to the Germans in the Atlantic. These "hunter-killer" task groups of escort carriers and DEs (sometimes DDs) broke the back of the Nazi U-boats threatening to cut our lines to England and Europe. The *Bogue's* planes definitely sank 10 subs, probably sank 8 others, and damaged 7. For a converted merchant ship (or any other), that's not bad.

Built on a C-3 hull, the *Bogue* was commissioned at Puget Sound on September 26, 1942. She had 8500 horsepower, displaced 13,890 tons, and was 495 feet long. Forty-four other C-3s were turned into carriers, 34 of them going to the British.

A series of sharply fought individual battles between the *Bogue* task group and German submarines in May, 1943 proved the worth of these early escort carriers. Engaging a German wolf-pack the *Bogue* dealt the U-boats the greatest blow delivered by a single ship until that time.

The *Bogue's* baptism in antisub combat came in the cold grayness of the North Atlantic, in a 600-mile stretch of open sea, beyond land-plane range. The conflict began at dusk, a favorite time for U-boat attacks. A torpedo plane returning from patrol attacked the first submarine 62 miles on the convoy's starboard bow. The pilot straddled the surfaced sub with four depth bombs and the U-boat disappeared.

At dawn the convoy was greeted by more subs and crews were at battle stations when another *Bogue* plane spotted a surfaced U-boat lying in wait dead ahead. But submarine lookouts had also sighted the plane, and the Germans opened fire as the Avenger dove in. Disregarding the enemy fire, the pilot dumped a depth bomb salvo near the sub and she went down by the stern, finally sinking. A fighter plane en route to aid the torpedo plane sighted a second U-boat and drove it beneath the surface with machine-gun fire.

Another sub, the one to get nearest the convoy, elected to fight it out with a *Bogue* Avenger in broad daylight. In the face of strong AA fire the torpedo plane charged in, landing a bomb forward of the conning tower. The U-boat rose suddenly, then settled slowly, stern first. The fifth submarine was sighted a few minutes later 25 miles off the starboard quarter. This one, too, fought back and though a four-bomb attack rocked the sub, she righted herself and submerged.

The rest of the wolf-pack stayed down during the afternoon, but at sunset a U-boat popped up 23 miles off the port quarter, running on an interception course. Again the *Bogue* was on hand and one of her Avengers, screaming down in a high-speed dive, straddled the sub with a well directed salvo. The German was knocked out of control and went under. The climax came an hour later when a seventh submarine, submerging after a heavy attack, was unable to stay under and resurfaced. The crew abandoned ship, with the German skipper and 23 others taken prisoner. The U-boat sank, presumably scuttled. In 24 hours the vaunted wolf-pack had been badly beaten.

A short time later Carrier B was in another dusk engagement when subs converged on the convoy from all directions. Two Avengers attacked, one to the northeast, damaging her, then within a minute of each other, two torpedo-bomber pilots were dropping depth bombs on surfaced U-boats on opposite sides of the convoy. The next morning a fighter and a torpedo plane strafed and bombed a final target.

The *Bogue,* which had been operating in this area with the British

Navy, returned to Argentia, Newfoundland. On June 1, 1943 she was underway again, and on June 4 she broke up a pack of U-boats lying directly across the path of an Africa-bound convoy, making four attacks in 48 hours. Three days later a sub only ten miles from the convoy was driven off badly damaged and four days after that 17 prisoners were taken in a successful U-boat sinking. Back in Norfolk, Captain Short was relieved by Capt. J. B. Dunn.

On her next cruise the *Bogue* encountered three new enemy developments in submarine warfare: "mother" subs, stronger AA batteries, and radar. Not long out of Norfolk the *Bogue* caught a mother sub refueling a smaller one and sank the "cow," taking 13 prisoners. The same day one of the DEs in the task group sent down a U-boat which had first been attacked by a plane from the *Bogue*. Carrier B continued to protect African convoys until late in August, and after a short rest began her seventh war cruise on September 5, 1943. No subs were sunk and only one attack was made on this cruise. On her next combat cruise the *Bogue* made five successful attacks, captured 46 Nazi prisoners.

The invasion of Europe was in the offing, and in January and February of 1944 the *Bogue* turned ferry, transporting Army fighter planes to Scotland. But the U-boats became active once more, and the *Bogue* went after them. The subs had changed tactics by this time and were remaining below all day, surfacing at night to charge batteries. This meant the *Bogue's* fliers had to operate around the clock. From May 5 to July 2, with Capt. A. B. Vosseller in command, the *Bogue* group scored three kills, two of them by surface craft. The strangest kill of all (by aircraft) turned out to be a Jap, the only Japanese submarine lost in the Atlantic. During this cruise the *Bogue's* planes set a new record, flying 3,230 hours, 893 of them at night. On the July 24-September 24 cruise, one sub was sent to the bottom and 42 Germans made prisoners. The Nazis were now using "schnorckel," a device which allowed them to charge their batteries under water, and they were spending less and less time on the surface. The wolf-packs were beaten, but individual subs were still dangerous.

Early in 1945 the Germans called in most of their undersea fleet for refitting, so the *Bogue* went in for pilot training off Quonset Point, Rhode Island. In March, when Capt. J. G. Dufek took over, another load of Army planes was ferried to England.

With their armies near collapse in April, the Germans made one last attempt in submarine warfare, sending a huge number of new and improved U-boats into the Atlantic in a final drive against Allied shipping. To combat these the Navy massed four escort carriers, including the *Bogue,* and 46 small ships. The *Bogue* and her sister ships made many attacks, sinking the U-546 and taking 33 prisoners, after that sub torpedoed the destroyer escort *Frederick C. Davis* with great loss of life on April 24, two weeks before the war ended.

From the Battle of the Atlantic the *Bogue* turned to the Pacific, but she got only as far as Guam when the Japs surrendered. In her three years the *Bogue* steamed over 200,000 miles, had more than 7,000 landings on her flight deck.

Ships and air squadrons which operated with the *Bogue* in her anti-submarine campaigns were the *Lea, Greene, Belknap, Osmand Ingram, George E. Badger, Clemson, Dupont, Willis, Haverfield, Swenning, Hobson, F. M. Robinson, Wilhoite,* and VC-9, VC-19, VC-95, VC-69 and VC-42.

The *Guadalcanal*

In 1815 the United States ship *Guerrière* boarded and captured the Algerian brig *Estido* in the Mediterranean. Sea warfare changed down through the years and although fierce battles between ships continued to be fought, rarely did two vessels come closer than gunshot range of each other. In the Battle of the Coral Sea in 1942 ships of the opposing fleets did not sight each other; the battle was fought entirely by carrier plane.

For one brief hour on the morning of June 4, 1944, the task group of the escort carrier *Guadalcanal* (CVE 60) reverted to the tactics of the Continental Navy. When the action was over the *Guadalcanal's* task group boarded and captured, for the first time in Navy history since the *Guerrière* did it in 1815, a foreign enemy man-of-war on the high seas. The prize was the 700-ton German submarine U-505.

Said Capt. Daniel V. Gallery of the *Guadalcanal:*

"I consider this capture to be proof for posterity of the versatility and courage of the present-day American sailor. All ships in this task group were less than a year old and eighty per cent of the officers and men were serving in their first seagoing ship. All hands did their stuff like veteran sea dogs, and airplane mechanics became submarine experts in a hurry, when the chips were down. I'm sure John Paul Jones and his men were proud of these lads and of the day's work when the US colors were run up on the U-505."

The *Guadalcanal,* sixth of the *Casablanca* line of escort carriers, was a Kaiser-built ship commissioned at Astoria, Oregon, September 25, 1943. She shook down on the Pacific Coast and then came through the Canal to make Norfolk her home port. On January 4, 1944, she was under way along the US–Gibraltar route for her first combat cruise in an anti-submarine task group with the destroyers, *Whipple, Ford, Alden,* and *Edwards.* January 16 planes from the *Guadalcanal* spotted three German U-boats in mid-Atlantic, a "mother" sub and two others. The mother boat and one being refueled were sunk by bombs and depth charges; the other escaped. Ten days later the task group put in at Casablanca and then returned to the States.

On the second cruise, which began March 7, the destroyer escorts *Forrest, Pillsbury, Pope, Flaherty,* and *Chatelain* replaced the DDs. Searches were conducted en route to Casablanca but the U-boats were scarce. On the way back a sub was sighted on April 8 but lost. On the 9th, after sighting another which got away, the *Pope* attacked a sound contact and forced a U-boat to the surface. The German was fired upon and sunk, and five prisoners taken. The submarine was the U-515, ten days out of Lorient, France. The next day planes attacked a surfaced sub which replied with heavy antiaircraft fire, but repeated strafing and depth charges finally exploded the vessel, the U-68, from which 17 prisoners were captured.

The *Jenks* replaced the *Forrest* for the third cruise, which got underway on May 14. Searches were unsuccessful until June 3, when a contact developed 150 miles off French West Africa. Next day the *Chatelain* picked up a sound contact and a few minutes later planes from the *Guadalcanal* sighted and strafed a sub running just below the surface. Following directions from the planes, the *Chatelain* raced to the scene and forced the sub to surface by depth charges. The U-boat came up in the center of the task group and immediately began fighting back, manning its deck and AA guns. Captain Gallery gave orders to capture the sub if possible, so that only light, anti-personnel ammunition was fired against the undersea vessel. The Nazis were soon driven overboard by the hail of machine gun bullets from the task group and abandoned the U-boat, leaving it circling at a speed of about six knots. Boarding parties from the *Pillsbury* and *Guadalcanal* raced after the sub in whaleboats, while the carrier dodged the one torpedo the Germans had been able to fire.

The group from the DE came alongside the submarine first and Lieut. Albert E. David, TM Arthur W. Knispel, and RM Stanley E. Wdowiak plunged down the conning tower prepared to fight it out with any Nazis still on board. They found only one dead man. Five other men from the *Pillsbury* and the boarding party from the *Guadalcanal,* led by Comdr. Earl Trosino and Lieut. D. E. Hampton, and including C PHo M C. V. Werlla and Cox. R. T. Sparks, went down into the sinking but still-underway sub. They found booby traps set and water pouring into the U-boat which the Nazis had attempted to scuttle. Working against time the boarders stopped the motors and closed the valves, checking the flooding just in time to prevent the sub from going under. Meanwhile the German survivors had been picked up and put aboard the *Guadalcanal.*

The submarine, the U-505, was taken in tow by the carrier, which conducted flight operations as usual in a continued search for other enemy vessels. The *Guadalcanal* towed the U-505 for four days until the fleet tug *Abnaki* arrived to take over and bring the sub into Bermuda. The technical and operational information obtained from the U-505 played a part in carrying out further anti-submarine missions which helped shorten the Battle of the Atlantic. The *Guadalcanal* and her task group received the Presidential Unit Citation for the feat.

The *Guadalcanal* made another combat cruise under Captain Gallery, with the *Neunzer* replacing the *Jenks,* and then Capt. B. C. McCaffree took over. Two more combat cruises were made, and although subs were attacked in August, October, and in May, 1945, no other definite kills were scored. The *Frederick C. Davis* was added to the task group and in October, while tracking a German sub in the North Atlantic, a terrific storm came up south of Iceland. Three days later the battered vessels were off Western Ireland, every ship damaged. Two attacks were made on submarines. After refueling in the Azores the *Guadalcanal* returned to Norfolk in November.

During the next cruise the *Guadalcanal* operated around Bermuda and in the Caribbean without contacting the enemy, but in April, 1945, while the ship was conducting carrier qualifications off the east coast of the United States, the Germans made their last great submarine thrust in the west and central Atlantic. The *Davis* was ordered north to join a DE and carrier group searching for the U-boats, and was torpedoed and sunk ten days before VE-day, only 36 men being saved. With German subs running loose in the Atlantic even after the war in Europe was over, the *Guadalcanal* figured in two more attacks before calling off the shooting for good. Until VJ-day, expecting to sail for the Pacific, the ship continued to qualify pilots for the Pacific fighting.

The *Tulagi*

The escort carrier *Tulagi* (CVE 72) was one of the few to take part in sustained action in both the European-North Africa and Pacific theaters of operations.

A Kaiser-built ship of the *Casablanca* class, the *Tulagi* was commissioned in December, 1943, and was en route to join the combined

American, British and Free French fleets in the Mediterranean in June, 1944. In July, while members of the Greek royal family were aboard, off Alexandria, Egypt, the *Tulagi* had to fight a determined German air attack. The next month the *Tulagi* was in on the Allied invasion of Southern France, and her fighter and bomber pilots scored impressively. Her fighters shot down 6 Nazi planes; 487 motor vehicles were destroyed, 23 locomotives and 195 railroad cars demolished; 2 forts, 4 gun emplacements and 7 coast guns wrecked; 16 barges and 5 other small craft sunk. With the European war drawing to a close, the *Tulagi* was ordered home. In a month she was on her way through the Panama Canal for the Pacific.

November 24 the *Tulagi* departed from Pearl Harbor in an anti-submarine task group, making sweeps around Saipan and Rota. Early in January 1945, the *Tulagi* had an opportunity to compare German and Japanese air attacks as Jap planes struck while the ship was passing through Mindoro Strait in the Philippines. Two planes were shot down but one got through to make a suicide crash dive on the cruiser *Louisville.* On January 6 the *Tulagi* and other ships commenced operations supporting landings on the Lingayen beaches, and many times during succeeding days the force had to drive off waves of attacking enemy planes. On the 13th a Kamikaze hit the *Salamaua* (CVE 96) steaming directly ahead of the *Tulagi,* and minutes later a second one closed in on the *Tulagi* but was brought down by the carrier's port battery. During the Lingayen action planes from the *Tulagi* flew 129 missions, made 548 sorties, shot down 2 Jap aircraft and damaged 1, and sunk 3 enemy ships.

January 30 the *Tulagi* was detailed to anti-submarine operations, and on the 31st two destroyers and a destroyer escort of the *Tulagi's* group sought out and sank an enemy submarine. In mid-February she put in at Ulithi to pick up planes for delivery to Guam and Iwo Jima, and then continued anti-sub patrols until early in March. Back at Ulithi on the 15th, she replenished in preparation for the invasion of Okinawa, and on the 29th began to furnish air support in connection with the landing of the Tenth Army and III Marine Corps. Early in April, while replenishing at Kerama Retto, the *Tulagi* was attacked by three Jap planes. Two were shot down and one crashed into a nearby LST. The *Tulagi* returned to Okinawa to continue air support operations until June 5, when she was ordered to Pearl Harbor, and then to the States. During the *Tulagi's* second engagement off Okinawa she was credited with 7 enemy planes shot down, 1 destroyed on the ground, and 1 ship sunk. By the time the *Tulagi* was overhauled at San Diego the war had ended.

CRUISERS

Cruisers are the light-heavyweights of the Fleet. Big enough to pack a murderous wallop, yet fast enough to flash through and around the enemy, they are always opponents to be feared. The long-range scouts of the Navy, their slim, graceful lines make them ships of deadly beauty.

Basic cruiser types are "light" and "heavy," although a third type, the battle cruiser, was revived by the Navy with the launching of the *Alaska*-class ships late in the war. The main difference between light and heavy cruisers is not in tonnage, size or speed, but in the ship's main batteries. Light cruisers (designated CL) carry ten to sixteen 6-inch guns. Heavy cruisers (CA) mount nine or ten 8-inch guns. Both types generally carry from four to eight 5-inch antiaircraft guns. *Cleveland*-class antiaircraft cruisers have twelve 5-inch guns in twin mounts.

Ships of the *Alaska*-class, while officially listed as large cruisers (CB), are actually pocket battleships, built as US replies to the German battle cruisers *Scharnhorst* and *Gneisenau*. The Nazi vessels carried nine 11-inch guns and had 80,000 horsepower Diesels with triple screws, rated at 28 knots. The 27,500-ton *Alaska, Guam* and *Hawaii* of the US Navy carry nine 12-inch rifles, have 150,000 horsepower turbines, and do better than 30 knots. These cruisers have catapults forward and carry four scout planes. Six large cruisers were contemplated by the Navy but three were cancelled.

Cruisers can make up to 33 knots, cruise over 15,000 miles without refueling. Normal crew complements of 450 to 800 men were often doubled during the war. Light and heavy cruisers are named for cities, large cruisers for territories and possessions. We entered the war with 18 heavy cruisers, had 7 sunk, ended up with 21. We had 19 light cruisers at the time of Pearl Harbor, lost 3, and had 49 afloat when the war was over.

The *Boise*

No cruiser had a finer fighting record than the *Boise* (CL 47). Commissioned in August, 1938, this light cruiser arrived in Manila with a troop convoy on December 4, 1941. She was in the Sulu Sea proceeding to Cebu when the Japs struck at Pearl Harbor. Immediately joining forces with the cruiser *Houston* and several destroyers, she spent the first month of the war in helping Allied shipping clear the Philippines.

In January the *Boise* became flagship of Task Force 5. On the morning of January 20, 1942 Jap forces appeared off Balikpapan and the *Boise* set out with four destroyers to attack, but the next morning she struck an uncharted reef and was consequently ordered to turn back. After minor repairs at Tjilatjap, Java, she went on to Bombay, India, with Capt. E. J. Moran in command.

Leaving Bombay on April 4 she returned to Mare Island for refitting and was back at sea on June 20 convoying troop ships to New Zealand. On July 2 the *Boise* left Pearl Harbor to carry out a feint in enemy home waters. This mission took her within 650 miles of Tokyo but she escaped enemy patrol planes and returned safely to Pearl.

On September 14 the *Boise* joined Task Force 64, supporting Marine landings on Guadalcanal.

The *Boise* along with the cruisers *San Francisco, Helena, Salt Lake City* and five destroyers was off Cape Esperance on the morning of October 12 when 15 enemy ships were sighted. Making an abrupt turn, the US ships "capped the Jap T," bringing the enemy under heavy and concentrated fire.

The *Boise* quickly engaged a Jap heavy cruiser which was set afire. However, the Jap slapped back hard, planting several shells into the *Boise,* and putting one of her 5-inch guns out of action. Under the combined pounding of the *Salt Lake City* and the *Boise,* the Jap cruiser finally sank.

Immediately the *Boise* turned her guns on a destroyer and after a few furious blasts, the enemy warship broke in two and disappeared. Switching her fire now to another destroyer, the *Boise* and the other ships sent down a third Jap vessel, and then the *Boise* took another Jap cruiser in a furious duel.

While the enemy tried to break off the engagement, the *Boise* opened on a third destroyer which disappeared beneath the water within two minutes. At this time the *Boise* was subjected to a fierce torpedo attack but expert maneuvering pulled her out of danger. Still looking for trouble, she found another target in a Jap light cruiser and was plastering this ship when an enemy heavy cruiser ranged in on the *Boise,* thudding shells into her with deadly precision. Turrets 1, 2 and 3 were hit and set afire with heavy casualties, and finally an 8-inch shell drummed into the forward magazine, killing every man there. Burning and helpless, the *Boise* fell out of line and retired to lick her wounds. She had lost 107 men in the fracas, but was officially credited with sinking or assisting in sinking a Jap cruiser and at least two destroyers.

After repairs at Philadelphia, the *Boise* put to sea on March 20, 1943 under Capt. Hewett Thebaud. She switched now to the North Africa Theater, convoying ships to the Mediterranean, and then joined the Eighth Fleet in the assault on Sicily July 10, serving with Task Force 88 until the end of the Sicilian Campaign. In September she joined the British 12th Cruiser Squadron and landed 788 men at Taranto as that Italian naval base was captured by British forces. From there the *Boise* went on to Salerno to replace the damaged *Savannah* and on November 15, after that engagement, returned to the States.

The *Boise* went back to the Pacific. Arriving at Milne Bay December 30, 1943 she served as a unit of the Seventh Fleet in the Southwest Pacific area until June 18, 1945. From January through September, 1944 she was in on the following bombardment and fire support missions:

(a) Aitape–Humboldt Bay–Tanamerah Occupation.
(b) Night bombardment of Wakde-Sawar Area.
(c) Wakde–Toem Occupation.
(d) Biak Occupation.
(e) Noemfoor Occupation.
(f) Cape Sansapor Landings.
(g) Morotai Occupation.

The *Boise* operated almost continuously in the Philippines from October, 1944, and participated in the following operations and engagements:

(a) Assault on Leyte Gulf, October 20-24.
(b) Battle of Surigao Strait, October 25.
(c) Covering operations with Leyte Gulf Security Forces until mid-December, 1944.
(d) Mindoro Operations, December 12-17.
(e) High-speed covering operation Leyte to Mindoro, December 26-29, incident to Japanese attack on Mindoro on December 26.
(f) Lingayen Occupation, initially as flagship for Commander in Chief, Southwest Pacific Area, January 4-13, 1945, en route to and in Lingayen Gulf; and January 14-31, with Cruiser-Carrier Covering Force off west coast of Luzon.
(g) Bataan–Corregidor Operation, February 13-17.
(h) Zamboanga Operation, March 8-12.

From April 24 to June 16, the *Boise* participated in operations in Borneo waters as follows:

(a) Tarakan Operation, April 27 to May 3.
(b) Brunei Bay Operation, June 10-11, coincident with carrying General of the Army Douglas MacArthur on a tour of the Philippines.

The *Boise* returned to Manila on June 15 with the general and his staff. She sailed from Manila on June 16 for Leyte, and from Leyte on the 18th for Pearl Harbor and the United States.

During the 44 months that the United States was at war, the *Boise* served 35 months overseas. She operated in the Netherlands East Indies Theater in 1941-1942, Pacific Areas in 1942, Mediterranean Theater in 1943, and Southwest Pacific Areas in 1944-1945. She engaged in two night surface actions (a) Battle of Cape Esperance, for which she is now credited with sinking or assisting in sinking 1 Japanese cruiser and 2 Japanese destroyers; (b) the Battle of Surigao Strait, for which she is credited with assisting in sinking one large Japanese unit. While in the combat areas the *Boise* underwent numerous air attacks and was credited with splashing seven Japanese aircraft. She participated in 14 major invasions and shore bombardments, and was damaged in action only once—at Cape Esperance.

The *Richmond*

One of the Navy's oldest veterans, the light cruiser *Richmond* (CL 9) has a record of combat missions any ship would be proud to possess. Launched in 1923, the 22-year-old veteran has taken part in 2 invasions (Attu and Kiska), 12 bombardments, and 3 surface actions with the enemy. Despite all these she has never suffered a scratch nor have any of her crew been battle casualties.

When the Japanese struck at Pearl Harbor the *Richmond* was engaged in patrolling off the west coast of South America. In response to orders received shortly afterward, the ship returned to the Gulf of Panama at high speed for a rendezvous with other naval units and was assigned the task of protecting the western approaches to the Panama Canal. During the first year of the war the *Richmond* steamed almost steadily escorting convoys carrying troops and supplies to the numerous South Pacific bases the Navy hurriedly built in order that vital sea lanes could be protected.

In December, 1942 orders were received detaching the *Richmond* from the Southeast Pacific Force. After a limited overhaul at the Navy Yard, Mare Island, the ship reported for duty in the Aleutian area. Upon arrival at Dutch Harbor in January, 1943 the ship commenced an almost uninterrupted tour of duty in this area, which earned her the title of "Queen of the North Pacific." Storms and fogs and bitter cold were a daily diet.

The mission of the *Richmond's* task force was to re-establish US bases on the Aleutian chain of islands and at the same time provide protection for our shipping.

In February, 1943 the ship took part in the first bombardments that softened up the Japanese garrison on the island of Attu for the landings soon to follow. Twice on February 10 she was attacked by enemy planes that dove out of the low-hanging clouds, but each time she escaped undamaged as her gunfire drove off the enemy.

On March 26 while operating a few miles southeast of the Russian Komandorski Islands in company with the heavy cruiser *Salt Lake City* and a few destroyers, she fought in what was probably one of the longest surface engagements of World War II. She and her consorts flushed a superior Japanese force headed north with supplies for Japan's Aleutian outposts. Under the command of Rear Admiral McMorris the numerically inferior American force turned back the enemy in a running battle. Time and time again the *Richmond* disappeared in smothering waves of spray as enemy salvos straddled her but each time she reappeared, her guns blazing at the Japanese. At one time during the long battle the *Salt Lake City* came to a dead stop, hit by enemy shellfire, and the *Richmond* turned back to shield her companion with a smoke screen while the destroyers made a desperate torpedo attack to halt the enemy.

In the reoccupation of Attu and Kiska in May and August the *Richmond* was part of a covering force which bombarded the islands before and during the landing of the troops.

With the Aleutians again secure, the *Richmond* turned to the Japanese-held Kurile Islands, jagged mountains jutting out of the cold waters of the North Pacific, from Russia's Kamchatka Peninsula to the northernmost Japanese home island of Hokkaido. The new mission was to destroy enemy installations in the Kuriles, seek out and destroy merchantmen and fishing vessels and keep open the sea lanes in the North Pacific. The constant pressure maintained by the *Richmond* and the other ships of this force on the northern flank of the enemy's homeland contributed materially to his eventual downfall.

The first blow of this operation was struck on February 4, 1944. The target was the Japanese base and airfield at Kurabu Zaki on the southern tip of the island of Paramushiro. Under command of Rear Adm. Wilder D. Baker the Americans steamed close inshore on a moonlit night and pommeled the area. Large fires were started and a Japanese freighter taken under fire by the *Richmond's* guns was turned into a blazing shambles that drifted ashore and burned into a gutted shell.

In November of the same year the ship again saw action. On the 21st, as flagship of Rear Adm. John L. McCrea, and commanded by Capt. H. L. Thompson, the *Richmond* participated in a bombardment of the Japanese plane base on the island of Matsuwa in the Northern Kuriles, only 960 miles from Tokyo. Again and again the *Richmond* and her force steamed back to the Kuriles, pounding every base within effective reach of their guns. On January 5, 1945 canneries and airbase facilities at Surabachi Wan were hit in a daylight bombardment, and on February 18 Kurabu Zaki was hit a second time despite Japanese snooper planes which harassed the formation.

As the pace of the war mounted in the South Pacific, events kept step in the north, and on March 15 the *Richmond* and her force of cruisers and destroyers plastered Matsuwa again with 160 tons of high explosives, sending flames billowing skyward as the Japanese shore installations blazed under the impact of the American shells. One salvo of the task force touched off a hidden enemy magazine that let go with a blast, sending pinwheels of explosives over six hundred feet into the air, a galaxy of tumbling light that rivaled a Fourth of July display. On the 10th and 11th of June Matsuwa was again pounded.

On June 25 a small Japanese convoy was spotted in the Okhotsk Sea. The lopsided engagement that followed was fought in a narrow, fog-enshrouded strait near the island of Onnekotan, a confined area, made more dangerous by uncharted rocks. Of the six Jap ships first spotted by *Richmond* lookouts, five were sunk and the sixth ran aground in efforts to escape.

The Japs lost their best chance for revenge when the *Richmond's* task force was caught on a clear day in narrow waters to the north of Matsuwa by a group of enemy planes which failed to press home their attack as the American vessels opened up on them. The enemy failure was rewarded by a visit of the task force to Surabachi Wan, where enemy installations were once more blasted to bits.

On August 11, in the last surface engagement of the war, combined forces of the Ninth and Third fleets, led by the *Richmond* as flagship, encountered and sank 11 Japanese ships off the coast of Paramushiro. The sinking of the largest enemy vessel and assistance in the destruction of another was credited to the *Richmond*. The engagement was fought under unlimited visibility and the sea was soon littered with the burning rubble of enemy shipping as the vessels of the task force closed to point-blank range. (One vessel came so close to the *Richmond* that part of the enemy crew could be seen dashing about the deck; one was seen shaking his fist from the stern of the sinking ship.) As our ships came within range, the guns of Kurabu Zaki opened fire but the *Richmond's* gunners immediately silenced the shore batteries. Then the force finished the day's operation with a three-way attack on Matsuwa, Kurabu Zaki and Surabachi Wan, final bombardment of the war.

The *Salt Lake City*

Aside from playing the leading role in the longest surface battle of the war, fighting 31 engagements against enemy sea, air and land forces in 45 months of warfare, sinking (or helping to sink) 15 enemy ships, damaging at least 10 other Jap vessels and destroying 12 planes, the *Salt Lake City* (CA 25) wasn't very busy.

The oldest heavy cruiser in the fleet, commissioned in 1924, she was returning from Wake Island when the war broke out and she figured largely as the Navy struck retaliatory blows in those early anxious months. In February, 1942 she bombarded Wotje and later the same month, in company with other ships, hammered the Japs on Wake Island. Eight days later she screened the *Enterprise* when that ship's planes bombed Marcus Island, and when Army planes from the *Hornet* raided Tokyo, the *Salt Lake City* was with that group. In August, 1942 she screened the carrier *Wasp* off Guadalcanal and the Russell Islands, within easy range of enemy airfields, saving 72 officers and 787 enlisted men from the *Wasp* when that carrier was sunk in September, 1942.

Off Cape Esperance in October she won the name of "The One Ship Fleet," helping to rescue the *Boise* in a ding-dong engagement against enemy units. While maneuvering to attack a Jap heavy cruiser which had ranged in on the *Boise,* the *Salt Lake City* took an 8-inch shell forward. But once in position she hit the target so often with the help of two other United States ships, that it sank almost immediately. Meanwhile the *Salt Lake City* had been struck again. Three enemy cruisers and 5 destroyers were sunk in the victory, while our forces lost only 1 destroyer sunk, 1 damaged and 2 cruisers hit. Moreover, this engagement assured the safety of Guadalcanal and prevented Jap reinforcements from landing.

After undergoing repairs the cruiser went to the North Pacific under the command of Capt. Bertram J. Rodgers. On March 26, 1943, along with the *Richmond* and 4 destroyers, she intercepted a Japanese force of 2 light and 2 heavy cruisers, 4 destroyers and 2 auxiliaries headed for the Aleutians. The longest US naval battle of the war followed. Although greatly outnumbered the American force closed and opened fire, with the *Salt Lake City* immediately engaging the two Jap heavy cruisers. Shells from her fourth salvo struck the leading enemy cruiser and shortly afterward she scored more hits on the other enemy cruiser, taking in return a Jap shell which caused some damage to one engine room. Ten minutes later she was straddled again and shaken badly. But the *Salt Lake City* continued to engage the enemy, and at 11 A. M. she took another hit on the starboard, followed by a dud hit soon after.

The battle had started at 9 A. M. and real disaster threatened at 11:25 A. M. when one engine room was flooded. Speed dropped, and the enemy fire grew increasingly hot. At this point a brilliantly executed torpedo feint by the destroyers caused the enemy to turn away long enough for the *Salt Lake City* to repair engines, and speed stepped up. By now her ammunition was running low and shells had to be run from bow to stern so that the rear turrets could continue to fire. Suddenly the flooding became almost uncontrollable. One by one the *Salt Lake City's* boilers went out and she lay dead in the water. Despite the protective smoke screen, shells began to fall around her like rain, but another daring torpedo attack by the destroyers again forced the Japs off course long enough for the cruiser to get under way. The battle ended a short time later as the Jap ships headed home, unsuccessful in their attempts to relieve the Aleutian bases.

After repairs at Mare Island the cruiser came back to the Aleutians in 1943 and stayed there until September, bombarding Kiska in the interim. Then with Capt. Leroy W. Busbey in command the *Salt Lake City* participated in the bombardment of Betio (at Tarawa), fighting off a Jap torpedo attack in the process. From there she went on to shell Wotje and Taroa early in February, 1944. Next came participation in raids on Palau, Yap, Ulithi and Woleai in March and April. Then in June she was back at Mare Island Navy Yard, and going on from there to Adak on June 8, she bombarded Paramushiro before returning to Pearl in August. In quick succession came bombardments and carrier operations against Wake Island, Eniwetok, Marcus and the Philippines. From November, 1944 to January, 1945 she operated against the Volcano Islands, protecting B-29 airfields on Saipan and Guam. Iwo Jima took the next pounding and on one "triple play" day, Iwo, Chichi and Haha Jima were all hit. After covering the raids on Luzon, the *Salt Lake City* went back for more blasting at Iwo Jima. Then she plunged into the holocaust of Okinawa for 66 days, repulsing numerous Kamikazes and slugging it out with enemy shore installations. Headed for repairs at Leyte in June, she returned to Okinawa for more duty and was en route to the Aleutians when word came of the war's end. After covering troop landings on Honshu, the *Salt Lake City* finally decided to call it a war.

The *Northampton*

Prominent in the ranks of the thin battle line which protected the Pacific during the earliest months of the war was the gallant cruiser *Northampton* (CA 26), sunk December 1, 1942 off Guadalcanal. On December 7, 1941 the *Northampton,* commanded by Capt. William D. Chandler, was approaching Pearl Harbor with a task force commanded by Admiral Halsey. Two of the *Northampton's* planes were immediately launched and attacking a Jap plane, they shot it down for an early victory. Early in 1942 she accompanied the *Salt Lake City* in the bombardment of Wotje, protecting the *Enterprise* as the carrier's planes attacked the island.

In February as part of the force under Admiral Spruance, she blistered Wake Island and although subjected to heavy return fire from shore batteries, escaped unscathed. April found the *Northampton* and *Enterprise* joining the *Hornet* group in the first bombing of Tokyo. At the battle of Midway in June, the *Northampton* was part of a screen for the *Enterprise,* and she was with that carrier on the morning of June 4 when United States planes smashed four enemy carriers. The next day she moved westward with the *Enterprise* and was on patrol as her planes inflicted the final losses on the Japanese. In mid-August she headed for Guadalcanal and at the end of that month was patrolling off San Cristóbal Island and the New Hebrides area.

Early in October she joined the *Hornet* group sent to attack Bougainville Island, and during the rest of the month operated with carrier and convoy forces off Guadalcanal. On October 26, under Capt. Willard Kitts, she acted as flagship for Rear Adm. Howard Good. Early in the morning of the 26th Navy flattops engaged in a deadly duel with Jap carriers and battleships located to the northwest. The *Northampton's* aircraft crews peppered the skies with bursts as enemy torpedo and dive bomber planes dove on the *Hornet.* Despite this barrage, the *Hornet* took several bad hits but the action was successfully concluded.

On November 30, 1942 the Japs sent a strong force sneaking along the coast of Guadalcanal in an attempt to relieve their battered troops.

Operating with the cruiser *Honolulu* and six destroyers the *Northampton* swirled into action at midnight, blasting a destroyer with her main battery.   But ten minutes later the ship reeled under the tremendous concussion of a torpedo hit, took water, and began listing rapidly. Fires raged throughout the cruiser despite the efforts of her damage-control personnel.   Three hours later she was abandoned.

Captain Kitts won the Legion of Merit when he rescued Stds. M. Francisco Macaraeg who, unable to swim, was clinging hopelessly to the keel of the sinking ship.   Captain Kitts swam back to the ship and towed the Filipino one hundred yards to a rescuing destroyer.

FC Milton P. Looney received the Navy Cross for organizing a section of men to fight the flames.   At great risk to his own safety, he labored in the midst of exploding ammunition and was later injured by a shell fragment as he attempted to rescue a wounded shipmate.

As the war ended, a new *Northampton* was being built.

The *Louisville*

The heavy cruiser *Louisville* (CA 28) was en route to Pearl Harbor when the first Jap bombs fell.   Delaying her cruise, the *Louisville* reached Pearl on December 16, when a heartsick crew viewed the havoc left by the Jap raid.   After that the *Louisville* was up front in every major engagement of the Pacific.

The "Lady Lou," as her crews liked to call her, was not a new ship. Commissioned at Puget Sound Navy Yard in 1931, she spent the decade before the war in routine training cruises, gunnery and tactical exercises.   The most dramatic event in Lou's prewar history was her cruise from Bahia, Brazil, to Simonstown, South Africa, in the winter just before the US entered the war.   With Comdr. H. J. Nelson as skipper, she traveled the submarine-infested waters with all lights aglow and her American flags carefully spotlighted.   At Simonstown she took aboard $148 million in British gold for deposit in the US and landed her precious cargo safely at New York City.

The *Louisville's* first war mission was landing troops on Samoa, and it was on her return from Samoa that she engaged in her first offensive action.   Operating with carriers, she made the opening raid on the Marshall and Gilbert Islands, under the command of Capt. E. B. Nixon. One of the ship's planes was lost during this action. Early in March, 1942 the *Louisville* found herself steaming toward Noumea, New Caledonia, as part of Task Force 11.   This carrier force, hastily assembled in an effort to stem the tide of Jap aggression, included every combatant unit then available.

When the enemy invaded the Aleutians, the *Louisville* was rushed to the dreary, fog-bound Dutch Harbor shore for a four-month stretch of duty, during which she engaged in shore bombardment of Kiska Island. It was on her next big assignment, when as a member of Task Force 18 she had the job of trying to stop the famed "Tokyo Express" from reinforcing Guadalcanal, that the *Louisville* ran into her first real trouble.

On January 29, 1943, as Task Force 11 was steaming off Rennell Island, a dozen Jap torpedo planes swooped in for a twilight raid. At one time six torpedo wakes ripped the water toward the *Louisville*. Gangs below decks heard one resounding crash against the hull—but there was no explosion. The single hit, the crew believed, must have been a dud torpedo. Steaming just ahead, the cruiser *Chicago* took two torpedoes on the starboard side which stopped her dead in the water. The *Louisville* braved destruction to take the disabled vessel in tow, and, thanks to the seamanship of the crew, was able to turn the *Chicago* over to a fleet tug the next morning.

Early in 1944 the *Louisville* became the flagship of Rear Adm. J. B. Oldendorf, who was to command the great naval Gunfire Support Group through all the epic amphibious operations ahead. The ship took her place in the tremendous force assembled for the invasion of the Marshalls, the momentous first operation in the relentless offensive that was to drive the Jap step by step back across the Pacific. One after another came the driving blows against Kwajalein, Eniwetok, Palau, Hollandia, New Guinea and Truk.

By summer the US was ready for its major campaign against the Marianas, and the *Louisville* led the shore bombardment group at Saipan and Tinian. For 11 days the Lady Lou kept her place in the firing line that rimmed the Saipan beaches, without a break except for the replenishment of ammunition. Admiral Oldendorf estimated that the ship had established an all-time gunnery record.

When the triumphant force lined up for the long-awaited invasion of the Philippines in October, the Lady Lou once again led the parade. It was while she was guarding troop landings on Leyte that word came that the Japs had assembled every available ship in a final desperate attempt to halt the inexorable advance of the Navy. Proudly the *Louisville* led her task group out of Leyte Gulf to meet the enemy at Surigao Strait.

By midnight Admiral Oldendorf had formed his units outside the Strait, and the force lay quietly waiting for the enemy fleet. When the Jap ships loomed up on the horizon, they were caught squarely by Navy broadsides which they were powerless to return except by forward guns. Firing the first salvo in that great night battle, the *Louisville* also fired more rounds from her main batteries than all the battleships of her force together. That night the Jap fleet ceased to exist as a real threat to the drive of the United States toward the Empire.

In December, 1944 Admiral Oldendorf hauled down his flag and Rear Adm. T. E. Chandler hoisted his. Seven days later Capt. Rex L. Hicks came aboard as commanding officer, relieving Capt. S. H. Hurt. The *Louisville* now headed toward the most disastrous days of the war when the Japs, powerless to halt the drive across the Pacific, turned to their last weapon—suicide planes.

Early in 1945 when the *Louisville* was moving on Luzon she met the Kamikaze pilots. A suicide plane, battered and blazing, drove straight into the ship, blasting open an 8-inch gun turret and sending flames shooting through the superstructure. Captain Hicks, directing crews from the bridge in a winning fight to save the power compartments below, was severely burned. In spite of the knocked-out turret and a badly jolted crew, the *Louisville* held her place in the task force as lead ship, entering Lingayen Gulf next day for invasion bombardments.

As the *Louisville* led her fire support group out of the Gulf that night, a swarm of suicide planes headed for the ships. Most of them were shot down, but one smashed into the *Louisville's* signal bridge and forward stack. Many *Louisville* men died in the flames, including Rear Admiral Chandler.

The two attacks kept the *Louisville* out of action at Iwo Jima, but she was back on the firing line at Okinawa. Bombarding Jap installations ahead of the advancing US troops, she sustained and weathered the third attempt to sink her. Coming in low over the water, a Kamikaze crashed into the *Louisville's* catapult and then into the ship's forward stack. Eight men were killed and another died later on a hospital ship.

But the *Louisville* proved able to take everything the Japs had to give. Her damages quickly repaired, she sailed as part of the victorious fleet to help clean up the tag ends of the war in Chinese ports after the Jap surrender.

The *Chicago*

The heavy cruiser *Chicago* (CA 29), commissioned in 1931 and commanded by Capt. Bernhard Bieri, was en route to Midway with a carrier task force when the attack on Pearl Harbor developed. After several months of patrol duty she was with the *Yorktown* when that carrier's planes attacked the Japs at Lae and Tulagi.

At 2:30 P. M. on April 7, 1942 the *Chicago* was about 110 miles southeast of South Cape, New Guinea, when 12 enemy planes were detected. The *Chicago* opened fire with her port 5-inch battery and the enemy formation broke and fled. A half-hour later waves of bombers and torpedo planes attacked the group and in the ensuing fracas, the cruiser dodged four torpedoes while shooting down three enemy planes. An attack by high level bombers followed immediately, but by taking violent evasive action the *Chicago* escaped damage.

In August the *Chicago* was at Guadalcanal when 25 enemy bombers came over, followed by a wave of dive bombers—but again the *Chicago* escaped. The next night forty more enemy planes came at the force and *Chicago's* strong antiaircraft fire kept her out of danger once more.

Early in the morning of August 9, 1942 the *Chicago* was in the channel between Guadalcanal and Savo Island when a destroyer sighted ships entering the bay. The *Chicago* was preparing to open fire when two torpedoes crossed her bow. She was turning to avoid these when another torpedo caught her. Despite the tremendous explosion that followed, she continued the action, firing several shells at what appeared to be enemy destroyers. She then cruised the area searching for enemy ships, although already badly hit.

Back in action in January, 1943 the *Chicago* ran into another night torpedo attack, this time from Jap planes which concentrated on the heavy cruisers in our task force. Jap flares lighted the wild scene and in the glare of a burning enemy bomber, the *Chicago* was silhouetted plainly. As a result the Japs were able to plant a torpedo in her, followed by another. All engines stopped and ship control was lost, but by 11:30 P. M. the attack was over and the cruiser's list had been stopped.

Next morning a tug arrived and took the *Chicago* under tow. At five in the afternoon, 12 enemy torpedo bombers plunged through an intense screen of antiaircraft fire and sent four more torpedoes into the damaged *Chicago*. She sank 19 minutes later.

A second *Chicago* (CA 136) was commissioned on January 19, 1945 under the command of Rear Adm. A. W. Radford. She joined the Third Fleet on July 10, 1945. From then until the end of the war the second *Chicago* supported nine air attacks against Honshu and Hokkaido, and participated in three shore bombardments of

Honshu. Following the cessation of hostilities, she supported the occupation of Yokosuka naval base before moving into Tokyo Bay.

The *Houston*

The heavy cruiser USS *Houston* (CA 30) disappeared on the night of February 28, 1942 off St. Nicholas Point on her way through Sunda Strait between Java and Sumatra. The previous day the *Houston* had taken part in the Battle of the Java Sea, in which the Japanese had scored some telling blows against an Allied force of British, Dutch and US ships in a Japanese invasion of Java. The Navy reported that its knowledge of the *Houston* ended on the night of the 28th, and no complete report of her fate came until September 1, 1945, when ninety-four *Houston* survivors were liberated from a Japanese prison. From them came the story of that fateful night off St. Nicholas Point. Here are the details.

The *Houston,* the British cruiser *Exeter,* the Australian cruiser *Perth,* and the Dutch cruisers *De Ruyter* and *Java,* screened by a small force of destroyers, had fought a great Jap fleet in the Java Sea, with the Allies taking heavy losses. The *De Ruyter, Java* and three destroyers were sunk on the 27th, the *Perth* and the *Houston* were lost on the 28th, and a sloop, three destroyers and the *Exeter* went down on March 1, with one other destroyer being damaged.

It was after dark on the 28th when the *Houston* and *Perth* were ordered to leave Tanjong Priok through Sunda Strait. About 11:15, with the open sea of the Indian Ocean in sight, the *Houston* and the *Perth* came upon the enemy—a dozen Jap destroyers, several cruisers, torpedo boats, and twenty or thirty transports. The *Perth* opened fire at once, and with no time to gauge the battle situation, the *Houston* followed. Jap searchlights and star shells caught the two ships in their glare, and the *Perth* was torpedoed and went down. The *Houston* fought on alone, her guns firing furiously at every target in sight. But her after engine room was hit and boiler pressure dropped dangerously. Then a torpedo struck in the starboard side. No. 2 turret got it next, then turret 1 and the small-arms magazine blazed. Her 5-inch guns completely out of ammunition, the *Houston* was listing badly. Just as the order was given to abandon ship, another torpedo crashed into the crippled cruiser.

Enemy shelling continued as the crew rushed topside to draw life-jackets. Men crouched in the lee of the turrets or dropped over the side. Captain Rooks was bidding his men goodbye as they left when a 5-inch shell struck a few feet aft, killing him instantly. Wounded men staggered down the deck. Then another tin fish hit, killing hundreds in the water. The *Houston,* battered and blazing, turned over on her side and went down, the sea hissing and foaming. (Survivors were scattered thirty miles along the Java coast; those whom the Japs rescued spent horrible years in prison camps; 75 died.)

Only six cruisers received the Presidential Unit Citation in World War II and the *Houston* was one of them. Here is her citation:

For outstanding performance against enemy Japanese forces in the Southwest Pacific from December 7, 1941 to February 28, 1942. At sea almost constantly, often damaged but self-sustaining, the *Houston* kept the sea. She maneuvered superbly and with deadly antiaircraft fire, repulsed the 9-plane Japanese bombing squadrons attacking a troop convoy under her escort. Later, in company with other Allied ships, she engaged a powerful enemy force, carried the brunt of the action with her two remaining 8-inch turrets and aided in damaging and routing two enemy heavy cruisers from the line of battle. On February 28, the *Houston* went down, gallantly fighting to the last against overwhelming odds. She leaves behind her an inspiring record of valiant and distinguished service.

On December 7, 1941 the *Houston* was in the Philippines, part of the Asiatic Fleet. But by the end of December the Asiatic Fleet had been forced southward to the Dutch East Indies. (Adm. William A. Glassford, as task force commander, had his flag on the *Houston,* later switching to the *Boise* and then the *Marblehead.*)

The *Houston* spent most of January, 1942 on convoy duty. But in early February an Allied striking force of Dutch and American cruisers and destroyers was formed, of which the *Houston,* commanded by Capt. Albert H. Rooks, was one. On February 3, just south of Kangean Islands, enemy planes appeared about 10 A. M. The ships scattered but the Jap planes concentrated on getting the cruisers. The *Houston,* zigzagging at top speed and furiously firing her antiaircraft guns, nevertheless took a hit from a single Jap plane. The bomb struck the mainmast, destroying the after turret. Forty-eight men were instantly killed and 20 injured. Early in the afternoon the Jap planes withdrew and the dead members of the *Houston* crew were buried at Tjilatjap. Captain Rooks had the ship patched up with some old rails and took her back to sea, her turret still disabled.

On February 15 the *Houston* was ordered to convoy fast troop carriers from Port Darwin to Timor. At 2:15 P. M. a Jap seaplane showed up, coming down from 10,000 to 4000 feet. The *Houston* opened up and scored almost immediately, the seaplane dumping its bombs and crashing into the water. But before it was splashed, the Jap plane had apparently been able to radio the location of the convoy, for four groups of Jap bombers appeared next day at 11 A. M.

The 36 heavy bombers were sighted to the North at 10,000 feet in perfect formation. The *Houston* swung into action with all her anti-aircraft batteries slapping a barrage across the Jap line of flight and breaking up the formation. Five minutes later the planes reappeared from all directions, each making for the *Houston.* As the Jap bombers came over the ship, each dropped a 1,000-pound missile. Twisting and turning, the Houston avoided being hit, meanwhile putting up a terrific curtain of antiaircraft. The attack lasted 45 long minutes as *Houston* gunners shot down 7 and damaged 8 Jap bombers.

Unable to damage the hard-hitting *Houston,* the Japs turned to the slower convoy vessels, showering them with 250-pounders, springing the seams of each ship, and causing many casualties from fragments. The attack finally died out, but the position of the convoy was now definitely known and with Jap surface forces in the area the troop carriers returned to Port Darwin, where the *Houston* refueled and headed west.

On the 25th information was received that Japanese invasion fleets were approaching Java and an Allied force of British, Dutch and US ships, including the *Houston,* was sent to intercept. On the 27th this force made contact with a superior Japanese force, headed by nine cruisers, between Java and Bawean Island, about four o'clock in the afternoon. The *Exeter* was hit, then the Dutch destroyer *Kortenear* went down. The action continued until early next morning and when the *Houston* and *Perth* reached Tanjong Priok, two British destroyers and two Dutch cruisers were gone. That was the *Houston's* last night.

The people of Houston, Texas, didn't take the loss without a show of patriotism. They immediately subscribed war bonds enough to build another Houston (CL 81), and over-subscribed enough to construct an additional carrier. At the same time, one hundred Houston men volunteered to replace those lost on the first *Houston.* The second *Houston* was commissioned December 20, 1943, with Capt. William W. Behrens in command.

This *Houston* took part in the carrier strikes against the Marianas and Iwo Jima, lent support to the Saipan landings, and then screened the strikes at Guam and Rota. She was fast becoming a veteran. In September, 1944 she bombarded Peleliu and Angaur. In October at Formosa she shot down six enemy planes, but another got through her AA fire to strike with an aerial torpedo. In bad shape, she was taken in tow by the *Boston,* and later by the Navy tug *Pawnee.* While being towed by the *Pawnee,* Jap planes attacked and the *Houston* was again hit by a torpedo with 4 officers and 51 enlisted men killed, many wounded. All except a 200-man salvage party were taken off the ship and transferred to other vessels, and in two weeks the *Houston* reached Ulithi. But her fighting career was over, and after drydock in Manus she limped back to the New York Navy Yard. She was ready for sea again in October, 1945, having been out of action a year.

The *New Orleans*

This heavy cruiser (CA 32) was another of the comparatively few ships which, although caught at Pearl Harbor, lived through the worst naval conflicts and was still going strong at the end of the war. Like the *Chicago,* the *New Orleans* was being overhauled when the Japs struck, and she too, could retaliate with only light guns. But that was the end of her weak defensive, for when she sallied forth in April, 1942 the *New Orleans* was ready for plenty of trouble . . . which she proceeded to get.

In the battle of the Coral Sea in May, she teamed with the *Lexington* to give the Japs the first decisive check of their career of conquest. Her guns spoke incessantly, protecting the Lex, but the enemy planes came through to rock the carrier with heavy bombs. Out of control, she drifted helplessly as fires burned with furnace-like intensity and the ship shook with explosions. Through this holocaust came the *New Orleans* rescuing hundreds of the Lex's crew from the water. *New Orleans* men and boat crews continually went overboard to grab weakening survivors, moving into an inferno of flames and deafening blasts.

After this rescue, the cruiser, commanded by Capt. Walter S. DeLany, screened the *Hornet* and *Enterprise* at the great Midway victory. August found her and the *Saratoga,* off Guadalcanal, in action during the Battle of the Eastern Solomons. And on November 30, commanded by Capt. Clifford Roper, she drove into the Battle of Tassafaronga.

Fought in the darkness of a tropic night, the half-hour action opened with a torpedo thrust by our destroyers at 11 P. M. The Japs, heading down towards Guadalcanal with troop transports and a destroyer-cruiser force, were intercepted between Savo and Lunga. The initial torpedo attack was followed by a successful engagement between the *New Orleans* and an enemy destroyer which blew up after the *New Orleans'* fourth salvo. Next the cruiser took a cargo vessel under fire and at that moment a smaller, faster Jap force made a sharp torpedo attack, hitting the *New Orleans* between turrets 1 and 2. All personnel in these turrets were killed and the entire bow of the ship was blown off by the explosion, yet she continued afloat, and after repairs was back in the line in September, 1943.

The three Rogers brothers, Jack, Edwin and Charles, lost their lives in this tragedy. A new destroyer, the *Rogers,* has been named in their honor. Ten of the *New Orleans'* crew received the Navy Cross. Comdr. Whitaker F. Riggs, Lt. Comdr. Henry S. Persons, Lt. Comdr. Oliver F. Naquin, Lt. Comdr. Hubert M. Hayter, Lt. Comdr. James H. Howard, Lieut. Richard A. Haines, Ens. Andrew L. Foreman, CCM. Erwin C. Parmalee, SF Gust Swenning and F. Alvin L. Marts were the men honored.

In September the *New Orleans* bombarded Wake Island with a raiding task force, following this with punches at the Gilberts, Kwajalein and Taroa, where she sank a cargo vessel. In January, 1944, she bombarded Kwajalein, supporting landings there with more pummelings of enemy installations. Then on February 13 she raided the bristling Jap base at Truk, as part of Task Force 58. (In this strike she ranged in on a *Katori*-class cruiser and a *Shiguri*-class destroyer, aiding in sinking them both.) In March, still with Task Force 58, she covered the landings on New Guinea and air strikes at Palau, repeating this performance at Hollandia, Wakde, Aitape, Satawan, Saipan, Tinian and Guam.

In June she came through the Battle of the Philippine Sea unscathed, shooting down several enemy planes. July found her bombarding Guam, then she patrolled off Saipan, and in August, now with the Third Fleet's Fast Carrier Task Force, she blasted Eniwetok, Iwo Jima and Chichi Jima, bombarding the latter area mercilessly on September 2, 1944.

On September 7 she was off Yap, bombarding that island before heading for air strikes at Okinawa and Formosa, October 10-13, where the *New Orleans* got two more planes. This was followed relentlessly by more strikes with Task Group 38.4, at Luzon and Leyte. The cruiser added two more notches to her guns by aiding in the sinking of an enemy light carrier and destroyer in October. Finally, after surviving continued operations in the suicide-plane belt off Leyte, and the typhoon of December, the *New Orleans* steamed for repairs at Pearl and Mare Island in January, 1945.

After overhaul and trials she headed back to the Pacific, joining the Fifth Fleet at Ulithi on April 18, 1945. Five days later she was in the thick of the Okinawa terror, and there she stayed until June 23. On May 26 the *New Orleans* fired on enemy troops on Okinawa. killing an estimated 400, and wrecking 6 tanks. She was at Subic Bay, readying for further duty in the Southwest Pacific, when the war ended.

The *Portland*

According to Navy records the heavy cruiser *Portland* (CA 33) is credited with having sunk 2 destroyers, assisted in sinking 2 battleships and 2 destroyers, rendered serious damage to 1 battleship, 1 heavy cruiser and 1 light cruiser, shot down 22 enemy planes and assisted in splashing another 11 planes in the Pacific. She participated in 24 major actions and has 15 battle stars to her credit—which puts her near the top of the batting list in World War II.

Commissioned in 1933, the *Portland* was headed for Midway with the *Lexington* to deliver planes when the enemy struck at Pearl Harbor. With Capt. Robert Thompson in command, she operated with a carrier task force during the early months of the war and screened the *Yorktown* in the battle of the Coral Sea, May 1942. In June 1942 she was with the *Yorktown* in the Battle of Midway and in August accompanied the *Enterprise* in the battle of the Eastern Solomons, going on from there to participate in the battle of Santa Cruz on October 26, 1942. During these battles, the *Portland* as part of the carrier screen was a constant target for Jap bombers and torpedo planes. Then followed the black night battle of Guadalcanal on November 12-13, during which the *Portland* won the Navy Unit Commendation, which read:

For outstanding heroism in action against enemy Japanese surface forces in the Battle of Guadalcanal in the Solomon Islands, November 12-13, 1942. As the third ship in a column vastly outnumbered by the hostile fleet force disposed in three savagely opposing groups, the USS *Portland* promptly countered the opening close-range fire of Japanese vessels and sent one powerful salvo after another from her main battery into the enemy. Immediately illuminated by hostile searchlights, starshells and the glare of enemy ships burning on both flanks, she fought a fierce independent action after losing contact with the Flag, sank one Japanese destroyer and quickly shifted fire to a heavy cruiser. Badly holed on the starboard quarter by hostile torpedo hits which disabled her steering control, two engines and No. 3 turret and forced her to steam in tight circles, the *Portland* fought on gamely, taking successive enemy ships under fire with her two remaining turrets as she circled and sinking another destroyer south of Savo Island as a climax to this historic 24-minute sea battle, one of the most furious surface engagements in the war with Japan. When firing had ceased, she dauntlessly loaded her whaleboat to capacity with survivors of the Task Group, and with her bouyancy increased by effective pumping and shoring, gallantly stood by, refusing tow in favor of the more seriously crippled *Atlanta*. This record of heroism in combat reflects the highest credit upon the *Portland's* fighting readiness and upon the superb seamanship, the courage and determination of the officers and men who kept her afloat.

After repairs to the ship, Capt. Arthur Burkens relieved Capt. Lawrence DuBose as commanding officer and in May, 1943, the *Port-*

land was sent to the North Pacific, patrolling off the Aleutians and bombarding Kiska.

In November, she was back with a task force attacking the Gilberts, firing on enemy batteries in the invasion of Betio and Tarawa. In December, 1945 she assisted in the bombardment of Majuro Atoll. In February the *Portland* left Majuro, returning to Kwajalein, where under Comdr. W. E. Guitar, she slammed shore installations until the island's capture.

At the end of March she screened carrier strikes at Palau, Yap, Ulithi and Woleai. In April she screened carriers during a major bombing attack on the Jap naval fortress at Truk. Then she steamed for Mare Island, liberty and a major overhaul, returning in time to blast Peleliu late in September. The whirlwind Philippine campaign came next, during which the *Portland* remained at sea for twenty weeks while actively engaged with every type of enemy opposition. The climax of this campaign was the battle of Surigao Strait on October 24, 1944.

Joining the left flank cruiser unit, the *Portland* waited near the mouth of the Strait as enemy ships drove into the trap. The right flank destroyers attacked first, pouring torpedoes into the enemy, and then the battleships and cruisers opened fire. The *Portland's* guns thundered at 3:52 A. M. at a range of nearly eight miles. Although straddled by several enemy salvos, she assisted in sinking two battleships and two destroyers, and inflicted heavy damage on an enemy cruiser in a dangerous pursuit down the Strait.

Following more air strikes on Luzon and attacks on enemy ships in the Visayan Sea, she returned to the Manila Bay area. Then after several days in the Leyte Gulf patrol, the *Portland* joined the force bound for the invasion of Mindoro, and later was assigned to help clear the way for the invasion.

During the progress of her formation through the Mindanao and Sulu Seas, the *Portland* was subjected to incessant attack by suicide planes. In February, 1945 she entered Manila Bay and bombarded Corregidor, preparing for paratroop and amphibious landings. Finally after five months at sea, she returned to Leyte Gulf for repairs, stores and recreation.

The *Portland* was to engage in two more combat phases before accepting the surrender of Truk and the Caroline Islands from Japan. Both engagements were at Okinawa, the first from March 21 to April 20, the second from May 8 until June 17. In between, it was replenishment at Ulithi and Leyte.

In the initial Okinawa assault the *Portland* bombarded Yontan airfield and while under heavy air attack shot down a Jap bomber and scored direct hits on a submarine which fired torpedoes at the *Pensacola.* Then the *Portland* turned to the shelling of Ie Shima in support of US troop landings and again was engaged heavily with enemy aircraft. In 24 raids her gunners accounted for 4 planes, shooting down 3 Kamikazes on April 6. The *Portland* also assisted in splashing eight more of the enemy.

The second Okinawa phase was less strenuous. The *Portland* bombarded southwestern Okinawa nightly until June 17 without being attacked and without bringing enemy aircraft under fire. During this time the cruiser's medical department received Army and Marine casualties aboard for hospitalization. On September 2 the Japanese at Truk boarded the *Portland* to surrender the islands under their domination, Vice Adm. George D. Murray accepting for the United States. The *Portland* made Guam and Pearl Harbor, then returned to the States carrying high-point servicemen.

The *Astoria*

It is ironic that the same heavy cruiser *Astoria* which carried the remains of Japanese Ambassador Hiroshi Saito back to Japan in March, 1939 was sunk by the Japs a few years later. But her successor came back to make another trip to Japan, this time to preside over the remains of the Japanese Navy.

The first *Astoria* (CA 34) was commissioned in April, 1934 and before she sank off Savo Island, had participated in three of the war's most decisive naval battles. First, she helped check Japan's southward drive toward Australia by screening the *Yorktown* and *Lexington* in the Battle of the Coral Sea. Then at Midway she helped administer the first decisive defeat suffered by the Japanese Navy in 350 years. Before she went down at Savo, the *Astoria* and her cohorts had stopped the threatened Jap attack on our troop transports off Guadalcanal.

En route to Midway under the command of Capt. Francis W. Scanland on December 7, 1941 the *Astoria* task force immediately began a high-speed sweep to the southeast in an attempt to intercept the enemy. Then until February she patrolled with the *Lexington,* joining a task force built around the carrier *Yorktown* on February 16, 1942.

Operating in the South Pacific, she participated in a series of operations which culminated in the carrier Battle of the Coral Sea, on May 7-8. (This was the battle in which not one shot was exchanged between rival surface forces.) The US task force was not attacked the first day of the action but when the weather front shifted on the 8th, the entire US force was exposed and enemy torpedo planes and dive bombers struck at our ships in waves. The *Astoria* stuck with the *Yorktown,* downing three torpedo planes and one dive bomber while maneuvering adroitly to escape the bombs directed at her.

In the Battle of Midway on June 3-6, the cruiser again screened the *Yorktown,* but Jap torpedo planes got through this time to send the carrier down.

Then in the Guadalcanal campaign in August, under the command of Capt. William Greenman, the *Astoria* was subjected to relentless torpedo attacks by forty Japanese planes which pressed in on the landing area. The *Astoria* and others set up such a furious barrage that at least 14 enemy planes were shot down and the remainder left in a hurry.

On the night of August 8 the *Astoria* was part of the column caught by the Jap units in the Battle of Savo Island. Although she sent several salvos into enemy ships, the *Astoria* was spotted in the glare of Japanese searchlights and took a merciless beating. Fires soon broke out, forcing the abandonment of the engine rooms, and the vessel began to lose speed. Then for five minutes the *Astoria* was "under the heaviest concentration of enemy fire." Helpless, the ship drifted while the crew worked desperately to save her. For some time there seemed to be hope but repeated explosions below decks settled the issue and a few minutes after noon on August 9 she sank.

The new *Astoria* (CL 90) is a light cruiser. She took her shakedown cruise in June, 1944, and dropped anchor with the Third Fleet at Ulithi in November, 1944, assigned to Cruiser Division 17.

In December she was with the Third Fleet during air strikes at Lingayen Gulf and a few days later the task force hit a typhoon off the Eastern Philippines. The storm tore two planes loose from her catapults, damaging them beyond repair. In January she was with the Third Fleet during air strikes on Formosa and South China Coast areas. In February, this time with Task Force 58, she accompanied carriers of the Fifth Fleet pounding the Tokyo area, Chichi Jima and Haha Jima. Then on February 21 she joined other ships in bombarding Iwo Jima. From then until the end of the war she was in on continued attacks at Tokyo, Okinawa, Kyushu, Shikoku and Nansei Shoto. She made one of the most daring rescues of the war in picking up Lieuts. (jg) J. F. Newman and D. O. Comb in Kagoshima Bay. All through the Okinawa campaign during which she shot down 11 Jap planes, the *Astoria* was under way continuously for 79 days, cruising 36,300 miles.

From July 1 until the end of the war the *Astoria* steamed along the Japanese coast with carrier task forces attacking inland cities. On the night of the 14th with Cruiser Division 17 she conducted a high speed sweep against shipping off Honshu, and again on the 24th. The *Astoria* remained with Task Force 58 until the signing of the surrender and then returned to California carrying servicemen to be discharged.

The *Minneapolis*

The "Minnie" (CA 36) should have gone down at Tassafaronga, but she didn't. She might have been fatally hit at Midway, or Tinian, or Surigao Strait, or Lingayen Gulf, or Okinawa . . . but she came through. This heavy cruiser lived up to the finest traditions of her class in proving a dogged, tough and rough sea raider from Pearl Harbor to VJ-day.

The Minnie, commissioned May 19, 1934, was off Pearl on December 7, 1941 engaged in gunnery drill under the command of Capt. F. J. Lowery. On patrol through January, she put to sea next as part of a carrier force raiding the Gilbert and Marshall Islands. The *Minneapolis* had her first brush with the Japs on February 1, 1942, when as part of the *Lexington's* screen, she fought off a prolonged air attack. In March she was with the Lex and *Yorktown* during strikes at Lae and Salamaua, and in May she steamed along with the force striking at Tulagi and Gavutu in the Solomons.

During the Battle of the Coral Sea on May 7-9, the Minnie threw up a curtain of flak to protect the *Lexington,* but the Japs got through and the Minnie stood by to pick up survivors. At the Battle of Midway she was with the *Hornet,* accompanying that carrier when it pursued the blasted Jap force westward. In July she sailed with the *Saratoga* and participated in the Guadalcanal campaign in August. The battle of the Eastern Solomons found the Minnie on hand again, flying the flag of Rear Adm. Carleton H. Wright as she screened the *Saratoga.* On August 30 the *Saratoga* was hit by a torpedo, and by taking her in tow the Minnie helped avert her complete destruction.

Capt. Charles Rosendahl relieved Captain Lowery in September. On November 30 the Minnie was part of Task Force 67 in the now famous Battle of Tassafaronga Strait. Opening up with her main battery, the cruiser scored many hits on a transport, then turned on a destroyer which soon sank. Another target was taken under fire when the men aboard the Minnie saw a blinding flash as a torpedo exploded on her port bow. At almost the same instant a second, deeper-running fish hit in the area of No. 2 fireroom. Tremendous walls of water were hurled up the side of the ship; flames, smoke and fumes engulfed her. Lieut. Allen W. Bain, WT Francis Irwin Coppage and GM William David Upshaw and other crew members all behaved with quiet valor in the ensuing moments.

With her bow practically gone, sinking, and losing steering control, the Minnie continued to send salvos after the retreating enemy. Somehow she staggered into Tulagi Harbor, 18 miles away. She fought her way back to Pearl, then to Mare Island for permanent repairs. And in October, 1943 she was back again, lamming shells into the Japs on Wake Island.

Later in October, under Vice Adm. Robert Giffen, she struck at the Gilberts, bombarding Makin during the invasion there. More invasion work at Taroa and Kwajalein followed from January through February 6, 1944. (Somewhere in this period she found time to move in with a force against Truk, pummelling a cruiser and destroyer in company with other units.)

Off Saipan and Tinian, the Minnie looked down the throats of the Japs as she poured it on the beaches in support of our troop landings. After this she turned to help soften up Guam. Two Jap bombers got through to drop their eggs so close to the Minnie's bow that it looked like cheesecloth. Her crew calmly patched up the two hundred holes in her plating and looked around for new prospects. July and August found her smashing enemy batteries on Guam and Rota, followed by more smack on Angaur, Ngesebus and Peleliu in September. When the Philippines were invaded in September, 1944, the *Minneapolis* was there, adding enemy planes to her brilliant gunnery record.

It was while the *Minneapolis* was operating with a task force off Leyte that the Japanese Navy essayed their now-historic counterattack which developed into the battle of Surigao Strait.

"That was one we'll never forget," one observer said. "There we were deployed across the Strait in the darkness. We knew the Japs were coming but we couldn't understand why. We could see the flashes of gunfire as the PT boats and destroyers rushed in to fire their torpedoes. They kept coming and coming right into our range without firing a shot. Then our whole line of cruisers and battleships let go at once.

"It was like drawing a flame across the sky with a paint brush—from broad to narrow that streak of flame converged. You could see it hit a Jap battleship before you could hear it. There was a tremendous flash—and the ship was gone.

"Others kept right on coming, though. And we kept right on picking them off. At one point in the battle enemy fire straddled us but we were never hit."

In November the Minnie screened carrier strikes on Manila Bay. While fueling in Leyte Gulf an eager Kamikaze hit the tanker from which Minnie was getting a drink, but the cruiser's luck held good. The New Year was ushered in by attacks at Lingayen Gulf, and after further attacks on Kerama Retto, she returned to the States for long-overdue repairs.

"Lingayen Gulf and Okinawa," said Commander Maginnis (the Minnie's exec.), "were the two most gruelling shows we were in. There were suicide swimmers with explosive charges on their backs, suicide boats and suicide planes day and night. On top of that, we were standing close to the shores for bombardment and those enemy shore batteries came perilously close sometimes. We were under frequent air attack in an enclosed bay with enemy batteries on both sides and at the mouth of the bay, and Jap airfields were far too close for comfort. We were in there a week ahead of the invasion and an enemy 11-inch gun chased us all over the bay. A large number of the bombardment force took hits, but Lady Luck was with us."

After her grooming at Puget Sound Navy Yard, the Minnie returned to the Far East in September, 1945. Her record: 25 actions, 16 Asiatic-Pacific stars, 40 killed and 31 wounded in action, 15 enemy planes destroyed, 4 enemy ships sunk.

The *Tuscaloosa*

Checking through the official naval records of ships like the heavy cruiser *Tuscaloosa* (CA-37) induces feeling that there must be a God of Battles who watches over the destiny of men and ships. The "Lucky Tuscy's" record of incredible adventure kept her in constant danger for six years, yet she had one of the lowest casualty records in the Fleet.

Commissioned in August, 1934 the Tuscy was an old favorite of President Roosevelt. She got into the war informally in 1939 on neutrality patrol duty off Iceland—not a dull assignment. Shortly before Christmas she arrived in New York with 589 survivors of the liner *Columbus,* scuttled in mid-Atlantic by the Nazis.

After more Presidential tours and patrols during 1940-1941, she received an exciting assignment in May, 1941 when she went on the prowl for the German battleship *Bismarck,* without success. Then in August, she took part in the famous Atlantic Charter meetings and began convoying US troops to Iceland. War did not find the *Tuscaloosa* unaware of its meaning. She had been near when the destroyer *Reuben*

James was sunk and when the tanker *Salinas* and destroyer *Kearney* were hit by torpedoes, all before Pearl Harbor.

On December 7, 1941 the Tuscy was at Vhalfjord, Iceland, on escort duty. From then until August, 1942 she made many trips deep into enemy waters—along the Barents Sea and in the fjords of Norway, swarming with Nazi planes and submarines.

This was the summer the Luftwaffe all but broke the vital Murmansk lifeline. On some of these patrols the *Tuscaloosa* saw as many as thirty merchant ships torpedoed in a single day—but miraculously she always escaped.

In August, 1942 a cruiser was needed to rush supplies to Murmansk and the Tuscy was chosen. For six days and nights, the Tuscy and a British destroyer pushed up the coast of Norway, through submarine traps and within easy range of land-based bombers. But again she arrived safely at Murmansk and brought home hundreds of survivors of sunken convoys on her return.

After a trip to New York in September, the Tuscy showed up at the invasion of Casablanca, where she shelled submarines, cruisers and destroyers and silenced enemy shore batteries. Meanwhile, retaliatory fire from these opponents missed her, as did 15-inch shells from the battleship *Jean Bart* and a torpedo that passed fifteen feet to port. At the end of nine hours her main-battery ammunition was all but exhausted and the Tuscy withdrew.

Following an overhaul late in 1942 the Tuscy made several trips to Africa on escort duty. Then in March, 1943, under the command of Capt. J. B. Waller, she sought contact with the German battleships *Tirpitz* and *Scharnhorst*. In October she was in on air strikes against German defenses in Norway, undergoing intense aerial attack in the process. In the same month she was with the forces relieving the air station at Spitzbergen, through ice-filled, submarine-infested waters. After one more sweep in Norwegian waters she returned to New York for overhaul in December, 1943.

Following overhaul, she returned to England and on the morning of June 6, 1944, the Tuscy was blasting shore installations in Normandy. For the next two weeks, she underwent constant enemy shore and air bombardment, coming unscathed through a literal rain of enemy fire. In July the Tuscy went to the Mediterranean for the bombardment of Southern France, and through August she continued to steam off Cannes and Nice rendering support to Army units.

After returning to Philadelphia for a grooming, the Tuscy, now under Capt. J. G. Atkins, headed for the Pacific, arriving at Pearl Harbor for Christmas, 1944.

She was in on the bombardment of Iwo Jima on February 16 and at Okinawa March 25 through June 28. The Okinawa period was one of the most harassing, with the crew at general quarters for days repelling suicidal air attacks. And always the Tuscy's guns were pounding—pounding the air and ground forces that sought to wipe her out in the war's very end. Some of the counterbattery fire was at such close range that the gunners themselves could see the shells hit—on one occasion the enemy gun, mount and crew went hurling down the hillside to land at the feet of Marine assault troops. During the month of July, the Tuscy was assigned to defend the Philippines in the Samar-Leyte and Manila Bay areas.

The Tuscy was in the war, informally and formally, for over six years. In the three years and eight months since Pearl Harbor, she lost three men in combat. Three men had been aboard since her commissioning in 1934. They were: CWT Erskin R. Ward, CMM William D. Martz, and CWT Ralph C. Conti.

The *San Francisco*

Few vessels in all Naval history can match the battle record of the heavy cruiser *San Francisco* (CA 38), commissioned in 1934. Under the command of Capt. Daniel J. Callaghan, she escaped damage at Pearl Harbor but was unable to strike back because she was being overhauled. Nevertheless her men grabbed rifles and machine guns wherever they could, and some scurried aboard the neighboring *New Orleans* to fight.

In January, 1942 she was in the South Pacific, part of a task force in the Samoa area. She met and repulsed the enemy for the first time on February 20, beating off air attacks near Rabaul. Then she screened the *Lexington* and *Yorktown* during raids off Lae and Salamaua in March. On patrol duty until the Guadalcanal campaign, the *San Francisco* was protecting the *Wasp* when that carrier was torpedoed near the Solomons on September 15.

The famous Tokyo Express—the Jap ship train which reinforced Guadalcanal, was upset on October 11 and 12 in the battle for Cape Esperance. As usual, these night engagements were wild melees but the *San Francisco* came through unscathed.

With Capt. Cassin Young in command, the *San Francisco* had her toughest fight on November 12 and 13 in the battle of Savo Island. The battle opened early in the afternoon of the 12th, as 52 enemy planes attacked the task force. *San Francisco* shot down 2 planes and damaged 2 but a burning Jap plane dived into the stern of the *San*

Francisco, smothering the area with burning gasoline, killing 15 and wounding 29.

On the night of Friday, November 13 Rear Admiral Callaghan took the "Frisco" task force into Savo Sound, engaging a large enemy force in four groups, including two battleships. The *San Francisco* fired seven salvos into a light cruiser which immediately blew up. She then set another cruiser afire before switching her attack to a battleship. Meanwhile she was under fire from an enemy battleship, a carrier and a destroyer. While the cruiser *Helena* silenced the Jap cruiser, the *San Francisco* and *Portland* took on the battleship. But the *San Francisco* was fighting under a heavy handicap, for the battleship's third salvo had smashed her bridge, killing Rear Adm. Callaghan and Captain Young. Firing as long as her main battery would bear, the Frisco lobbed a 5-inch shell into the magazine of a Jap destroyer, which immediately exploded and sank. The enemy battleship stopped firing and its destruction was completed the next day by US planes. Meanwhile, 25 separate fires were burning on the Frisco but all were brought under control.

For her part in this fight the *San Francisco* received the Presidential Unit Citation. She had 189 men killed, missing or seriously wounded from this action. "In this engagement," says the citation, "the *San Francisco* silenced and disabled an enemy battleship at a range of three thousand yards, sank 1 enemy destroyer and damaged 2 other vessels. Although heavily damaged by 15 major caliber hits, she lived to fight again."

After repairs at Mare Island the Frisco went to the Aleutians from April to September, 1943. Then in October she went on to bombard Wake, following this with raids on Makin, and carrier strikes in the Marshalls, Taroa, and bombardments at Kwajalein.

In February, 1944 she was in on attacks at Truk and Yap, repelling constant attacks by enemy planes. More carrier strikes at Palau, Woleai, New Guinea and the Carolines followed in April. Then in July she participated in the amphibious operations at Saipan, Tinian and Guam before returning to Mare Island for an overhauling.

Returning to sea in December, the *San Francisco* joined a fast carrier task force and for the remainder of the war she slashed at the enemy in raids on the Philippines, Formosa, Iwo Jima, and Okinawa. On September 2, the date on which Japan formally surrendered, she was operating off Korea. It had been a long road to Tokyo—281,757 miles.

The *Quincy*

The old heavy cruiser *Quincy* (CA 39) fired the first gun in the Guadalcanal campaign and her successor, also a heavy cruiser, was one of the first ships to bombard both Europe and Japan.

The old *Quincy,* commissioned June 9, 1936, was in the Atlantic under command of Capt. Charlton E. Battle when the war formally began. After a navy-yard overhaul she proceeded to San Diego, where the late Rear Adm. Norman Scott hoisted his flag. In June, she proceeded to the South Pacific and on August 7, 1942 the *Quincy* fired the first shot in the battle for Guadalcanal, bombarding Jap installations west of Lunga Point.

In the early hours of August 9 the *Quincy,* along with the *Astoria* and *Vincennes,* was steaming on a circular patrol of Tulagi harbor. In the pitch-black dark, the force failed to detect the approaching Japanese ships, whose presence was announced by blasts of gunfire. Simultaneously, the US ships were illuminated by Jap flares and searchlights. Accurate Jap gunnery pounded the *Quincy* to a pulp and she burst into a mass of flames. Still she turned, first to port, then to starboard, and her forward turret continued to fire. Then No. 1 turret was hit and after two salvos, turret No. 2 exploded and burned. A hit on the bridge killed almost everyone in the pilot house. The 5-inch battery was put completely out of action. Another hit wrecked Battle Station II. The last communication from the bridge said, "We're going down between them—give them hell!" With the *Quincy* dead in the water and her decks a blazing inferno, the order was finally given to abandon ship.

The new *Quincy* (CA 71) was commissioned on December 15, 1943, and after months of training actively entered the war by bombarding enemy batteries on Utah Beach on D-day. (Her pin-point firing against enemy batteries and concentrations was so accurate that one Army colonel, whose unit had been saved by *Quincy* gunfire said: "I'm gonna kiss that ship the first time I see her!") The *Quincy* also displayed her marksmanship off Omaha Beach and at Cherbourg before leaving to cover landings in Southern France. On August 19-24 the cruiser engaged enemy heavy batteries at Toulon, and when vital minesweeper operations were halted off Marseille, the *Quincy* swept through twelve miles of thickly mined waters to demolish a heavy enemy battery. She then returned to the States on September 8, 1944.

After being fitted out for a Presidential cruise, the *Quincy* carried President Roosevelt and his party to Malta, Suez, Alexandria and

Algiers, receiving many dignitaries aboard during this diplomatic mission.

The *Quincy* left Norfolk, Virginia, on March 5, 1945 and on April 11 joined the Fifth Fleet at Ulithi. On April 16 she joined Cruiser Division 10 of the First Carrier Task Force under Vice Adm. Mitscher. During the next months she supported carrier strikes at Okinawa, Amami Gunto, Minami Daito Jima, Kyushu, Tokuno Jima and Kikai Jima. The *Quincy* safely rode out the severe typhoon in June, and anchored in the Gulf of Leyte on June 13, 1945. Here Capt. John A. Waters relieved Capt. Elliott Senn.

Then the *Quincy*, with Task Force 38, began the period of Empire strikes against Hokkaido, Honshu, and Shikoku including the bombardment of the Imperial Steel and Iron Works on July 14. After more strikes, the *Quincy* bombarded Homamatsu on the night of July 30, rejoining the carriers at daylight for strikes at Tokyo and Nagoya. After bombarding Kamaishi Steel Works, the carrier strikes were suspended pending peace negotiations. On August 27 the second *Quincy* anchored off Sagami Wan. The war was over.

The *Brooklyn*

Soldiers from New York's famed borough who fought in the African, Sicilian, Italian and French invasions no doubt muttered to themselves on those occasions, "I'm glad that baby's here."

"That baby" would have been, of course, the light cruiser *Brooklyn* (CL 40) whose guns wiped out many an enemy position which otherwise would have made things even tougher for the men on the beachheads.

The *Brooklyn*, commissioned in November, 1936 saw the war through, from the neutrality patrol until shortly before VE-day. If she retired from the conflict a little early, it can be said that she got in a little early, too. In June, 1941, while most of us were still reading about the war, the *Brooklyn* was convoying troops to Iceland and later, escorting the carriers *Wasp, Ranger* and *Yorktown* across the submarine-sprinkled Atlantic. Her first actual war mission began on December 10, when in company with the *Wasp* and the destroyers *Stack, Wilson* and *Sterett,* she steamed for Martinique to neutralize French warships there. During the operation her scout planes sank a German U-boat.

Next she convoyed the First Marine Division to Panama, and on the way back, broke up a submarine wolf pack lying in wait off the New Jersey coast, rescuing a merchant ship engaged in a surface action with one of the subs. Until September, 1942 she convoyed troops to

Ireland and Scotland, and once, when the transport *Wakefield* burst into flames in mid-ocean, came alongside and took off one thousand three hundred passengers and the crew of the burning ship without serious injury to a person. The Commander-in-Chief of the Atlantic Fleet commended the *Brooklyn* for that.

The *Brooklyn's* first great role came in November, 1942 in the dramatic amphibious North African operation. As one of the principal units of the Western Naval Task Force, the cruiser played a key part in the invasion of Fedala, 14 miles northwest of Casablanca. Fedala had to be secured to protect the important harbor of Casablanca, and it was the heavy Port Blondin battery near Fedala that was knocked out of action by the *Brooklyn* on November 8. The *Brooklyn* was opposed by French warships which attempted to prevent US troop landings, and the guns of two of the largest French units which sortied out of Casablanca, a cruiser and a destroyer, were silenced. Many other French vessels sunk in the engagement were sent down with the help of the *Brooklyn,* which was struck once by a French shell. A French submarine fired a spread of five torpedoes at the *Brooklyn* but skillful maneuvering by Capt. Francis C. Denebrink brought the cruiser through safely.

By December 1, the *Brooklyn* was back in New York, and until April, 1943 her assignment was convoying troops to Africa. In June she was in the Mediterranean at Oran to prepare for the assault on Sicily, and in July she led the Fire Support Group in the invasion bombardment as the flagship of Rear Adm. Laurence T. DuBose. She neutralized enemy gun positions at Licata and gave fire support for Army forces at Porto Empedocle. Later she cruised the Mediterranean giving fire support to advancing ground troops, and protecting Allied convoys. Once while escorting merchant vessels into Naples harbor she was caught in a heavy night air attack but escaped undamaged.

The Anzio landings came in January, 1944, and there the *Brooklyn* took shore targets under fire, at the same time fighting off numerous large-scale air attacks. In ten days off Anzio she was the target of enemy planes 32 times, sustaining the heaviest attack on the night of January 24 but again coming through unscathed. In May, with the Fifth Army still trying doggedly to fight towards Rome, the *Brooklyn* was joined by the US cruiser *Philadelphia* and the British cruisers *Phoebe* and *Orion* in pounding ammunition dumps and railroad guns on the army's left flank.

New units of the Atlantic Fleet were on the scene in August to add to the *Brooklyn's* fire power for the invasion of Southern France.

In the armada were the battleships *Texas, Nevada* and *Arkansas;* the cruisers *Tuscaloosa, Quincy, Augusta, Concord* and *Cincinnati,* several escort carriers and numerous destroyers. On the 15th the *Brooklyn* began lobbing shells into Cannes to soften up the beach for the 45th and 36th Infantry Divisions and the French First Army. German torpedo planes attacked the cruiser and were answered by antiaircraft salvos. On the 22d the *Brooklyn* entered La Napoule Gulf for the purpose of drawing enemy fire from concealed batteries, then opened at close range to blast the German positions. The maneuver forced the enemy to withdraw from the area and Cannes subsequently fell.

In October the *Brooklyn* sailed for Corsica, then made Bizerte and Oran, finally receiving orders to return to New York for overhaul, the first time in the States in 15 months. It was April, 1945 before she left the yard, and by the time she was ready to sail for the Pacific, the war was over.

The *Brooklyn* could point to three years of combat duty, to four major operations, to Navy and Marine Corps and Air Medal winners like Pvt. Henry M. Flati, Cox. Matthew P. Giordanella, ARM William J. Hoban, and to Purple Hearts on men like Sgt. Samuel H. Donavan, GM William Proudfoot, and Sea. Floyd Howard.

The *Philadelphia*

The USS *Philadelphia* (CL 41) was commissioned on September 23, 1937 and from September, 1941 until our entry into the war the cruiser engaged in neutrality patrol. Pearl Harbor found the *Philadelphia* in the Boston Navy Yard and she was assigned to North Atlantic convoy duty, which continued well into 1942. On November 8 the *Philadelphia* entered her first action at Safi as she earned her initial combat star in the invasion of North Africa.

The next few months were taken by alternate convoy runs to Casablanca and short stays in New York, after which a complete job of modernizing was done in Brooklyn Navy Yard. In June, 1943, the *Philadelphia* was on her way to Sicily as part of a cruiser and destroyer task group. The invasion is history itself—the storm which threatened to ruin all the plans, the storming ashore at Scoglitti, and the establishment of a successful beachhead. The days following the landing were spent in supporting the Army along the southern coast of Sicily, and then acting as heavy artillery for General Patton's Army along the northern coast. The *Philadelphia* destroyed bridges, aided "leapfrog" movements, knocked down enemy planes which attempted to silence her guns, and tangled with coastal batteries.

On September 5 the *Philadelphia* was underway for Salerno and the bloodiest landing in the Mediterranean. Her job was to keep the Army from being pushed back into the sea. The *Philadelphia* plied up and down the coast, supporting the troops where support was needed, blasting artillery concentrations, destroying tanks, and stubbornly fighting off German planes. A radio-controlled bomb came near ending the *Philadelphia's* career, but it missed by a few feet, lifting her stern out of the water. She left Salerno proud of a job well done.

On January 19, 1944 the *Philadelphia* again headed toward the Mediterranean, and by early February was off the Anzio beachhead, giving much-needed support. Shore bombardment became almost a daily routine, and although there were few air attacks, the German coastal batteries were extremely dangerous. With occasional rest periods in Oran and Palermo, the *Philadelphia* continued to support the Army through May, 1944, proceeding then to Malta for overhaul. On August 11 she got underway for the invasion of Southern France, which turned out to be the quietest in the *Philadelphia's* history, though not without its difficult times. Later the *Philadelphia* accepted the surrender of the German garrison on the Fortress Islands off Marseille. In the fall the *Philadelphia* headed back to the States at the end of her active war duty. After returning to sea in May, 1945 she remained in the Atlantic.

The *Savannah*

The light cruiser *Savannah* (CL 42), commissioned in 1938, was one of the few ships in World War II to take a direct hit from a Nazi radio-controlled glider bomb and survive. On D-day plus 3 at Salerno, the cruiser was bombed repeatedly in high-level attacks which showered her with tons of water. But no hits were made until a Dornier came over and circled well out of range. As the men aboard the *Savannah* watched, the black glider-bomb began its dive. The cruiser took evasive action but the Dornier, circling like a huge buzzard, guided the rocketing bomb straight into the *Savannah's* No. 3 turret.

With a terrific crash the bomb penetrated the turret and passed completely through the ship, exploding and blasting a hole big enough to drive a truck through. Over two hundred men were killed instantly and scores injured, but excellent damage-control work enabled the stricken ship to make Malta for temporary repairs. She went on from there to Philadelphia Navy Yard, emerging after eight months of rebuilding that made her into a practically new ship, ten feet broader and equipped with the latest radar and antiaircraft weapons.

This action climaxed the *Savannah's* war career, which started early in the autumn of 1941 on convoy duty in the North Atlantic. On December 7 she was just out of Brooklyn Navy Yard after a quick overhaul, and assigned to duty off Bermuda, she patrolled Martinique from time to time, under the command of Capt. Andrew C. Bennett.

In late October, 1942 she sortied from Hampton Roads under the command of Capt. Leon S. Fiske, en route to the invasion of North Africa. On November 7 she was off her targets at Mehdia and Port Lyautey, and opened fire on the French forts at 7:55 the next morning. Enemy planes and fierce counterbattery fire from the shore failed to drive her off and at 4:21 that afternoon the enemy batteries were silenced. On November 9 the *Savannah* opened fire on enemy tanks opposing our forces, smashing three and causing the remainder to disperse. And on November 10, one of her scout planes located an enemy battery northeast of Port Lyautey, dropping two bombs directly on the target. Later in the day the cruiser shelled tank and troop concentrations, concluding her role in this operation.

By mid-November the cruiser was under way for a period of South Atlantic patrol duty, and on February 7, 1943 Capt. Robert W. Carey assumed command. In early May she sailed with a convoy for Africa and on July 6 left Algiers escorting transports to Gela, Sicily. Landings began early on the morning of July 10, as the cruiser slammed shells into the beaches. A Junkers 88 attacked and was shot down at 5:14 A. M., and persistent attacks followed, chiefly directed at the landing craft. Nevertheless the operation proceeded, with the *Savannah* alternately patrolling and bombarding.

The next morning 12 Italian planes swept over the transports as tanks of the Hermann Goering Division drove toward Allied beachheads in a strong counterattack. The crew spent 20 of the next 24 hours at battle stations, firing at shore targets and chasing off enemy planes. Only at 10:35 that night did the determined Nazi thrust break before the concerted fire of our ships and tanks. By noon the next day the Gela landings were safely established and after more fire support on roads and other targets, the *Savannah* was sent to Algiers.

Late in July she was back off Sicily, helping drive German troops into the Messina Corner by bombarding their retreat along coastal roads. On August 8 she was again ordered back to Algiers.

On September 9, 1943 the *Savannah* was part of a fire-support group commanded by Rear Adm. Richard L. Conolly, charged with covering the landing of the British 46th Division at Salerno. The landing successfully accomplished, ensuing days saw some of the wildest fighting of the war as the Nazis threw everything against the thin line of troops on the beachhead. What those days were like was ably described by Cy Peterman, Philadelphia war correspondent then on the *Savannah:*

Seven terrible days have passed since the Allied invasion fleet nudged through the mine-seeded waters of Salerno Gulf. Yet the battle for a bridgehead rages unabated today.

I have just left a battle scene that surpasses everything I saw during the entire Tunisian and Sicilian campaigns—and I thought El Guettar the hottest ever and Hill 609 the top assault. But what is happening on the slopes of Naples these days, with five German divisions surging repeatedly against Allied forces, is writing in vivid muzzle flashes one of the great battle stories of the war.

I have been aboard an American cruiser ever since troop convoys approached the shore and I am wondering how we have survived. We've been bombed night and day by the deadliest German devices, including Dornier bomber planes heavily armed. I have seen our naval guns blow Germans sky high with their batteries, tanks and railway guns—Nazis with orders to die in their tracks.

I have seen Nazis hurled off the beaches where on D-day they stood shoulder to shoulder blazing into our landing craft until cruisers and destroyers, ploughing through lanes cleared by courageous minesweeper crews, literally blew tanks to fragment and gun emplacements to dust.

I have seen German planes penetrate the steady cover of our fighters and pelt the gulf with bombs that raise a sheet of flame a hundred feet high and columns of black smoke that rise domelike among our ships.

I have seen bombs splash within twenty yards, lifting warships from the water, and have heard such ack-ack defense that the concussion cracked bulkheads and knocked us around like flies. Meanwhile, constant dogfights raged in the skies while ashore the slopes sprouted dust and shell fragments as Americans and British soldiers hurled back as many as five and six German counterattacks daily. Men who were at Dieppe say this is infinitely worse. They say Dieppe lasted only nine hours, this has continued for a whole week.

The actual landings began under a waning half-moon about 2:00 a. m., but they were temporarily halted because of the presence of many mines offshore. By daylight, dauntless sweepers cleared a lane through the mines, and the infantry dashed in to seize two beaches, suffering considerable casualties.

Daylight revealed a German railway gun firing at the Yanks in tank barges. There was an immediate request for naval gun support, and then, not before, the cruiser's six-inch persuaders opened up.

I have seen some shooting in my day, I have seen the boys with 105s in the Djebel country, and those with the famed Long Toms. But what took place next curled my hair and shriveled the Germans to cinders. On the third volley from our cruiser, the railway gun glinted through the morning sunlight as it was blown hundreds of feet high. A couple tanks followed the same path of destruction in a few minutes.

When the German bombers got through, the whole harbor became a milling mass of ships. This became particularly ghastly at night when, in addition to dodging bombs, the ships tried to escape the blazing light of countless flares.

Once I saw our prow miss a cargo vessel by no more than two feet and again we scraped our catapult platform against the rail of a speeding destroyer. Nobody even bothered to think about traffic matters, however, as antiaircraft practically stunned the senses.

I cannot describe the sensation created by this ack-ack. Our 5-inchers, with a bark like 105s, seemed to slap the eardrums together while a hail of falling fragments drove everyone under cover.

It was impossible to distinguish the muzzle-flashes from the sheet of bomb-flame, except when a cruiser threw a shell. In such moments the ship reacted like a picador's horse wincing under the horns of a plunging bull. This has continued night and day, with all hands at general quarters from Wednesday evening until we withdrew.

It was during this action that the *Savannah* was hit.

After long months of repairs, she made a second shakedown cruise, then accompanied President Roosevelt on his trip to Malta in February, 1945, holding memorial services for the *Savannah* dead buried there after Salerno.

From then until the war's end she saw little action, but she wrote a final happy chapter to her service by acting as one of the greatly welcomed "Magic Carpet" ships carrying troops back to the States. Typical of the Navy spirit was her generosity in treating one thousand two hundred Army men to a delicious Thanksgiving dinner—paid for by the ship's own special service fund.

The *Honolulu*

This light cruiser (CL 48) was one of the few ships of the war to take two torpedo hits and live to fight on. The first, suffered during the Battle of Kolombangara, July 13, 1943, caused only slight damage, but the second killed 65 men and wounded 47 when it smacked into the *Honolulu* in Leyte Gulf on October 29, 1944. But these were not the first injuries to the famous "Blue Goose," for she was one of the ships to go into action at Pearl Harbor, where she was damaged. In between she miraculously managed to escape unscathed in some of the hottest naval battles of the war. She had been commissioned in 1933.

The first of these escapes came during the bombardment of Kiska, in August, 1942 when several enemy fighter planes dropped bombs ahead and astern. The next came in the Battle of Tassafaronga, November 30, 1942. On that black night, the *Honolulu* furiously shelled a Jap destroyer, which broke and sank. During the next hectic minutes, filled with confusion and lighted by the glare of burning ships, the *Honolulu* sighted several torpedoes headed her way, and by taking violent evasive action, escaped.

On January 5, 1943 she was attacked by three Aichi dive bombers off Guadalcanal. Three bombs fell close by and no serious damage was done. Her next big-time encounter came on July 4-5-6, when after bombarding enemy positions on New Georgia, she was ordered to speed to the Kula Gulf area, joining other ships in an effort to intercept the "Tokyo Express." At 1:36 A. M. July 6, the *Honolulu* contacted enemy vessels off the northeast coast of Kolombangara. In the action that followed, again typified by sudden intense exchanges, the Blue Goose and her sister ships sank two destroyers and damaged at least five others. Five nights later she was the flagship during the Battle of Kolombangara, during which she took several enemy ships under fire before being hit by her first torpedo. (She returned to base under her own power.)

On January 8, 1944 the *Honolulu* bombarded the Shortlands and in February, she was in on the occupation of Green Island, north of Bougainville. The Guam, Tinian and Saipan engagements of the summer are in her log book.

Under the command of Capt. H. R. Thurber, the *Honolulu* moved into position off Leyte on October 14, and for two days hurled shell after shell into enemy positions. Meanwhile determined enemy plane attacks continued. On the afternoon of the 20th, a Jap "Kate" raced towards the ship from the direction of Leyte. The cruiser spotted this threat and began to dodge and weave, but the enemy skillfully maneuvered into position and dropped two torpedoes, one of which caught the *Honolulu* solidly. The destroyer *Richard P. Leary* and tugs *Potawatomi* and *Menominee* moved in to remove the injured and assist in repairing the damage. By performing one of the classic damage-control jobs of the war, they were able to stop the flooding and the *Honolulu* limped back to an advanced Navy base. Here the famous SRUs (Ship Repair Units) went into action, cutting away wreckage and placing such an excellent temporary patch over the gaping hole in her side that the Blue Goose was able to steam twelve thousand miles home under her own power, and at normal cruising speeds.

The *Atlanta*

Less than a year after her commissioning on December 21, 1941, the light cruiser *Atlanta* (CL 51) third ship of that name, was sunk off Guadalcanal. Sixty days after the announcement of her loss the residents of Atlanta and other Georgia communities raised $63,000,000 to build her successor. That was the spirit the men who fought on the "Mighty A" and her successor could understand.

Under the command of Capt. Samuel P. Jenkins, the Mighty A soon got into action at the battle of Midway, in June, 1942 as part of the group screening the *Hornet.* After this initiation she headed for the Solomon Islands campaign, where along with the *Enterprise* and *North Carolina,* she was attacked by about 75 enemy planes on August 24, at 5 P. M. Heavy fire from the *Atlanta* and other ships drove off the attackers.

Eleven weeks later, the *Atlanta* swung into the Battle of Guadalcanal (the third Battle of Savo Island) on the night of November 12, 1942. The late Rear Adm. Norman Scott was in command of the *Atlanta,* part of a force assigned to protecting the landing-force transports. Suddenly the flash came—the Japs were coming in three groups between Florida, Savo, and Guadalcanal Islands. Rear Admirals Callaghan and Scott, with 5 cruisers and 8 destroyers, advanced to meet the enemy. The boiling, thunderous battle that followed was epic in its swiftness and ferocity.

The Japs had 2 battleships, 7 cruisers and about 10 destroyers. The two forces collided in the inky blackness off Lunga Point, the *Atlanta* leading a destroyer group. The Mighty A pummeled a Jap destroyer, and was caught herself in the searchlight beam of an enemy cruiser. Another enemy cruiser dropped several shells on her conning tower, killing Admiral Scott and ruining her control system. At almost the same instant a torpedo caught her and with her rudder jammed, she began circling towards the enemy. A hail of 8-inch and 5-inch shells pounded her, and she lay helplessly out of control as the battle waned.

Fires raged everywhere, but her crew extinguished them and she was taken under tow to Tulagi. Water continued to pour in through her wounds and she was finally sunk. For this action the Mighty A received a Presidential Unit Citation, which read:

For outstanding performance . . . struck by one torpedo and no less than 49 shells, the *Atlanta,* after sinking an enemy destroyer and repeatedly hitting a cruiser which later went down, gallantly remained in action . . . with one-third of her crew killed or missing, her engine room flooded and her topsides a shambles . . .

Among the awards to her crew were the Navy Cross to CWT Thomas J. Maloy and Lt. Comdr. James Stuart Smith, both of whom died in action.

The fourth *Atlanta* (CL 104) joined Admiral Spruance's Fifth Fleet in May, 1945 and served later with Admiral Halsey's Third Fleet before the war's end. Many men from the Mighty A asked and were granted transfers to her successor.

The fourth *Atlanta* took a beating in the June 5 typhoon off Okinawa, but after repairs at Leyte, she went to sea and began to work over the Jap homeland from Kyushu to Hokkaido. She was present as a support ship for the carriers during all the strikes on the Jap homeland from early July until the war's end.

The *Helena*

For her outstanding heroism against Jap forces in the Solomons-New Georgia area, the light cruiser *Helena* (CL 50) became the first ship to win the new Navy Unit Commendation. The price she and her men paid for this honor was high—for the gallant *Helena* was sunk—but hundreds of her crew survived to fight on. Few will ever forget the *Helena*, whose blazing guns gave more than she received before her death.

On December 7, 1941 the *Helena* was moored at Pearl Harbor, alongside the wooden minesweeper *Ogala*. By pure chance the cruiser was occupying the battleship *Pennsylvania's* normal berth, thus becoming a primary target for Jap attacks. The call to General Quarters had just sounded when low-flying torpedo planes skimmed in over Ford Island and cut loose. Several fish missed the *Helena*, but one aimed at the *Ogala* freakishly dived under that ship's shallow keel and exploded in the cruiser's forward engine room. The tremendous force of the explosion turned the *Ogala* over, her bottom completely crushed. Despite this hit and many casualties, the *Helena* manned her guns against continued enemy attacks.

Following repairs at Pearl and Mare Island, the cruiser escorted a detachment of Seabees to the South Pacific, then joined the carrier *Wasp's* force off Guadalcanal, in August, 1942. On the afternoon of September 15, 1942 the *Helena* was under the command of Captain Oliver M. Read when the *Wasp* was attacked and sunk by a submarine pack. Disregarding the danger of further attacks, the *Helena* stood by to take aboard nearly 400 *Wasp* survivors.

On October 11-12, under the command of Capt. Gilbert C. Hoover the *Helena* and other cruisers and destroyers slammed into an enemy force off Cape Esperance. The *Helena's* guns were first to speak, as she opened fire on two different targets. In several minutes the main battery's target sank, so fire was shifted to a *Kako*-class cruiser. Other ships also smacked shells into this ship, which soon rolled over and sank. The *Helena* then took a light cruiser and destroyer under fire, shelling the latter for fully ten minutes until it went down, burning fiercely.

Eight nights later the Japs were back again, trying to disrupt our communications lines and to land reinforcements on October 20. A submarine pack caught the heavy cruiser *Chester,* and though several fish exploded near the *Helena,* she was not hit. On November 4, 1942 the cruiser bombarded Jap forces on Guadalcanal and on November 10 she shot down four Zeros in repelling determined enemy air attacks.

On the night of November 12-13 the *Helena* was with Rear Adm. Daniel Callaghan's force which tackled a greatly superior enemy unit. The *Helena* soon scored hits on a heavy cruiser and as this target burst into flames, she shifted her main battery to bear on a light cruiser then firing on the *San Francisco.* While this threat was being silenced, her secondary batteries concentrated on a destroyer. We lost the destroyers *Laffey, Cushing, Barton,* and *Monssen* and the cruiser *Juneau* in this carnage, but the Japs also took heavy punishment and the *Helena* escaped with moderate wounds.

Early in January, 1943 the *Helena,* under the command of Capt. Charles P. Cecil, went into action in a series of bombardments off Munda Point, important enemy airbase on New Georgia.

In March, the cruiser headed for Sydney, Australia, but by the end of that month she was back again in her patrol spot off Guadalcanal. At the end of June the Solomons fighting shifted to the Vila-Stanmore area and the *Helena* bombarded that sector and Bairoko Harbor.

On the night of July 6 the *Helena* took part in the battle of Kula Gulf, part of the cruiser-destroyer force under Rear Adm. Walden Ainsworth. Moving up the slot to intercept the Tokyo Express, the *Helena* opened fire with ordinary smokeless powder (all her flashless powder had been consumed in the preceding bombardments). The cruiser's stacatto fire was so rapid that she was brilliantly lighted by her own gun flashes, an excellent target for prowling subs. As she was about to execute a turn, several torpedoes caught her and she sank in twenty minutes. Deadly to the last, her main battery had sunk a large enemy ship and her secondary guns had sent two destroyers to the bottom before she went down! Her Presidential Citation for this action read:

For outstanding heroism in action against enemy Japanese forces afloat in the Solomon Islands-New Georgia area. Gallantly carrying the fights to the enemy, the USS *Helena* opened the night Battle of Cape Esperance on October 11-12, 1942, boldly sending her fire into the force of enemy warships, sinking a hostile destroyer and holding to a minimum the damage to our destroyers in the rear of the Task Force. She engaged at close quarters a superior force of hostile combatant ships in the Battle of Guadalcanal (Third Savo) on the night of November 12-13, 1942, rallying our own forces after the flagship had been disabled and contributing to the enemy's defeat. In her final engagement in the pre-dawn battle of July 5, 1943 the *Helena* valiantly sailed down the restricted and submarine-infested waters of Kula Gulf under the terrific torpedo and gun fire of the enemy to bombard Kolombangara and New Georgia while covering the landing of our troops at Rice Anchorage, and 24 hours later, her blazing guns aided in the destruction of a vastly superior enemy naval force before she was fatally struck by a Japanese torpedo. Her brave record of combat achievement is evidence of the *Helena's* intrepidity and the heroic fighting spirit of her officers and men.

A new cruiser *Helena* (CA 75) was completed in September, 1945.

The *Juneau*

Like the story of most great ships, the story of the light cruiser *Juneau* (CL 52) is most of all the story of her gallant crew. When the *Juneau* sank in Iron Bottom Bay during the Battle of Guadalcanal, 34 officers and 648 enlisted men went down with her. Among them were the five Sullivan brothers who had enlisted together, trained together at the Great Lakes Naval Training Station, and asked to be assigned to the same ship. Said one of the Sullivans: "We will make a team together that can't be beat."

The *Juneau* disaster was marked by many an act of spectacular heroism, most of them unchronicled. Among the handful of survivors, SM Joseph P. F. Hartney got the Legion of Merit for "exceptionally meritorious conduct in the performance of outstanding services." Said Secretary of the Navy Frank Knox: "After swimming a considerable distance through shark-infested waters to obtain a life float which had been dropped by a plane, Hartney, as a courageous volunteer, set out against the perils of the sea to secure medical attention for a critically wounded officer and to expedite rescue of the injured and helpless. Although both his companions were irrational at times and could offer little assistance, Hartney, by his tenacious determination and extraordinary resourcefulness, fought his flimsy craft through mountainous waves, terrific storms and hazardous coral reefs without food or water for seven terrible days until, haggard and weak, he brought his comrades to an island and consequent safety . . ."

The 6,000-ton *Juneau* was commissioned in March, 1942 under the command of Capt. Lyman K. Swenson, Provo, Utah, who went down with his ship at Guadalcanal. After a few months' service in the Atlantic, the *Juneau* proceeded to the Pacific where she was attached to a task force commanded by Rear Adm. Leigh Noyes. Within a week after joining this force, while steaming in support of a transport group bound for Guadalcanal, the *Juneau* witnessed the sinking of the carrier *Wasp*.

On Guadalcanal the enemy had thrown everything it had into a land offensive against Marine positions. During the night of October 25 the Japs achieved a temporary breakthrough along Lunga Ridge and this short-lived victory was evidently a signal for Jap naval forces to converge on the island.

At dawn 16 US carrier planes took off to search for approaching enemy ships. While they located and then bombed the Jap force, 27 planes battled their way past the American fighters to unleash a co-ordinated dive bombing and torpedo plane assault on the carrier *Hornet,* just off Santa Cruz.

The *Juneau* and other ships screening the *Hornet* immediately threw up a heavy barrage of antiaircraft fire, and about 20 of the attackers dropped, but not before the *Hornet* had taken several bomb and torpedo hits. As she started to burn fiercely, a cruiser took her in tow. Just before noon the *Juneau* left the *Hornet's* escort and steamed to where the carrier *Enterprise* was a target of unremitting Jap attack. Adding her fire power to help repel the dive bombers and torpedo planes, the *Juneau* again escaped disaster.

But the decisive Battle of Guadalcanal, which followed two weeks later, was the *Juneau's* last fight. Escorting a transport group, the *Juneau* reached Guadalcanal early in the morning of November 12, and stood guard while troops and cargo were unloaded in the teeth of shelling from Jap shore batteries. Just after the shore guns were silenced by close fire from US destroyers, an alert sounded. Some 25 Jap torpedo planes, accompanied by five Zeros, zoomed in to attack. The *Juneau* opened fire immediately and her devastating antiaircraft gunnery knocked six Japs from the sky. Antiaircraft fire from other ships and dog-fighting Navy planes picked off all but one of the enemy aircraft, and unloading was resumed.

Late in the afternoon word came that a strong surface force was headed for the island. An American attack force of cruisers and destroyers including the *Juneau* was hastily formed and stood out to meet the enemy. Just after midnight this relatively small force met some twenty powerful Jap ships, including two battleships. Outnumbered and outranged by the enemy's guns, the little group determinedly slugged it out at close range. During the action the *Juneau* took a torpedo in her port side. Nineteen men were killed by the blast and the damaged ship heeled over. About noon on November 13, the *Juneau,* limping along with two other damaged US cruisers, was torpedoed by an enemy submarine and sank in less than a minute. The gallant ship had met her end scarcely eight months after her commissioning.

The *San Juan*

Commissioned in February, 1942 the light cruiser *San Juan* (CL 54) arrived just in time for the war, which she got into very quickly, convoying troops to the Guadalcanal invasion in June, 1942. From there she went on to steam 286,000 miles (comparable to twelve trips around the world), and the range of her activity was so varied that a list of her engagements would look like a war history.

During the bombardment of Tulagi, a gun mount blew up through overheating, killing 5 and wounding 12, but the *San Juan* didn't return to Pearl for several weeks. After Pearl and repairs, she headed for Funa Futi, then raided the South Gilberts, sinking two Jap patrol vessels and taking sixteen prisoners. From there she headed into the battle of Santa Cruz, along with the *Enterprise* and *South Dakota*. During this action the *San Juan* knocked down a number of Jap planes, but during the last enemy dive-bombing attack several planes dove from behind a low-hanging cloud and plunged a bomb through her stern. Passing entirely through the ship it exploded, flattening the rudder and flooding two compartments. Battered but still seaworthy, the *San Juan* proceeded to Noumea for repairs, then on to Sydney.

From December, 1942 to June, 1943 she based at Noumea. During the occupation of New Georgia the *San Juan* prowled the Coral Sea in an unsuccessful search for enemy vessels.

At the end of July she moved to Efate Island, then based at Espíritu Santo before going on to neutralize Buka airfield with the *Saratoga* during the landings on Bougainville. During mid-November she was called to the Gilberts, went on to raid the Marshalls, repulsing seven solid hours of night torpedo attacks en route. The *San Juan,* incidentally, splashed the only enemy plane downed during the fracas. Then came the "best trip of the war"—a quick dash to 'Frisco for renovating and Christmas liberty in the States!

Back in the Marshall Islands campaign, a rejuvenated *San Juan* dashed around with the Fast Carrier Task Force during action against Roi, Kwajalein, Wotje and Eniwetok, to the New Hebrides for strikes at Palau, Yap and Ulithi. Next came MacArthur's landing at Hollandia, on New Guinea, and a smack at Truk on the way back from that. Early in June she went again with the carriers to Iwo and Chichi Jima in the Bonins, then covered the capture of Saipan and Guam, before overhaul. At Ulithi in November, the *San Juan* headed into the last furious months of the war. In December she covered strikes on Formosa and Luzon, pulling the unenviable duty of being "Jap-bait." This meant steaming around near Jap airfields, without any protection but her own guns, guts and speed. Very fortunately, that trick ended without any mishaps! Even the typhoon that sank three destroyers brought the *San Juan* no undue terror, for although caught in its fury, excellent seamanship pulled her through.

After Christmas in Ulithi, air strikes were made at Luzon, Formosa, Okinawa, and the occupation of Iwo Jima was covered. During this last stint the *San Juan* scouted within one hundred miles of Tokyo without sighting a Jap. In March she went back to Ulithi, then operated off the Jap home islands through April. During this time the *San Juan's* antiaircraft continued to score bull's-eyes, and once had the satisfaction of seeing a "Betty" vanish into thin air when hit. In May and June she was in Leyte Gulf, where she became flagship of her force on May 27, and on June 5, she rode out her second typhoon.

During July and August she was with Admiral Halsey's Third Fleet, hitting Japan relentlessly. After 59 days at sea without sighting land, she anchored in sight of Mount Fujiyama as the war ended. Her final assignment was repatriating war prisoners, and when the formal surrender was signed, she was 15 miles from the *Missouri,* still evacuating prisoners. Following that she went on the Magic Carpet assignment until January, 1946, then headed for San Pedro and retirement.

The *Columbia*

The first two ships bearing the name *Columbia* were burned at Washington Navy Yard; the first (a 44-gun frigate) by the British in 1814, and the second (a 50-gun frigate) by panicky Union forces in 1861. The third was a captured blockade runner, wrecked off North Carolina in 1862, and the fourth saw duty in the Spanish-American and First World Wars before being placed out of commission in 1921. The fifth *Columbia* was a troop transport (originally the *Great Northern*), but the sixth *Columbia,* commissioned June 20, 1942, was a fightin' light cruiser that saw more action alone than all her predecessors put together. Wherever she went, things seemed to happen.

Early in January, 1943, patrolling off Guadalcanal in her first action, four dive bombers plunged at her group. The *Columbia* (CL 56) emerged unhit, but HMS *Achilles* was hit and the *Helena* straddled. In April, Capt. F. E. Beatty relieved Capt. W. A. Heard, the *Columbia's* first commanding officer. Back to New Hebrides, she covered operations in the Solomons area; here torpedo bombers bored in, badly damaged the heavy cruiser *Chicago.* In June the *Columbia* shelled shore positions in New Georgia, and two weeks later repeated these tactics at Munda, in the face of strong counter-fire. After liberty in

Sydney, Australia in September she joined Task Group 39.2, shelling airfields in the Shortland Islands, and covering the Bougainville landing in October, 1943.

With Cruiser Division 12, the *Columbia* intercepted a superior enemy surface force off Empress Augusta Bay on November 2. Rear Admiral Merrill sent his destroyers in to attack, and in the action that followed off Bougainville two separate enemy groups were taken under fire by the cruisers. An hour of furious, swirling fighting followed, with the *Columbia* straddled at least four times. The destroyers *Foote* and cruiser *Denver* were hit badly, but the enemy suffered worse casualties and turned back.

In the ensuing week the *Columbia* was under incessant air attack. At one point the division saw ten splashed Jap planes in the water at once, with seven more crashing outside the formation! Buka was raided by the *Columbia* in December, and in February, 1944 she assisted in covering landings on the Green Islands in the northern Solomons. Then, after over a year in combat zone, she returned to the States in April 1944 for an overhaul. Here Capt. M. E. Curtis relieved Captain Beatty.

On September 6 the *Columbia* was back in the party, this time destroying ground installations with her fire at Angaur, Peleliu and Ngesebus Islands in the Palaus. During supporting work in the landings on the Philippines in October, her sister ship the *Honolulu* was torpedoed but again the *Columbia* escaped. Then came the battle for Leyte Gulf, which encompassed the naval victories of Surigao Strait, Samar and Cape Engaño. When the firing was quieted at Surigao, *Columbia* was credited with assisting in the sinking of two battleships, a cruiser and a destroyer.

She remained in the Leyte area under continuous air attack from Kamikazes, during which the *St. Louis, Maryland, Nashville* and destroyer *Haraden* were hit close by. En route to Lingayen Gulf on January 3, Kamikazes repeatedly bored in. The carrier *Ommaney Bay*, hit by a Kamikaze, had to be sunk by our torpedoes; the *Columbia* picked up survivors. On January 4 the attacks continued, with the destroyer escort *Stafford,* cruiser *Louisville,* carrier *Manila Bay* and two Australian ships hit in quick succession despite desperate antiaircraft fire in which the *Columbia* got two planes. On January 6 the ship was literally "shaved" by a bomb, but stood by to bombard Santiago Island. The destroyer *Leary* was hit, then the *Walke.* A Kamikaze plunged so close to the *Columbia* that gas from its tanks sprayed the superstructure. On through the narrow, mined channel plunged the formation, with little opportunity to take evasive action. On the 5th and 6th, 21 ships had been hit, and at last the *Columbia* caught hers.

Plane, pilot and engine plummeted through the main deck and No. 4 turret, the 800-kg. bomb penetrating the third deck before exploding. The deafening blast ruined turrets 3 and 4 and flooded 9 compartments, killing 17, with 20 missing. But within five minutes the ship was firing again, and in 15 minutes had accounted for an enemy plane.

The force retired to the South China Sea, with *Columbia* experiencing steering difficulties and hampered by fires. Still, on January 7, she recommenced bombarding, although down four feet at the stern. Then on January 9 another suicide plane plunged into her forward main battery director, killing 8 and wounding 97. Gasoline fires raged but were brought under control in 39 minutes. Vice Admiral Oldendorf then detached the ship and she returned to California for repairs.

The sixth *Columbia* was awarded the Navy Unit Commendation for her heroism and refusal to drop out though badly crippled.

The *Santa Fe*

The *Santa Fe* (CL 60) won public acclaim when she ran alongside the blazing carrier *Franklin* more than two hours, saving over 800 men with a daring piece of seamanship. This performance was nothing unusual for this light cruiser which had been in the thick of things since early 1943, following her commissioning in 1942. She had sunk 7 Jap ships and downed 7 planes while participating in 42 air strikes, 12 shore bombardments and 4 surface actions, during a long combat tour. Nevertheless, she did not lose a man nor suffer any serious battle damage.

Assigned to patrol and bombardment duty off the Aleutians in April, 1943, she stayed in those waters under the command of Capt. Russel Berkey until September, when she headed for Tarawa, following that battle with an assault on Wake. Moving off to the Southwest Pacific she patrolled the Solomons area until November, 1943, returning then to bombard Bititu (Betio) Island in the Tarawa conquest. The following month she moved with a carrier group on Kwajalein Atoll in the Marshalls and on January 30, now under the command of Capt. Jerauld Wright, she bombarded Wotje, successfully completing this mission despite heavy opposition. From here she went on to smash at Kwajalein, Wotje, Palau, Yap, Hollandia, Wakde, and by July, 1944, she had also been in engagements at Truk and Saipan and patrolled off Ponape, Pagan, Iwo Jima, Guam and the Philippines.

In August she caught a Jap destroyer in the Bonins and sank her, then in September she sent four cargo ships to the bottom off Mindanao. The next month saw air blows at Leyte, Luzon, Samar, Okinawa and Formosa. And later in October she caught a Jap escort carrier and light cruiser off Cape Engaño in the battle of Leyte Gulf. Both had been damaged by air strikes and the *Santa Fe* finished them with vigor and dispatch. During the next four months she accompanied the fast carriers in smashes on the Jap home islands before returning to the west coast and a major overhaul.

Her rescue work in the *Franklin* disaster ended this tour. When the *Santa Fe* moved in on the stricken carrier, ammunition was exploding furiously and the *Santa Fe's* crew was caught in the deadly shower. Still they persisted, even passing hose lines to the carrier's forward deck to bring the flames under control. CSF Richard Kemp and CM Clarence R. LaFontaine saved one group personally. With over two hundred men treated for injuries, medics like Harold M. Haugen got less than three hours' sleep in three days. BM Joseph J. Lupo swung down a line between the two grinding ships to assist in the transfer of stretchers. Sea. Ray Hilly dived overboard into a sea of flames to rescue a badly burned man. Tales of individual and collective heroism were common.

In 25 months of combat the *Santa Fe* fired more than 1,645,000 pounds of shells at the enemy, steaming 221,000 miles in the process.

The *Birmingham*

Battle-scarred is the way to describe the light cruiser *Birmingham* (CL 62) which was skip-bombed, torpedoed, blasted by the exploding *Princeton* and hit by a Jap suicide bomber. Yet at the final bell she was in there swinging. One of her proudest possessions is a plaque which says simply: "In Appreciation." It was given the cruiser by the 1,400 survivors of the ill-fated *Princeton,* in memory of the 237 *Birmingham* men killed during rescue operations when the carrier was hit by a Jap bomb. And beside it, on the cruiser's quarterdeck, hangs another, inscribed: "Greater Love Hath No Man."

Commissioned on January 29, 1943, the cruiser's first action was in the invasion of Sicily on July 10, 1943 with Capt. John Wilkes in command. Operating five miles off Licata, her guns protected landing craft while working over enemy shore batteries. Although operating impudently within 25 miles of a large enemy airport, she escaped with nothing more than a few near misses.

Switching to the Pacific, the *Birmingham* hit Wake Island with a carrier task force on October 4-6, 1943. Enemy shore batteries straddled her, but she again came through unhurt. Proceeding to the Solomons area, she received her first wounds off Bougainville Island on November 8, 1943. Attacked by a heavy force of night raiders, the cruiser took a torpedo hit forward and bombs on No. 4 turret and astern. The torpedo blew a hole 14 by 15 feet in the hull, but the Jap plane which had delivered the aerial tin fish went down in flames. Before the night attack was over, the cruiser had officially downed 3 more planes and assisted in splashing 7 others. *Birmingham* casualties were 1 killed and 31 wounded. Badly hurt, she returned to the States for repairs.

Back in the lineup again in June, 1944, she was in on the Saipan assault, covering demolition work as she stood defiantly within two thousand yards of shore batteries to pound the beaches. On June 20 she was assigned to Task Force 58, participating in the Tinian and Guam assaults. In August she was marauding through the Palaus and eastern Philippines. At Hinatuan Bay her guns destroyed 3,000 tons of enemy shipping, aided in sinking 3,000 more when a convoy was intercepted. On October 9 she aided in the raids on Nansei Shoto by Task Force 38, the first heavy smashes at the Nip homelands.

Three days later she was with the Third Fleet as it hammered Eastern Formosa. During this operation the fleet was hunted continually by enemy planes, and suffered incessant heavy air attacks. The *Houston* and *Canberra* were hit by torpedo planes and badly damaged; when the *Houston* was hit, a second time the *Birmingham* stood by to pick up survivors.

On October 24 the *Birmingham* was off the eastern coast of Luzon with the *Princeton*, supporting landings. At 9:40 A. M. a single Jap plane popped out of the overcast and dropped a bomb in the center of the *Princeton's* flight deck. Twenty minutes later there were two violent internal explosions and the carrier lay dead in the water, wreathed in smoke and flames. The "abandon ship" order was given and hundreds took to the water.

Then Capt. Thomas B. Inglis used a daring maneuver, running the *Birmingham* close alongside the *Princeton* to bring the cruiser's fire hoses into play. "The entire carrier aft the bridge was in flames and heavy clouds of smoke," said Captain Inglis. "Minor-caliber ammunition was exploding everywhere and there were heavier explosions occasionally." But the fire control crews kept at it and by 1:30 P. M. only a small fire was burning aft. Suddenly Jap air raiders and submarine contacts were reported and regretfully, the *Birmingham* cast off and joined the circling screen.

An hour later this danger had passed and the *Birmingham* again drew near, ready to wind up the job. The cruiser had approached to within fifty feet of the carrier when suddenly the *Princeton's* magazine exploded. The terrific blast from the exploding bombs and torpedoes rained death on the crowded decks of the *Birmingham*. Men on other ships saw the stricken vessels leap apart from the spur of the explosion. The carrier was enveloped in orange flames, and columns of smoke poured forth. The *Birmingham* presented a scene of horror and agony. Blood ran so freely sand had to be scattered for safe walking. In addition to the 237 killed, 426 were wounded and 4 were missing. Captain Inglis remained on the bridge to move the cruiser away before collapsing from severe burns and a broken arm. The cruiser *Reno* and destroyers *Irwin, Cassin Young,* and *Gatling* stood by throughout to aid survivors and protect both ships.

The *Birmingham* lay at Mare Island, California, until January, 1945, and in February steamed for Okinawa, under the command of Capt. Harry D. Power. She was credited with destroying two 5-inch shore batteries there in preliminary bombardments.

On May 4 the *Birmingham* was bombarding the stubborn Jap garrisons in support of the Tenth Army and had been under three direct attacks during 26 raids. Then, after thirty days of almost continuous operation in the area, the *Birmingham* was hit by a Kamikaze making a long dive out of the sun. Heavy antiaircraft fire was unable to unnerve the Jap pilot and the plane crashed, along with its 500-pound bomb, just aft of No. 2 turret. Penetrating three decks, the bomb wiped out the sick bay and blew a five-foot hole in the starboard side. Forty-five were killed, 6 missing and 83 wounded. Both medical officers were killed, together with 19 of the 24 hospital corpsmen. Gasoline from the plane's tanks spread and caught fire. Yet in a short time everything was under control and the *Birmingham* headed for Pearl Harbor. She was sent to Brisbane, Australia, as the war ended.

The *Vincennes*

The Jap first team sank the first cruiser *Vincennes* (CL-64)) in August, 1942 at Savo Island, but her successor came back in June, 1944 to complete the job of knocking out the Jap Navy in approved one-two fashion.

The first heavy cruiser *Vincennes* (commissioned in 1937) landed patrol duty in the Atlantic during the summer of 1941, and Pearl Harbor Day found her at Capetown, South Africa. Immediately recalled to New York, she was overhauled and speeded to the Pacific in time to accompany the *Hornet* on its famous April Tokyo raid, and to screen the *Yorktown* in the decisive Battle of Midway in June, 1942. In the Midway action her gunners shot down four enemy planes, including one suicide pilot intent on crashing her. Her next action was at Guadalcanal when the Marines invaded that island early in August, 1942.

After bombarding the landing area the *Vincennes* patrolled outside the transports on D-day, splashing two Jap planes from the hordes that swept in at the force. The next day more waves of enemy torpedo bombers veered in from Florida Island, and the cruiser opened up with everything she had, even using her 8-inch guns to send up splashes in front of low-flying torpedo planes. Narrowly escaping several hits, the *Vincennes* rang up seven bull's-eyes and three probables in this dangerous skeet-shoot.

Then came the fateful night of August 8-9 and the first Battle of Savo. The *Vincennes* was serving as guide-ship for the group guarding the north channel. Suddenly, at 1:45 A. M. enemy aircraft dropped flares over our ships. Meanwhile a force of enemy cruisers and destroyers churned in, headed in the direction of the comparatively defenseless transports and supply ships. After feinting at a force headed by the Australian cruiser *Canberra* (which was sunk), the Japs changed course and headed for the cruisers *Vincennes, Quincy* and *Astoria,* and the destroyers *Helm* and *Wilson.* The Japs had the advantage of surprise and a neatly coordinated flare attack to silhouette our ships. Moreover, they caught the *Vincennes* with their searchlights and displayed superb marksmanship in sending 57 shells into her in quick succession. A torpedo hit completed the dirty work as the *Vincennes,* now burning badly, lost steering control. Battered but still game, her turrets continued to fire on auxiliary power.

At 2:00 A. M. she was dead in the water and a half-hour later Capt. Frederick Riefkohl passed the word to abandon ship. Comdr. Robert Craighill, a survivor, described her end as follows:

The ship listed and was going over at an increasing rate. The top decks were brightly lighted by numerous fires. When we were about two hundred yards away, she finally reached her beam ends, seemed to hesitate before the stacks went under, and with burning planes and cranes crashing into the water, she slowly turned over and went down bow first.

Rescue operations were dangerous that night, but somehow, through all the murderous fire, 730 survived. Thirty-six were killed.

With Rear Adm. Wilder Baker in command, the second *Vincennes* joined Task Force 58 in June, 1944 and during the next twelve months she scoured the Pacific much to the regret of the Japanese Navy and air force.

During the bewildering series of punches our growing forces threw at the enemy in that period, the *Vincennes* was in on air strikes and bombardments on Saipan, Pagan, Guam, Tinian, Rota, the Bonins, Palau, Ngesebus, Peleliu, Angaur, Mindanao, Leyte, Cebu, Bohol, Luzon, Samar and Negros islands. That occupied her from June through September.

Operating off Okinawa with Task Force 38 in October, she headed next for Formosa, where she shot down several Jap planes. Off Visayas in the Philippines on October 20 she was in on more strikes and retaliatory raids, escaping without damage.

At 3:25 A. M. on October 25 an enemy force of four battleships, eight heavy cruisers and 13 destroyers was detected heading for our landing vessels in Leyte Gulf. The *Vincennes*, in company with battleships, destroyers and other cruisers, steamed south towards San Bernardino Strait to cut the enemy off. Shortly after midnight a radar surface contact was made and the *Vincennes, Miami* and *Biloxi* closed in to attack. Firing commenced about 1:00 A. M. and ceased in a few minutes. An enemy cruiser was burning and sinking as two destroyers rushed in for the kill. No more contacts were made.

In November the *Vincennes* task group commenced air strikes on Luzon, in the face of fanatic attacks from the first Kamikaze units. Within the space of a half-hour suicide planes crashed into the carriers *Hancock, Cabot* and the *Intrepid,* but again the cruiser went untouched. Following further strikes at Luzon in December, the *Vincennes* tackled another formidable opponent on the 18th, weathering a typhoon.

She wound up her career with strikes against Luzon, Formosa, Okinawa and the China Coast before heading into the carrier strikes against Tokyo, Chichi Jima, Okino Daito Jima, Kyushu and Okinawa. The going off Kyushu and Okinawa was especially rugged, with one Kamikaze crashing fifty feet astern. Seaman Joe P. Hines won special commendation and the gratitude of his shipmates by being "the first to detect and report enemy aircraft on five separate occasions."

On June 16 after brilliant counterbattery work at Okinawa, the *Vincennes* returned to the states for overhauling. She was at Mare Island when the war ended.

DESTROYERS

About six hundred destroyers were in service during the war and several hundred others were building when the last shot was fired. The tough little DDs saw plenty of action in every theater; 80 were sunk, including 9 destroyer transports.

Destroyers range from the 1,020-ton *Manley* commissioned in 1917 to the 2,400-ton *Gearing* class which came off the ways in 1945. The *Manley* was 315 feet long, the *Gearing* 390. Destroyer speeds do not vary much; the DDs' function is to protect the larger ships, to kill submarines, to attack large enemy surface craft with torpedoes, to pursue merchant ships, and to patrol, and for all these tasks speed is essential. The *Livermore* class of 1941 could make 37 knots, while the *Manley,* built 24 years earlier was rated at 32 knots.

Destroyers are unarmored but are well armed with 3-, 4-, and 5-inch guns, torpedo tubes, depth charges, and antiaircraft guns. Their AA fire is tremendous. They depend more or less on speed and agility for defense. Cruising ranges are long, and their crews of from 200 to 350 live in cramped quarters but are usually singing the praises of the "tin can Navy." If these sailors must go to sea, they'll take a "can" every time.

Destroyers work in divisions and squadrons, usually attached to larger fleet units. They screened escort aircraft carriers in anti-submarine hunter-killer task groups, and escorted convoys. They were particularly valuable in amphibious landing operations, and took some of their heaviest punishment in these engagements.

Destroyer escorts are smaller models of destroyers, much slower, with less armament. They were designed to be constructed rapidly, and more than 500 were built during the war. Ten were sunk, most of them in the Atlantic, where they were used extensively in the anti-submarine compaign and in convoying. They ranged from 1,100 to 1,300 tons, were about 300 feet long, carried torpedo tubes and 3- or 5-inch guns, and a crew of 220.

The *Sterett*

Little was reported during the war about the destroyer *Sterett* (DD 407) but this ship sank 2 Japanese destroyers unaided, shot down 14 planes, and sent hundreds of Japs in sampans and barges to watery graves. She also managed to play a pretty large part in the sinking of an enemy battleship, a cruiser, and another destroyer, while participating in 14 engagements and operations. The *Sterett* never made the headlines but she was selected for this book as representative of all those fighting ships which should be included but are not.

The *Sterett* was commissioned in August, 1939 and was at Bermuda when the Japanese struck at Pearl Harbor. During the next four months she was on escort patrol in the Atlantic, going to England in March, 1942 in the first US task force sent there. Early in May she escorted the carrier *Wasp* when it delivered planes to beleaguered Malta in the Mediterranean. She returned to the States in June and was ordered to the Pacific, arriving at Tongabatu on July 8, 1942. Here are the cold facts of the record of one Navy ship:

1. Atlantic anti-submarine duty	December 1941 - March 1942
2. USS *Wasp* operations in reinforcement of Malta	14-21 April - 3-17 May 1942
3. Guadalcanal—Tulagi Landings (Including First Savo)	7-9 August 1942
4. Capture and Defense of Guadalcanal	10 August 1942 - 8 February 1943
5. Guadalcanal (Third Savo)	12-15 November 1942
6. Consolidation of Southern Solomons	8 February - 20 June 1943
7. New Georgia Group Operation:	
(a) New Georgia-Rendova-Vangunu Occupations	20 June - 31 August 1943
(b) Vella Gulf Action	6-7 August 1943
8. Treasury-Bougainville Operation	27 October - 15 December 1943
(a) Rabaul Strike	5 November 1943
(b) Rabaul Strike	11 November 1943
9. Gilbert Islands Operation	13 November - 8 December 1943
10. Marshall Islands Operation	26 November 1942 - 2 March 1944
(a) Air attacks designated by Cincpac on defended Marshall Islands Targets	
(b) Asiatic-Pacific Raids	1944
11. Truk Attack	16-17 February 1944
Marianas Attack	21-22 February 1944
12. Marianas Operation	10 June - 27 August 1944

(a) Neutralization of Japanese bases in Bonins, Marianas, and Western Pacific — 1 June - 27 August 1944

(b) Capture and Occupation of Saipan — 11 June - 10 August 1944

(c) First Bonins Raid — 15-16 June 1944

(d) Battle of Philippine Sea — 19-20 June 1944

(e) Capture and Occupation Guam — 12 July - 15 August 1944

(f) Capture and Occupation Tinian — 20 July - 10 August 1944

(g) Palau, Yap, Ulithi Raid — 25-27 July 1944

13. Liberation of Philippines — 7 December 1944 - 1 February 1945

(a) Supply and protection of Leyte
(b) Resupply of Mindoro

14. Luzon Operation — 12 December 1944
(a) Lingayen Gulf Landing — 4-18 January 1945

15. Okinawa Gunto, Nansei Shoto Operation — 17 March - 11 June 1945

Enemy surface units sunk by *Sterett* or with assistance of *Sterett:*

Battleship	13 November 1942	Assist
Cruiser	13 November 1942	Assist
Destroyer	13 November 1942	Unassisted
Destroyer	6 August 1943	Unassisted
Destroyer	6-7 August 1943	Assist
Numerous barges and sampans		

Here is the official transcript of the *Sterett* in the famous night battle off Guadalcanal in November, 1942:

At 0148 the *Sterett* received orders to open fire to starboard, and although she had been tracking a target on the port bow, took under fire a cruiser on the starboard bow at a range of four thousand yards. Numerous hits were observed on the bridge and forward part of the superstructure.

At 0151 the *Sterett* received her first hit, which cut the starboard cable to the steering gear and caused the rudder to jam momentarily making it necessary to maneuver by engines. The range was fouled by a friendly destroyer at this time so the *Sterett* ceased firing. At 0205 the foremast of the *Sterett* was hit, disabling the SC radar, the emergency identification lights, and TBS transmitting antenna. Temporary emergency lights and antenna were rigged.

At this time a *Kongo* class battleship was visible to port and the *Sterett* closed range to three thousand yards and fired a full salvo of four torpedoes. Two torpedoes were definitely seen to hit, causing two large explosions aft. A number of direct 5-inch hits were also observed, but these sounded like peas hitting against a window pane. These 5-inch hits caused numerous fires in the superstructure. During this period the battleship was being hit on the bow and forward superstructure by large caliber shells and part of her crew was observed abandoning ship.

At 0220 an enemy destroyer of the *Fubuki* class was silhouetted on the *Sterett's* starboard bow at one thousand yards and she immediately took the enemy under fire with the main battery and torpedoes were launched. Only two salvos had been fired when two torpedoes hit, lifting the destroyer out of the water. This destroyer did not get a chance to open fire and sank immediately. The explosion of this destroyer illuminated the entire area causing heavy cross fire to be concentrated on the *Sterett*.

At 0227 the *Sterett* received numerous hits on port quarter. Enemy salvos struck the port side of No. 3 handling room, gun shelter, and No. 4 handling room. These hits started fires in each of these stations causing detonation of several 5-inch ready service power tanks in each handling room and inflicting severe casualties to both personnel and material. Both after guns were thus put out of action. This area received three 5-inch and three 14-inch hits.

A second salvo of five struck the ship in quarterdeck area. One pierced the port inboard torpedo tube while the others pierced the midship clipping room causing damage to the starboard torpedo tube nest.

Both after magazines and handling rooms were flooded, all power to guns No. 3 and No. 4 was cut off, ready service ammunition, much of it on the verge of explosion from the heat of the fires, was thrown overboard. The fires were brought under control and at 0230 the *Sterett* retired, burning fiercely aft, both afterguns disabled, and with two remaining torpedoes to be fired.

The *Sterett* had received eleven direct hits, including three 14-inch hits and fragments from many near misses. Serious fires had been started in No. 3 and No. 4 handling rooms and up through the gun mounts. Several compartments were on fire. Over twenty per cent of the ship's company had been killed or seriously wounded. The fighting efficiency of the ship had been reduced about eighty per cent, yet the *Sterett* managed to retire at flank speed. A short time later boilers No. 1 and No. 2 had to be secured, limiting speed to twenty-three knots and at about 0600 the *Sterett* joined up with the remainder of the re-tiring force. This can be attributed only to the high state of training for battle, the prompt action of the gunnery officer in flooding all magazines aft and ordering all power to mounts three and four cut off, the prompt and efficient action of the damage control officer and his repair parties and the coolness and efficient cooperation of every man aboard.

The men who sailed the *Sterett* knew what it was like.

The *Borie*

The battle which led to the sinking of the first destroyer *Borie* (DD 215) in November, 1943 is one of the epic encounters of all time between a surface ship and a U-boat. The *Borie* was an old destroyer; she was launched on October 4, 1919; she drew the nasty North Atlantic patrol assignment during the early war months. Merely to cruise in those icy, storm-tossed waters aboard the old cans was an ordeal. To endure the rigors of constant patrol, subject to attack at any instant, was the toughest kind of duty.

One black and blowy night in the autumn of 1943 the *Borie,* along with the destroyers *Goff* and *Barry* and the escort carrier *Card,* suddenly found herself in the middle of a Nazi wolf-pack. Fighting a 40-mile wind her commanding officer, Lieutenant Commander Charles Hutchins, soon flashed the *Card,* "Scratch one pigboat. Am hunting for more." He soon found "more," and the *Borie* moved in to attack.

Splattering the sea with dozens of depth charges, she forced the sub to surface. When the huge grey shape popped into view, the *Borie's* 4-inch batteries cut loose, blasting the sub's heavy deck gun. Determined Germans poured out of the conning tower and dove for machine guns to retaliate, but the *Borie's* machine gunners cut them down with murderous accuracy. But the battle had just begun. Suddenly the sub began to twist and turn, trying to bring her torpedo tubes to bear. The *Borie* shifted quickly, meanwhile trying to blast the Nazi with her 4-inch guns as 30-foot waves tossed the old destroyer about like a matchbox.

A desperate game of tag followed, climaxed by the *Borie's* attempted ramming of the sub. The can drove her sharp prow in towards the Nazi, when a huge wave lifted her and the destroyer dropped harmlessly on the sub's deck. Locked together, the two craft pounded in the swelling seas, as the *Borie's* crew used rifles, automatics, shell cases, beer cans and knives to stem the flood of Nazis sweeping toward her decks. It was a slaughter, for the Germans were like sitting ducks in the beams of the *Borie's* searchlight.

Still the dogged Nazi sub refused to give up, and breaking loose she circled and drove relentlessly in. This time her intentions were plain. The sub was trying to ram the destroyer! At the last minute the *Borie* evaded disaster as her quick-thinking commander splattered the sub with depth charges. Shaken, the sub shuddered to a halt just short of the destroyer. A few moments later the *Borie's* heavy guns found the range and the U-boat exploded and sank.

But the *Borie* herself was mortally wounded and sinking, far from her companion ships in waters so cold that brief exposure meant death. To make matters worse, the storm continued and rain fell in sheets. Water poured into the engine room but Lieut. Morrison R. Brown stayed at his post and (in the words of his Navy Cross citation), "as the flooding increased . . . he calmly ordered his men to safety while he stayed below, standing neck-deep in water at the throttle."

In the battle to save the ship that followed, MM Irving Randolph Saum also won the Navy Cross when, according to his citation: "He voluntarily entered the debris-filled water of the forward engine room of the heavily rolling ship. He descended about ten feet below the surface, located and closed the secondary drain valve, enabling increased pumping capacity to be diverted to the after engine room. His tenacity and endurance, together with an utter disregard for his personal safety, contributed greatly to the seaworthiness and power of the ship . . ."

CMM W. J. Green and MM Mario James Pagnotta won the Silver Star Medal for similar daring acts. But despite such valor, the *Borie* seemed doomed to sink without hope of rescue, for radio communications were dead. At 11:00 A. M. the next morning the crew succeeded in rigging a weak temporary set, using cigarette lighter fluid and alcohol from the sick bay to run the generator. Capt. Arnold Isbell, then commander of the carrier *Card* (later killed in action) told of the rescue in the magazine *Sperryscope*. Said Captain Isbell:

"It wasn't until 12:30 that one of the planes located the destroyer, and we came up to find her wallowing in the trough of the sea, a gallant old warrior bleeding from a hundred wounds—back broken, engine room flooded, all electric power lost. A tow was out of the question, even had weather permitted, for Hutchins had jettisoned his anchor chains along with guns, ammunition and everything movable in order to keep afloat. With the storm increasing in fury, I put the decision up to Lieutenant Hutchins, although pointing out that the gale was growing in intensity. Reluctantly enough, for it's a heart-breaking thing for any commander to do, he gave orders to abandon ship."

Thanks to the clever rescue efforts of the *Goff* and *Barry* only twenty-seven men were lost in the frigid, pounding seas. Throughout these operations German subs dogged the US ships but were driven off. The next morning a search continued for survivors but the bodies that wallowed in the waves were frozen hard as chunks of ice. The old *Borie* was still afloat, but inspection showed she must be sunk. Finally three planes from the *Card* sent her down with direct bomb hits. The entire group, the *Borie, Goff, Barry* and *Card,* received the Presidential Unit Citation.

The second *Borie* (DD 704) was commissioned in September, 1944 at New York, and operated with the Atlantic Fleet as an escort for the ammunition ship *Wrangel* from New York to the Canal Zone. In December she was ordered to Pearl Harbor with the battleship *Nevada* and minelayer *Gwin.*

In January the *Borie,* en route to the invasion of Iwo Jima with the *Gwin* and *Indiana,* was attacked on January 24, 1945 by Japanese bombers attempting to break up the ship formation. The *Borie's* first salvo sent the lead plane bursting into flames and the other enemy aircraft were driven off. The *Borie* and the task group continued in for the bombardment of Iwo, and a fierce duel with the shore batteries began which was only broken off when overcast made observation impossible.

After returning to Ulithi, the *Borie* joined Task Force 58 for carrier strikes on Tokyo in February. In March, when Kyushu was being hit, the *Borie's* gunners helped bring down an attacking dive bomber. Late in the month she furnished star shell illumination for the bombardment of southern Japan by a big battleship force.

In April while transferring mail to the carrier *Essex,* the *Borie* was damaged in heavy seas and again made Ulithi for repairs. She rejoined the force on May 1 to stand picket duty at Okinawa, a hazardous occupation, and then took part in strikes at Minami Daito and Kyushu. In the latter operation the *Borie* splashed one Jap plane and was credited with an assist on another. Late in May she returned to Okinawa to resume picket duty.

The carrier *Ticonderoga* had to put in to Guam for repairs and the *Borie* was assigned as escort, but joined Task Force 38 in the blasting of the Japanese Empire on her return. On July 10 strikes began on Honshu and Hokkaido, and then the *Borie* and other ships conducted an anti-shipping sweep into Tokyo Bay. A typhoon broke up operations early in August.

August 9 was bad news for this second *Borie.* While on picket duty off Honshu, a Jap bomber popped out of the clouds on the starboard bow and came in low on the water, turning down the port side to come in astern. The *Borie* attempted to come left, but before she could get around the Kamikaze pilot crashed into the bridge, his 500-pound bomb exploding forward and causing large fires to break out. Radars and main battery were wiped out and steering control lost. During the trial of the *Borie,* while fire control parties tried to extinguish the flames, four more suicide planes attacked, all being shot down by the after guns. Casualties were 34 dead, 13 missing, 66 wounded. The *Alabama* and *Abbot* assisted with medical supplies and the hospital ship *Rescue* took off 34 of the wounded next day. Another typhoon prevented the *Borie* from leaving the force, but on the 13th she was detached for repairs. She reached Saipan on the 17th and made San Francisco on September 8.

The *Preston*

The first *Preston,* a coal-burning destroyer, 289 feet in length, was launched July 14, 1910 and was stricken from the Navy list on September 15, 1919 after seeing heavy duty in the First World War.

The second *Preston* was an oil-burning destroyer of 1,215 tons displacement, 510 feet in length. Launched August 7, 1920, she was stricken from the Navy list November 6, 1941.

The third *Preston* (DD 379) was launched April 22, 1936 and sunk by enemy action during the battle of Guadalcanal, November 13-15, 1942.

Ens. Theodore Marx described the death of the third *Preston:*

"Most of the ships fought their way out, but we were between a Jap battleship and a cruiser and were hit by two 14-inchers and a salvo of eights. Before we went down six minutes later we got a cruiser and set another on fire." (When that salvo of shells hit the length of the *Preston,* those which landed directly below the bridge turned out to be duds, luckily for Marx.)

"I had a friend back aft who had a real narrow escape. Lieut. W. W. Woods was in charge of the repair party there when he saw splashes on the port side and knew the enemy was lining up on us. The next salvo got us and he was pinned against a bulkhead. Flames broke out over him. He was going to shoot himself when the *Preston* lurched over and he fell free. The only way he could get to the side and overboard was on one remaining beam. He started across, the beam crashed and he fell into the engine room, among steam pipes and with the water pouring in on him. He was going down again when he drifted out through the side of the ship. We picked him up and gave him a shot of morphine."

Marx remembers being showered with bread and onions as the shells struck the full length of the ship.

"The battleship behind us couldn't change its course in time. There was nothing to do but come through over us. I never saw anything as big in my life. I could have reached out and touched its bow, it missed me that close. The bow wave picked me up and I rode it out, getting just beyond the reach of the suction in the ship's wake. They didn't have time for much on the battleship but some quick-witted soul tossed a life raft overboard to us. There was a Japanese battleship burning near us and it exploded four times before going down about 4:00 A. M. All the while it was as light as day. Then a Japanese submarine came up in the middle of us and flashed a little blue-green light. They picked up a couple of the fellows, but when they found out they weren't Japs they threw them back in and submerged. There were about thirty of us. Some of the men drifted away and I never saw them again."

The fourth *Preston's* (DD 795) first major duty was in a convoy of Navy transports with destroyer screen bound for Eniwetok. After that she was underway to Guam, again part of the antisubmarine screen for transports. She left Guam with the *Wichita, New Orleans, Farenholt,* and *Wedderburn* to return to Eniwetok. She later got underway as a unit of Task Force 38, en route to the Palau Islands. From this area the task force proceeded south and operated off the southern Philippines.

In 1945 she departed with Task Force 58 to carry out operations against Tokyo and support of the Iwo Jima campaign. On April 12 a detachment of Marines trapped by the Japanese on Motobu Peninsula was liberated as a result of fire delivered by the *Preston.*

After the armed truce with Japan was effected the *Preston* was on air-sea rescue station for aircraft flying from Okinawa to Tokyo.

The *Blue*

Four ensigns were sitting in the wardroom of the destroyer *Blue* (DD-387) at Pearl Harbor. It was a quiet Sunday morning, December 7, 1941. Suddenly from the men on deck came a startled cry. The Japanese were attacking. Where was the commanding officer? Where was the rest of the crew? It hardly mattered now. The ensigns and the few men would have to see it through. The senior officer on board, Ensign N. S. Asher, said later that he thought of other honors he would much rather have had.

Within five minutes the *Blue's* cold machine guns were rattling away, and the blasting of the 5-inch guns was not far behind. Engines were turned over by inexperienced hands, painfully and slowly, and forty-seven minutes later the harassed *Blue* steamed out of the harbor at 25 knots.

Already she had a number of Jap planes to her credit.

Ordered by the cruiser *St. Louis* to screen her from submarines while the larger ship maneuvered evasively in the harbor, the *Blue* began to get into position. Hardly had she done so when her sonar gear picked up the track of a submerged raider. The *Blue* unloaded three 600-pound depth charges, to no effect, and then three more of the same. Quickly a 200-foot oil slick attested to the accuracy of the last charge and a submarine was added to the *Blue's* aircraft kills.

The *Blue* was in the war in earnest now. For thirty hours her young commanding officer stood at the "con" while his even younger aides stuck to their posts. Out of the holocaust the *Blue* came with no damage to herself—no casualties except a couple of broken eardrums.

Two months later she was in the fight again; this time as a screen for the *Enterprise* near the Marshall Islands. Here she encountered five 2-engined Jap bombers heading for the great carrier, opposed by one apparently badly over-matched American fighter. While the fighter pecked at the enemy, the *Blue* maneuvered into position to join the scrap. By the time she was ready one of the bombers had crashed trying to hit the *Enterprise,* and the others had turned away. Still the *Blue* had time for one four-gun salvo at five thousand yards which exploded a Jap plane in midair.

August found the *Blue* on antisubmarine patrol in the Battle of Savo Island; her most important contribution was the rescue of many men from the stricken Australian cruiser *Canberra.* Here the *Blue* had an interesting experience when she rescued a downed Zero pilot, and took off three others from a battered torpedo plane. The *Blue's* commanding officer reported later that all were terribly frightened, expecting to receive drastic and inhumane treatment.

Later the same month, engaged in the first great American offensive against Tulagi and Guadalcanal, the *Blue* operated in advance of a Navy formation. She entered Lunga Channel in the Solomons, and after having one unfortunate experience in firing on small American high speed transports, she kept on the prowl for enemy submarines. At four o'clock the morning of the 22d, the *Blue's* sonar gear picked up the sounds of fast propellers, and soon the wakes of two torpedoes were spotted in the phosphorescent waters. Before the *Blue* could maneuver out of the way there was a terrific explosion at her stern. The ship rocked madly and the engines stopped, the propeller and rudder knocked out of commission. Men and gear were catapulted fifty feet from the stern; 5 were killed, 22 wounded and 6 missing.

At daylight, the destroyer *Henley* took the *Blue* in tow; a difficult job which eventually had to be abandoned because of enemy action. A large Jap task force was heading for the area and all surface ships were ordered to sea. But the *Henley,* making only five knots with the *Blue,* could not possibly get out of the way. Accordingly, she asked permission to scuttle the *Blue* in order to move freely when the enemy attacked. At 11:00 P. M. August 3, 1942 the *Blue's* water-tight compartments which had saved her from foundering earlier were opened and she was left to sink.

Like other US ships heavily damaged in combat the *Blue* survived everything sent at her by the enemy, only to be forced down by our own hands to save other Fleet units.

The second destroyer *Blue* to see action in World War II was commissioned at Brooklyn in March, 1944, and was the first of the new 2200-ton DDs to pass through the Panama Canal for the Pacific. She joined the Third Fleet as it was getting underway for the initial attacks on Palau and the Philippines, and served throughout the Leyte, Luzon, Iwo Jima, Okinawa and Empire campaigns.

During the carrier sweeps from the southern Philippines to Hokkaido in Japan, the new *Blue* (DD-744) steamed over 150,000 miles, repelled numerous Kamikaze attacks and shot down four enemy planes. On 18 occasions following carrier plane crashes she conducted rescue operations, never losing a man. She rode out three typhoons, in one of which the destroyers *Hull, Spence* and *Monaghan* were lost.

Twice the *Blue* took part in shore bombardments, at Okino Daito and Minami Daito, islands between Okinawa and Japan. With destroyer Squadron 61 she attacked an enemy convoy emerging from Tokyo Bay on the night of July 22, 1945, and sunk two ships and damaged two others.

After the cessation of hostilities but before the surrender, the *Blue* overtook and captured the largest submarine in the Japanese Navy, a 5500-ton plane-carrying vessel which was steaming for the Honshu coast. The *Blue* entered Tokyo Bay on September 2, anchoring near the *Missouri* for the surrender ceremonies.

The *Ralph Talbot*

The men of the *Ralph Talbot* (DD-390) claim, and with a good deal of justification, that she saw as much action against the enemy "as any ship in the Fleet."

Time alone would tend to bear out this claim. The *Ralph Talbot*, commissioned at Norfolk Navy Yard in 1937, was moored at Pearl Harbor on December 7, 1941. Her score there was two enemy planes shot down and one damaged. Then, after coming through hell and high water everywhere in the Pacific, she turned up in 1945 for the surrender of the great Japanese naval base at Truk.

On September 19, 1945 she carried Rear Adm. Morton L. Deyo to Sasebo on the west coast of Kyushu to make arrangements for the dissolution of the remaining fragments of the Japanese fleet. She was the first foreign ship to touch Sasebo for several decades.

The *Ralph Talbot* earned her honors. In January, 1942 she participated in the Marshall and Gilbert Island raids; in February and

March, she was at Wake and Marcus; in June, she brought desperately needed aviation fuel to Midway; in August, she was at Guadalcanal and Tulagi and Savo Island. So it went; she was later at the Solomons, New Guinea, New Georgia and Bismarck Islands, at Saipan, Tinian, Guam and the Marianas. In the fall of 1944, with Task Force 38, she raided the Volcano and Bonin Islands and made the first strikes at Formosa, Okinawa and the Philippines. Later still she was at Leyte, Iwo and Okinawa again for the conquest.

To her credit the *Ralph Talbot* has 20 Jap planes splashed and 5 damaged. She has taken on cruisers, destroyers and groups of smaller vessels. She covered more than twenty major amphibious landings while engaging coastal batteries of the enemy. All told, she expended over five hundred tons of high explosives to good effect.

Moreover, the *Ralph Talbot* participated in more than twenty aviation rescue operations. She also saved and treated more than four hundred survivors of damaged and sunken ships, including the torpedoed *Indianapolis.*

There is no better way to tell of the *Ralph Talbot* than to summarize her wonderful record. If ever a ship speaks for herself, this one does:

Officers and men of the *Ralph Talbot* won 2 Navy Crosses, 4 Silver Stars, 2 Legions of Merit, 1 Bronze Star Medal, 20 Commendation Ribbons, 50 Purple Hearts and 5 Meritorious Promotions.

The *Benham*

Ships and men die in naval warfare, but their names live on. The Japanese torpedoed the destroyer *Benham* (DD 397) off Savo Island in the South Pacific on November 15, 1942, but less than two years later they found another *Benham* (DD 796) carrying the fight to them—to the Marianas, Palau Island, Philippines, Leyte, Mindoro, Lingayen Gulf, Iwo Jima, Okinawa and the home islands themselves.

Some ships have only murderous missions. Thus the very first of the *Benhams,* in World War I won for its Skipper, Comdr. Jesse B. Gay, the Navy Cross for "offensive and defensive action, vigorously and unremittingly prosecuted against all forms of enemy naval activity." Other ships find more merciful actions. A number of enlisted men of the second *Benham* (the first of World War II), were cited for displaying "outstanding courage in manning a motor whaleboat and dropping it into the water, well knowing that the falls were cut, and that the boat hull and engine were holed by shell fragments. The crew were able to keep the boat afloat and running and as a result of their efforts, saved many men in the water who were in urgent need of assistance."

As a result of the same action, the *Benham's* medical officer, Lieut. Seymour Brown, was cited when, "for five days and nights, he attended 83 seriously injured and 153 injured personnel rescued by the *Benham*. By his tireless and unselfish devotion to duty and by his skill in his profession, he saved the lives of many of these officers and men."

These operations in enemy infested waters were carried out during the battle of Midway, June 4-6, 1942 when the 1500-ton *Benham*, which had been launched in April, 1938, was acting with other destroyers as a carrier screen in the South Pacific. Subsequently she helped turn back twenty enemy aircraft that unsuccessfully attacked the carrier *Enterprise* and the battleship *North Carolina*. In August, 1942 the *Benham* formed part of the naval and air forces which rebuffed the Japanese attempts to recapture Guadalcanal and Tulagi.

The *Benham's* final participation in the war took place in November, 1942, during the night action in the battle for Guadalcanal. In company with other destroyers, notably the *Walke* and *Preston*, the *Benham* attacked several Japanese cruisers in the vicinity of Savo Island and helped set fire to one of them. But she received a torpedo herself which, with consequent explosions, carried away the forward part of her bow and flooded all forward compartments below the water line.

Fortunately there were no casualties and though badly crippled the *Benham* strove valiantly to rescue survivors of the *Preston*, which had been sunk in the fight. Enemy action, however, forced the *Benham* to turn reluctantly back to Guadalcanal. Then a tremendous explosion convulsed her, and with the *Gwinn* standing by, the order was given at 4:00 A. M., November 15 to abondon ship.

The second World War II *Benham* (DD 796) participated in several operations rating battle stars, from the invasion of the Marianas to the Third Fleet strikes against Japan. She had been commissioned at Brooklyn in December, 1943.

Screening escort carriers in the Marianas engagement, the *Benham* splashed two attacking bombers in her first scrape with Japanese aircraft. En route to the invasion she had depth-charged a submarine. Throughout July and until August 6, 1944 the *Benham* blasted Marpi Point and northern Tinian so effectively that enemy ground operations were slowed down.

The *Benham* was next assigned to the fast carrier task forces preparing to hit Palau and the central Philippines, and after those strikes she took part in the blows at Luzon. The carriers, with the *Benham* and others screening, assaulted Okinawa on October 10-11, and on the night of the 12th the *Benham* was credited with a "probable" in a nine-plane enemy raid on the force. To support the Leyte invasion, the *Benham* and the carriers neutralized Mindanao and Luzon by strikes until December 16. On the 18th she weathered the big typhoon.

The *Benham* had not long to wait in 1945 before returning to action after repairs at Ulithi. On January 3 Formosa was a target, and then came the China Sea operation. During February when Task Force 58 struck Tokyo and other Japanese cities, the *Benham* was a radar and scouting picket for main fleet units. The Iwo Jima campaign followed, and then the bombardment and invasion of Okinawa. On April 17 a suicide plane attacking the *Benham* was destroyed by accurate gunfire, but the plane exploded close astern of the destroyer and killed one man and wounded eight. Another raiding plane was later knocked down and assists were scored on two others. On May 14, after two months at sea, the *Benham* put in at Ulithi.

From July 21 until the end of the war the *Benham* took part in intermittent strikes against the Japanese homeland, and on August 27 began the occupation of Yokosuka, anchoring in Tokyo Bay on September 2 for the formal surrender.

The *O'Brien*

The first destroyer *O'Brien* in World War II was sunk in September, 1942 while escorting a convoy to Guadalcanal. She had been commissioned in 1940. Soon after the *Wasp* was hit on September 14, the *O'Brien* (DD 415) was steaming ahead protectingly when two torpedo tracks were seen heading dead for the destroyer. While the destroyer was maneuvering to miss one torpedo, the other crashed into the *O'Brien* near the bow, throwing up a great spout of water and crushing the bow plates, but miraculously not killing one crew member. After making temporary repairs, the *O'Brien* was proceeding to a Navy base when she began to take water badly, foundered and sank. No lives were lost.

The second destroyer *O'Brien* (DD 725) in World War II entered the arena late, commissioned in 1944, but exacted more than retribution for her predecessor. Some *O'Brien* enthusiasts claim she was the fightingest destroyer in the Navy. From D-day at Normandy to Pacific landings at Okinawa on the doorstep of Japan, her combat assignments carried her at express-train speed from one battle action to the next, sometimes with a whole skin and sometimes patched up.

First action for the *O'Brien* was shepherding a fleet of fifty large infantry landing ships into flaming Omaha Beach at Normandy on D-day. This done, she bombarded Nazi coastal gun positions at

Cherbourg. On June 25, 1944 the *O'Brien* was well inshore, screening minesweepers and slamming away at the German batteries with her 5-inchers. The famed old battlewagon USS *Texas* was standing farther off shore, pumping her 16-inch projectiles into the Cherbourg area directly over the *O'Brien.* The little destroyer, however, was scoring so effectively on the Nazi gun positions that the Germans switched their attention from the bellowing *Texas* to the *O'Brien.* Once the snouts of the Nazis' long rifles were concentrated smack on the *O'Brien* it was just a matter of time until the weaving, dodging destroyer was straddled and one shell lit on the after part of the bridge. This happened about noon of the 25th and although badly battered, the *O'Brien* stayed on the job, hurling shells ashore until 3:30 P. M.

The *Texas* also was hit by a shore battery and the *O'Brien* was ordered to make smoke to cover her. In spite of her grievous wounds, the gallant little ship laid a thick screen in front of the *Texas,* and undoubtedly saved her from more hits from shore.

In August, 1944, in company with a new carrier, the *O'Brien* joined the Third Fleet in strikes against Luzon in the Leyte landing operations.

In Ormoc Bay on December 7, 1944 the *O'Brien* had her first experience with Jap suicide planes. As the troops started ashore, the Kamikazes began swarming over the escorting destroyers.

The *O'Brien* next participated in the invasion of Mindoro. Back to Leyte from Mindoro, she was dispatched to join in the pre-invasion bombardments of Lingayen Gulf.

On January 5, 1945 the destroyer was gingerly threading her way around the Gulf, escorting minesweepers and demolition teams in small boats. The next day, under terrific Jap suicide air attacks, the *O'Brien* was hit by a Jap "Zeke" in a suicide dive. The plane exploded, opening a large hole in the destroyer's side. With mattresses and odd bits of lumber jammed in the gaping hole, the *O'Brien* steamed back into the fray on the morning of January 7—and she stayed at her job until the troops arrived and took over on January 9. She returned then to Leyte for temporary repairs.

She joined a carrier group for the first raid on Tokyo and approached within ninety miles of the Jap capital while on picket duty far ahead of the rest of the fleet.

From that raid, the *O'Brien* made all available knots to Iwo Jima with a fast carrier force to give that invasion air and ship fire support. On March 26, 1945 the *O'Brien* was standing off the strategic Kerama Retto, about 25 miles from Okinawa, where Army troops were about to force a landing. Suicide planes were again in evidence. Nothing happened to the *O'Brien* until the following morning, March 27, when a little after six o'clock a Jap suicide plane skimmed out of low clouds and before the *O'Brien* gunners could fire, hit just aft of the bridge, exploding a magazine and spreading death and destruction through the ship.

Twenty-eight men were killed outright, 22 were missing and more than 100 were injured.

Following temporary repairs at an advanced base, the battered destroyer set out on the long voyage home. Putting in at Mare Island Navy Yard for repairs after her ordeal in the Pacific, she required more than 298,000 man-hours of work to make her ready for Fleet duty.

The *Meredith*

Three destroyers carried the name of *Meredith* through World War II. The first (DD 434) was sunk off San Cristóbal Island on October 15, 1942, as more than 30 Jap planes attacked her. Three torpedoes and two bomb hits delivered the death blow as the *Meredith* stood by to escort barges of high-octane gas for our planes on Guadalcanal.

Lieut. (jg) Charles J. Bates gave a graphic eye-witness account of the tragedy in which 177 men lost their lives. The ordeal of the 61 survivors who lived three days in the water before being rescued is a chilling tale, made nightmarish by the sharks which swarmed about them. Here is Lieutenant Bates' story:

At 1215, radar contact was made on a large group of planes 45 miles away. Just as I started to report to Capt. Hubbard, I was thrown up into the air and landed in a heap on the deck of the flying bridge. I looked up and saw planes going overhead and at the same time felt an explosion below.

I saw one bomb hit in the water about 10 feet from the port bow; the bow went up and then settled down with a small list to port. I noticed about one foot from where I had been standing a hole in the deck where the bomb that had knocked me had gone through, exploding somewhere below.

Six torpedo planes came in from starboard. The 20mm's hit the third and fourth planes, setting fires in their wings. The first four torpedoes missed ahead; the fifth I saw was going to hit so I ducked. I looked up and saw that it had hit just forward of Gun 1, bending the bow to port. The sixth torpedo missed. As each of the planes dropped its torpedo, it flew on over the ship, machine-gunning the deck. From my station I could see the Japs looking at us, some staring curiously, others grinning.

I went from my station to the bridge and saw the captain. He was badly burned about the face and hands. The captain, who appeared dazed, asked what was happening so I told him we were going down by the bow. He then told us to pass the word to abandon ship.

I was just climbing up on a raft when a bomb, dropped by one of the planes, hit the water. The concussion hurt a little. As I sat on the raft I saw the ship disappear beneath the waves; gun No. 4 was twisted and torn, the depth-charge racks and part of the stern gone, one propeller shaft hung brokenly, and at No. 3 20mm gun, Joe Oban, F1c, was still in the harness (he once made the statement that he would never leave his gun until he shot down a plane).

Looking up, I saw 6 Jap planes coming in low and strafing everyone in the water. As they headed my way I slipped off the raft and, holding onto a life line, ducked under the water each time they headed my way. When they left, I climbed back on the raft and looked for the tug and barge. As the planes flew by, I counted 27, 3 being shot down.

After the planes had left, I looked around and saw Lieut. T. Shriver (gunnery officer) struggling in the water. He seemed to be in trouble so I swam over and brought him back to the raft and put him on board. Next I saw Ensign Miller (second assistant engineering officer). He called and said the Captain needed help. I swam over and helped get the Captain aboard the raft. We then had the most seriously wounded men put aboard, filling the raft.

The Captain kept talking for a while, asking questions. I explained to him the procedure I had instituted and answered his many questions. The doctor, who was on the raft, was holding the Captain's head out of the water. After a while, the Captain was quiet so the doctor tried to find signs of life, but there were none.

In the meantime, the fuel and Diesel oil had drifted and come up about us, covering everyone and everything. In the life rafts it was five inches thick, outside about three inches. We took inventory of supplies. All the gear from one raft was gone, blown off by a bomb explosion. In the other raft was 1 canteen, 1 five-gallon water cask, 1 box of provisions and a first-aid box.

Later on when the wounded got very thirsty, we passed the canteen around. They each got about one-half teaspoon of water, all that anyone was to have for the next three days and nights.

During the night men would lose hold of the raft and be carried away by the current. Those who could not find strength to swim back would cry and call for help but no one dared go after them because it would have been virtually impossible to locate them and then after reaching them to find the raft again. I never saw such black nights.

It was about noon on the 16th when we had our first casualty from sharks. From that time on we could see the sharks circling the raft anywhere from 10 to 50 yards away. During the balance of the day and evening there were four or five more men bitten by sharks. On the second evening, several of the men became delirious; they would request permission to do such things as go below to close the main steam line or to go to the scuttlebutt (water fountain). Again, this night, several became exhausted, floated away and would come to, when several hundred yards away.

Late in the afternoon of the 17th, a B-17 went over too high to see us. Sharks continued occasionally to bite a man. Once a shark struck at the raft, and going right over my shoulder, slid into the raft. It took a big bite out of the thigh of one man. One of the men and myself caught the shark by the tail and pulled him out of the raft. By this time, with a little crowding everyone could get on the raft. It rained that night; the shower lasted about five minutes. We all held our heads back and mouths open to relieve our dry throats. I held a meat tin up to catch some rain but a wave came over and filled it with oily salt water.

I have no recollection of the dawning of the morning of the 18th (third day). I just noticed that I was warm and that the sun was out. About an hour later a PBY (Navy patrol plane) flew over very low and dropped a smoke float about fifty yards away. We knew we were spotted.

The *Meredith* started war work early in neutrality patrol in the Atlantic. After Pearl Harbor, she joined the meager Pacific force and starred in convoy duty until her sinking.

The second *Meredith* (DD-726) in World War II was commissioned March 14, 1944. She had one of the shortest lives of any ships, being sunk after hitting a mine off Normandy on June 8, 1944. The third *Meredith* (DD-890) is still afloat, having been commissioned in 1945, too late to get into combat.

The *Monssen*

The first destroyer *Monssen* (DD-436) affectionately dubbed the "Little Swede" by her crew, went down in the Battle of Guadalcanal on November 13, 1942. She had been commissioned in 1941. Her commanding officer, Lieutenant Commander Charles E. McCombs, was trapped by fire and forced to jump from the bridge to escape. McCombs tells the story of the *Monssen's* sinking as follows:

"The battle had just started when we observed the silhouette of an enemy battleship in the blackness," he said. "It was a rough free-for-all that followed . . . a barroom brawl after the lights had been shot out. Within a few seconds we saw one of our destroyers or cruisers being fired on by an enemy cruiser or battleship. We opened up on the new target and within 45 seconds the vessel had ceased firing. Then an enemy destroyer appeared and we sprayed her superstructure with point-blank fire. No shots were returned and the Little Swede had still not been hit.

"Two searchlights suddenly beamed on us and we fired at them. Soon the *Monssen* began to be hit by medium-caliber shells. Lookouts reported several torpedoes heading close at us. We maneuvered quickly and they passed by our bow. Two others passed directly under us. Our remaining guns fired on the second searchlight and made numerous hits on its ship. We were being shot at from both sides by large and small vessels; many were large-caliber shells. Fires started as hits became too numerous to count but able hands continued to man the guns until one by one, each weapon was crippled. With the ship defenseless, drifting and aflame, I gave the order to abandon."

Lieutenant Commander McCombs did not say that his doughty tin can had taken on a Jap battleship, two destroyers and two cruisers before sinking, damaging them all. Several of the vessels, including the battleship, were later reported sunk.

The next *Monssen* (DD-798), a gleaming 2100-ton destroyer, was commissioned February 14, 1944 at the Brooklyn Navy Yard. Four months later she joined a fire-support unit of the Fifth Fleet operating off Saipan.

For two days the *Monssen,* lying-to within slingshot range of the beach, shelled enemy positions. During the evening of the second day, the *Monssen* opened up on what its spotter believed to be an ammunition dump. His guess was right. Three salvos into the area set off a tremendous explosion followed by smoke and flames which billowed four thousand feet into the air.

Taking time out only long enough to reload ammunition, the *Monssen* followed the advance of the Marines northward until Saipan was secured.

On July 21 Comdr. B. A. Fuetsch, skipper of the second *Monssen* since she was commissioned, was relieved by Commander C. K. Bergin. The ship moved in on the second phase of the operation—the invasion of Tinian. During the two-island campaign the destroyer fired a total of 5,200 rounds of 5-inch projectiles, a record high for destroyer support fire at that time.

Sandwiched between these two phases of the Marianas campaign, the *Monssen* participated in the Battle of the Philippine Sea. For this—the greatest single air battle of the war—the crew of the *Monssen* had a ringside seat.

Assigned to the fast battleships, the *Monssen* took a picket station ten miles to the west of the main force. Many enemy planes headed for the main force passed over the destroyer but out of range of her guns. Of the two planes which did attack the *Monssen,* one which dropped a bomb within 500 yards of the ship was shot down, and hits were scored on the second which turned away and eventually crashed.

Throughout the days, wave after wave of enemy planes came through only to be turned back by carrier fighters. Of the few planes shot down by ship's fire, the *Monssen* and three other picket ships accounted for almost half of them.

Following the Marianas operation the *Monssen* moved south, and during the following month she participated in the invasion and occupation of Angaur Island in the Palaus.

The highlight of the *Monssen's* jam-packed career in the Pacific was her participation in the clash of naval forces in the historic Battle for Leyte Gulf in October.

During the landings at Leyte, the *Monssen* was one of five destroyers assigned to guard the southern entrance to the Gulf. First indications that the Japanese fleet was on the move alerted all ships. As it became evident that one force would try to attack through Surigao Strait, these five picket ships were designated to launch the initial attack, a two-way squeeze with torpedoes.

As the distance between the two forces closed and it was certain that contact with the enemy would be made, Commander Bergin ordered the ship to General Quarters. The time was 2:07 A. M., October 25, 1944.

As the five ships moved in for the attack, they split into two units. The *Monssen* was the second of two ships in the western unit.

Radar contact with the enemy force was made at twenty miles range. Leading the force were two battleships in column, two other ships, possibly cruisers, and an undetermined number of destroyers.

It was 3:00 A. M. when the eastern group let go their torpedoes. Immediately, Jap guns began to bark. Seconds later the two ships of the western group, which included the *Monssen*, were spotted and taken under fire. Six salvos hit close to the *Monssen* as she closed in for the attack. Several shells passed overhead and one burst within two hundred yards of the *Monssen*.

Then came the order to fire, and both ships let loose a full spread of torpedoes. With the torpedoes away and clear, both ships turned from the enemy force. At the same moment, they were picked up by searchlights. A moment later the torpedoes found their marks, and the searchlights went out.

Three explosions were observed, and one of the enemy battleships was seen to drop astern of the formation.

As the destroyers cleared the enemy force, heavy units waiting in the mouth of Surigao Strait opened up. This fire, observed from the *Monssen*, was terrific. Said one of the crew: "It looked like the Golden Gate at night."

The defeat of the Jap force begun by the *Monssen's* squadron was finished by the heavy units of the Seventh Fleet. A later evaluation credited the five destroyers with six to eight direct torpedo hits. Sinking of the Jap battleship *Fuso* and one destroyer was among the damage credited to the torpedo attack. Not one of the destroyers received a scratch.

On December 8 Lt. Comdr. Everett G. Sanderson assumed command of the *Monssen*, relieving Commander Bergin.

At Luzon the *Monssen* received her first taste of Jap suicide planes.

Operating with a reinforcement convoy, the *Monssen* was scheduled to arrive at Luzon following the initial invasion. The ship arrived in the area on the morning of January 12. After many alerts, enemy planes singled out the *Monssen* and her group. Three planes approached the group to attack. Two of these planes actually came in on the ships.

Only the aggressiveness of the *Monssen* saved her from serious trouble. Gun crews had their guns going full blast as the first plane came into range. Fire from the *Monssen's* automatic guns sent the plane crashing into the water just short of an ammunition ship. The second plane, diving, twisting and dodging, went down in flames. Exposed to numerous attacks and alerts throughout her stay at Luzon, the ship again weathered the best the enemy could offer and came through without damage.

From mid-February through mid-May the *Monssen,* operating with Vice Adm. Marc A. Mitscher's famed Task Force 58, roamed the enemy coast from Tokyo to Okinawa. During this period she served in many capacities, received only one 48-hour break for reprovisioning. Air alerts, picket duty, mail deliveries, flight operations, storms, submarine attacks, fueling exercises—all of these became routine during the 90-day period. During this time the *Monssen* was credited with assists in bringing down more suicide planes, and along with another destroyer, sank a Jap submarine.

In June the *Monssen,* with other units of the fleet, spent two weeks in San Pedro Bay, Leyte. From here she got underway for the last all-out drive against Japan.

The *Fletcher*

The scrappy destroyer *Fletcher* (DD-445) is credited with being the only US destroyer which challenged and sank a Jap heavy cruiser without assistance from other ships. This victory was just one star in the *Fletcher's* war crown—which boasted 11 star engagements— won as she steamed 200,000 miles during her two and one-half years of combat service, shooting down 11 enemy planes and assisting in splashing eight others. Not content with that, she added a light cruiser and an enemy submarine, rescued survivors from six ships, then to wind up the score, heavily damaged two enemy destroyers!

Commissioned June 30, 1942 the *Fletcher* was hauled into the war while on her shakedown cruise, when word was received that German submarines were attacking an allied convoy bound for Europe. Steaming full speed to the rescue, she pulled from the Atlantic over 100 survivors of a torpedoed merchant ship and chased off at least one German submarine in a rousing depth-charge attack.

Ordered to the Pacific, the destroyer fired her first shot against the Japanese while covering the landings of Marines at Guadalcanal. From November 3 to November 12, 1942 she was under gruelling air attacks, knocking her first six Jap planes out of the air.

Smashing into the thick of the wild battle of Savo Island on November 13, the *Fletcher* won acclaim as she sunk a heavy cruiser unassisted and aided in sending a light cruiser to the bottom. Said Admiral King, "This action, which lasted 24 minutes and was one of the most furious sea battles in history, was terminated when the *Fletcher* torpedoed a heavy cruiser." Of all the allied vessels engaged this destroyer alone escaped undamaged.

That melee was followed on November 30 by the Battle of Tassafaronga. In the boiling night battle the *Fletcher* flashed in to send ten torpedoes at Jap units. That accomplished she stood in to rescue 742 survivors of the sunker cruiser *Northampton*.

After a short rest at Noumea, New Caledonia, she was again engaged in bombardment operations at Munda and Guadalcanal, destroying numerous Japanese landing craft during the latter engagement. And on the afternoon of February 11 she claimed her first undersea victory, destroying a Japanese submarine spotted by a cruiser plane.

The succeeding months were taken up with routine bombardments and air attacks and in July, 1943 the *Fletcher* returned to San Francisco for an overhaul. But after a month she was on her way out to the Pacific again.

By this time our forces were moving northward and the *Fletcher* left her familiar haunts around Guadalcanal and Tulagi for the Gilberts. The Marshalls were next and here the *Fletcher* was under continuous air attack for eight hours. Then came the New Guinea campaign with the *Fletcher* underway continually, escorting amphibious forces to their beachheads and offering a few bombardments besides.

On the night of June 8 a task group was snooping around the north coast of Biak Island off New Guinea in search of Jap ships. About 11:00 P. M. the *Fletcher* gave chase to five Jap destroyers. It wasn't long before she opened fire at extreme range, and as the range slowly closed, a large explosion was observed on one of the enemy ships. For two and a half hours the race continued until it was necessary to break off because of the proximity to enemy bases. Following this brief engagement, the *Fletcher* participated in landings at Noemfoor Island, Cape Sansapor, and Morotai and Halmahera islands in the Moluccas.

At the invasion of Leyte Gulf, the *Fletcher* arrived early on the morning of October 20 in company with a huge force of destroyers, attack transports, and amphibious craft. The enemy made sporadic air attacks at first, but later nightly air raids were common occurrences.

Landings at Ormoc Bay and Mindoro Island followed with the usual bombardments. Then came the invasion of Lingayen Gulf where the *Fletcher* patrolled with a carrier force to the northwest for 30 days in rough seas.

After Lingayen was secured, the *Fletcher* participated in the landings at San Antonio, Nasugbu, and Subic Bay. The *Fletcher* claimed the distinction of being the first major war vessel to enter the old naval base since the beginning of the war, only 500 yards behind the minesweepers. Later the *Fletcher* was part of a large force assembled to bombard enemy positions on Corregidor and in Mariveles Harbor.

During that operation the *Fletcher's* record was marred when a 6-inch shell from a hidden Jap battery struck the ship, putting both forward guns out of action.

The DD ignored her own losses and proceeded to pick up survivors from a minesweeper which had been hit by another shore battery.

Puerto Princesa on the Island of Palawan followed, then Zamboanga. After the successful invasion of Mindanao the *Fletcher* supported the Australian landing at Tarakan, Borneo, silencing several shore batteries.

On May 2, 1945 the *Fletcher* was ordered to return to the United States for overhaul and her career was terminated by the cessation of hostilities before she was able to leave drydock.

The *O'Bannon*

Rushed into the Pacific cauldron with a crew made up largely of inexperienced men, the destroyer *O'Bannon* (DD-450) found herself in the middle of a Solomon Islands campaign almost before the paint was dry on her hull.

Her first assignment was the routine but dangerous work of convoying, patrolling and shelling enemy shore installations. The *O'Bannon* (known as the "Little Helena") landed smack in the middle of the Battle of Guadalcanal on the night of November 12-13. While our out-numbered cruisers traded punches with Jap battleships, the *O'Bannon* stormed into the middle of what has been termed one of the most furious sea actions ever fought. The cruisers *Atlanta* and *Juneau* were sunk in this melee, but the *O'Bannon* slammed three torpedoes into a Jap battleship of the *Kongo* class, and splattered a cruiser with shells to help win the battle. The other destroyers in the action were either sunk or badly damaged but the *O'Bannon* escaped with but slight injury.

In January the *O'Bannon* bombarded enemy airfields on New Georgia and Kolombangara and struck heavily at enemy shipping in a number of raids. In April Capt. Donald MacDonald won a second Legion of Merit award for a bold *O'Bannon* thrust into enemy waters. June found the *O'Bannon* on convoy duty off Guadalcanal, coming safely through a determined air attack, in which the *Aludra* and *Deimos* were sunk.

Meanwhile the Tokyo Express was continuing its nightly runs. Task Group 36.1, consisting of the cruisers *Helena, Honolulu* and *St. Louis* and destroyers *O'Bannon* and *Nicholas* was ordered to intercept the Express off Kula Gulf. In the ensuing action, the Japs again took a trouncing, but the cruiser *Helena* was torpedoed and sunk. After picking up *Helena* survivors, the *O'Bannon* stood in under fierce enemy shore fire to rescue survivors of the destroyer *Strong,* sunk during the action.

The *O'Bannon* ran into the Express again on July 12-13, 1943 and was credited with sinking a destroyer. Then on August 18 the *O'Bannon* and three other destroyers encountered four enemy cans escorting a number of barges to reinforce the Jap garrison. Two enemy destroyers were sunk, the other two retired badly damaged and the barges were sent under. And still the furious pace did not let up. On the night of October 6, with the destroyers *Chevalier* and *Selfridge,* she intercepted and turned back a superior enemy force, sinking a *Ubari*-class cruiser.

In December the overworked destroyer returned to the States for repairs, where she was awarded a Presidential Unit Citation. But a few months later the *O'Bannon* was back again shelling enemy positions at Aitape, New Guinea, on April 22, 1944. From then until September 15 the *O'Bannon* was on convoy patrol duty, going on to support the landings on Morotai Island.

When the attacks on the Philippines began in October, the *O'Bannon* was in there slugging with all her usual vigor. On the morning of October 26 she fought off three separate formations of enemy planes and off Mindoro the *O'Bannon* got her first close shave from suicide planes when she saw the nearby cruiser *Nashville* take one on her main deck. From then until January 10 she was off the Philippines, snooping around for enemy submarines and doing the thousand-and-one duties that only a first-class destroyer could perform. In February she was off Mariveles Beach as our troops stormed in to recapture the town, and in the ensuing days she steamed boldly through mine-filled waters to work over stubborn Jap coastal batteries near Cavite. In March she was in on the landings on Mindanao and Cebu. April found her slamming shells at Carabao and Tarakan Islands as Australian and New Zealand troops went to work. From June until the end of the war the tireless *O'Bannon* accompanied our carriers on their strikes against the northern Honshu and southern Hokkaido areas of the Jap home islands. After operating in Tokyo Bay area with the Third Fleet at the end of the war, she was assigned to the Nineteenth Fleet (inactive), to be laid up on the West Coast.

The *Pringle*

The destroyer *Pringle* (DD 477) got her first look at enemy planes off New Guinea, in May, 1943. From then until the war ended for her, this "can" cut a swath right up to the Jap home islands.

On the night of July 17-18 the *Pringle* was screening a transport division landing supplies and reinforcements at Enogai, when three Jap destroyers were reported off Vanga Point, Kolombangara. The *Pringle* joined the *Waller* (DD 466) and her sister ship, *Saufley* (DD 465) and moved in. At 1:42 A. M. the *Waller* opened fire, followed closely by the *Saufley*. When her comrades turned away, the *Pringle* closed in, fired ten torpedoes at 5400 yards, then retired at 35 knots. Four minutes later two violent explosions were felt. The radar operator reported the targets disappeared from the screen entirely.

The formation returned to patrol off Kula Gulf and promptly encountered a beehive of Jap dive bombers. Several sticks of bombs landed near the destroyers but the *Pringle* weathered the raid and shot down one enemy float biplane in the process.

Operations off Efate Island produced several lively moments on August 15, when Jap torpedo bombers attacked the *Pringle,* dropping one torpedo close aboard.

On August 24 the destroyer covered a daring minelaying operation off Kolombangara. While the *Pringle* stood guard, a small group of minelayers planted a minefield. The operation was being conducted successfully until a collision between *Preble* (DM 20) and *Montgomery* (DM 17). The ships retired at only 10 knots, hugging the coast for concealment. The force was not spotted until it rounded Tuki Point, where a plane dropped a stick of bombs close to the *Montgomery.* Shore batteries, thus alerted, promptly roared out in anger, but a rain storm shielded the passage across Kula and saved the vessels.

While leading an echelon of LST's through Gizo Strait on September 21 the *Pringle* encountered another Jap plane attack. Two torpedo bombers and one fighter picked her out from under the gathering smoke screen and attacked. The two torpedo planes were close, but the fighter was closer, making several strafing runs across the decks, to explode the depth charges. More than two hundred 20mm hits and a large number of .30 dents were scored on the ship in five passes. One man was killed, 26 wounded, and some of the ship's ammunition was set afire.

On the night of September 2-3 a sweep of Jap barges was conducted with the *Dyson* (DD 572) between Choiseul and Kolombangara. Several barges were intercepted and three were definitely destroyed.

Escorting a task group into the Empress Augusta Bay area of Bougainville on November 11, the destroyer ran into a Jap air formation. One of the Jap planes apparently failed to see the *Pringle* until he was nearly upon her. The destroyer's guns opened up and sent the plane down in flames.

On December 15 Jap reconnaissance planes led an enemy force into Empress Augusta Bay to attack the *Pringle's* task unit. Radar-controlled fire was successfully used to repel the raid. One contact was fired upon until it disappeared from the radar screen.

On March 1, 1944, the *Pringle* swept the southwest coast of Bougainville, bombarding enemy installations. Enemy barges were given no rest as the *Pringle* continued her prowls up and down the coast during March.

The Marianas operation produced another long period of bombardment, screening, and antisubmarine missions. During the initial phase of the assault on Saipan, starting on June 17, the *Pringle* served as a fire-support ship. Straddled by enemy shore batteries on June 18, she repelled several air attacks in her patrols there till July 8. On July 24 the *Pringle* was again called, this time for the occupation of Tinian.

The Philippines operations brought on some of the fiercest fighting the *Pringle* experienced. Following the assault the ship retired to sweep the channel between Leyte and Ponson Islands. A Jap submarine was taken under fire and sunk in a combined assault launched by the destroyers.

While in Leyte Gulf on November 27 the *Pringle* saw five enemy planes break through an overcast sky as her fire assisted in destroying one of them. One of the planes in another attack strafed the destroyer heavily. But the most intense airplane attack came on December 28 as the *Pringle* escorted sixty ships, most of them cumbersome landing craft. Three "Zekes" attacked the formation at 10:20 A. M. One crashed into the SS *John S. Burke,* which blew up. Another dove into the SS *William Sharon* (later abandoned) and the third dove into the USS *Porcupine* (IX 126). At twilight, four enemy aircraft reappeared for another try and the *Pringle* shot down a "Betty."

As the vessels moved into Mindoro on December 30, Jap planes continued to press their attack. At 3.48 P. M. that day a Kamikaze crashed into the *Pringle's* after deckhouse, totally destroying one 40mm mount and damaging two 5-inch mounts. Alert damage control quickly extinguished the fires and the ship patched up its damage and joined the convoy on its return to Leyte that day. Five were killed, 20 wounded, with 6 missing.

The battle-scarred "tin can" steamed to the assault on Iwo Jima on February 17. Alternating between the transport screen and fire-support stations, the *Pringle* went through the familiar process of shelling the beachheads and guarding transports against submarines and airplanes. On February 22 she was sent in search of carrier pilots; several bodies were recovered and proper burials given.

On March 1, 1945 the destroyer was sent to rendezvous with a task unit en route to Ulithi, where plans were laid for the next invasion.

The landing on Okinawa started out as just another assault. Operating with Destroyer Division 90, the *Pringle* screened transport areas, repelling air attacks with boring regularity. Then at noon on April 14, the *Pringle* left on a new assignment—radar picket duty. She arrived on station at 4:30 that afternoon and saw the day pass by without incident. But the men sensed the calm before the storm and the hunch was unhappily right. On April 16 a single Zeke came in early but was promptly splashed.

Ten minutes later, with the *Pringle's* air cover off in a grand melee a trio of Nip planes approached the area just outside of effective firing range. Cunningly the planes dropped low, alternately opening and closing the range from nine to eleven thousand yards to draw fire while weaving around.

Finally the Nips picked their opportunity and moved in. The lowest hit into a shell splash and crashed. Another feinted, and a third kept coming, weaving radically through the heavy bursts of antiaircraft fire. The ship swung hard right and increased speed, but the determined Jap hit, splitting the vessel in two at the forward fireroom.

With immediate flooding and total loss of power, the men could do little to save the shattered hulk. The crew went over the side and even as the men lay in the water, the Japs continued to attack. The

Pringle's commanding officer, Lt. Comdr. J. L. Kelley, Jr., reported 62 men missing in action.

A unit of the *Fletcher* class, the *Pringle* measured 377 feet overall, 39 feet in beam, and had displacement of 2,050 tons. Her main battery consisted of five 5-inch 38-caliber (barrels 190 inches long) single guns and ten 21-inch torpedo tubes.

The *Buchanan*

The United States began to move forward against the Japs in August, 1942, when we made our first landings in the Solomons near Tulagi. The destroyer *Buchanan* (DD-484) was there then, blasting at shore installations, helping to cover our initial landings. This was the *Buchanan's* first taste of battle, and she smelled smoke up until August 29, 1945 when she made her triumphant entry into Tokyo Bay, three years later almost to the day.

The *Buchanan* started moving forward when our Pacific offensive did; she continued to move forward to the end. Her job was to remain the same during the entire war; to blast shore installations, to harass enemy shipping; to cover our landings. These activities she carried out at Guadalcanal, Cape Esperance, New Georgia, Treasury-Bougainville, Bismarck Archipelago.

Some ships are lucky ships; they go through the hottest fighting, kill their quarry, come out unscathed. Others, freshly commissioned, go to the bottom almost before they have a chance to try their guns. In between are ships like the *Buchanan*. She must be considered lucky, since with all the tough fighting she saw over 180,000 miles of water, she was alive to see the final victory. But the *Buchanan* had her casualties, her close calls, her terrible emergencies.

The *Buchanan* was commissioned at the Brooklyn Navy Yard on March 21, 1942. In May, she headed for the Pacific. In her second major engagement at Guadalcanal in November, 1942 a 5-inch shell from an enemy shore battery killed five of the crew.

On April 30, 1942 while convoying transports with other ships of the Twelfth Destroyer Squadron to which she was attached, the *Buchanan* ran aground in Sealark Channel off southern Guadalcanal as an enemy air attack developed. Fortunately, the aircraft never reached her there nor was anyone hurt in the accident. But enough damage was done to the *Buchanan* to put her out of commission for months.

More serious was the hit on the *Buchanan* on February 25, 1944. That morning, in broad daylight, Destroyer Squadron Twelve raided

Japanese shipping in strongly fortified Kavieng Harbor at New Ireland. A 6-inch shell struck the *Buchanan* in this action, costing her eight injured and one killed.

But the *Buchanan* gave much better than she received. Her most notable conquest was over an enemy cruiser which the destroyer engaged on October 11-12, 1942. At a range of 3500 yards she fired with main and torpedo batteries. Two torpedoes and a rain of 5-inch shells found their mark and in nine minutes the cruiser broke in two and sank.

To her credit, the *Buchanan* also had three merchantmen and another plane.

When she steamed victoriously into Tokyo Bay, the *Buchanan* and her crew were the proud possessors of a Presidential Unit Citation.

The *McCalla*

The *McCalla* (DD-488) was commissioned on May 27, 1942 and by the end of the war this hard-working destroyer helped send to the bottom 1 heavy cruiser, 2 destroyers, 40 landing craft and barges, and 8 aircraft, while engaging the enemy in 15 separate operations.

The ship's outstanding performance came in her first engagement at the Battle of Cape Esperance October 11, 1942 when she hit an enemy cruiser and two enemy destroyers. The cruiser went down from the combined fire of other ships, but the *McCalla* sank one destroyer unaided.

After the crippled enemy had broken off the battle, the *McCalla* searched in vain for the damaged cruiser *Boise*. One vessel, gutted with fire, was sighted drifting close to Savo Island. The smoldering mass was not the *Boise* but the destroyer *Duncan,* which also had been heavily damaged in the night battle.

No sign of life was found on the burning vessel, but a *McCalla* salvage party worked steadily, attempting to restore power. When the *McCalla* returned, the report was received that the damaged destroyer could be successfully towed by the stern and salvaged, but a decision was made to pick up survivors first.

Most of the *Duncan* personnel were picked up without incident, but while one man was being rescued another, two hundred yards away, was under vicious attack from sharks. Several other survivors reported that they were closely investigated by these man-eaters, and three were actually attacked.

Returning to take the *Duncan* in tow, the *McCalla* found that the destroyer had developed several additional leaks and had foundered.

In the trip back to base the destroyer threw a line to several Jap seamen who were struggling in the water. To a man, they refused to grasp the line. The destroyer lowered a boat, captured them and departed.

While on patrol in the Guadalcanal area on November 3, a submarine was sighted. It appeared to be lying dead in the water. Guns were ordered to train on the target and speed increased with an intent to ram, but the submarine submerged in a crash dive. A heavy depth charge attack followed; no evidence of destruction was observed, however, except a strong odor of fuel oil.

On November 9, the *McCalla* was part of a task group covering unloading operations at Lunga Point, Guadalcanal, when the Japs launched a dive-bombing attack.

A second raid of 28 twin-engined bombers came in high and fast; no hits were obtained. Similar screening operations were conducted on the 12th when another force came in to bomb the transports. The commanding officer observed that two planes fired upon by his ship's gunners crashed into flames and a third was damaged.

At the end of the month the *McCalla* was detailed to wipe out a nest of Jap landing craft and barges in the vicinity of Tassafaronga, near Guadalcanal. The destroyer charged in for a bold daylight attack. The enemy ships were caught by surprise and by the time resistance could be organized, the fast destroyer was on its way out, leaving in its wake an estimated forty splintered landing craft and barges.

Following this, the destroyer spent six months of comparatively uneventful escort duty in the Southwest Pacific.

On the last day of June, 1943 the *McCalla* formed part of an anti-aircraft screen about a group of transports. Twenty-five torpedo planes were spotted and immediately engaged by our own fighters. Fifteen planes left the formation and headed in.

All ships opened fire, but three torpedo planes managed to drop their "fish" and bracket the *McCalla*. One passed ahead, another astern, and one sped under the ship as the destroyer evaded all successfully. One plane got through and strafed the *McCalla*, spraying her with 20mm projectiles and armor piercing bullets. The ship's torpedo director was put out of action and two officers and one man were wounded. The *McCalla* shot down one of the enemy planes and damaged two.

After the planes dispersed, the *McCalla* went alongside the *McCauley* (APA-4) which was sinking as a result of torpedoing, to rescue survivors. Sixteen officers and 82 men were removed a few minutes before the transport blew up in a violent explosion. Shortly after, two torpedo tracks were observed heading for the *McCalla;* the ship went to flank speed and left full rudder to avoid a torpedo which passed five yards ahead and another which sped by fifty yards astern.

On the morning of July 5 the *McCalla* participated in a landing at Rice anchorage on the north coast of New Georgia and early on July 9 the force of four destroyers entered Blanche Channel for an hour's bombardment of Munda airfield.

With no help from the Japs, the career of the *McCalla* was temporarily halted on the night of September 29 when a steering casualty resulted in a collision with the *Patterson* (DD-392). Twenty-four frames of the bow were sheared off, but quick action by the damage-control crew saved the ship.

With a month's overhaul in Purvis Bay, Florida Island, the injured vessel started for Pearl Harbor via Samoa. On November 12, while en route, she picked up 600 survivors of the torpedoed merchant vessel *Cape San Juan* and delivered them to Suva, Fiji Islands. The *McCalla* then proceeded to Mare Island Navy Yard, California, and remained there until January 8, 1944.

By the end of January the *McCalla* was back to pick up the war where she had left off and on March 20 she softened Ailinglapalap Atoll, where Marines were landing.

The *McCalla* operated with a fast carrier task group during the month of June, hitting the Bonin Islands and repelling an air attack west of the Marianas.

At daybreak on August 4 the destroyer lashed out with a Task Group on enemy installations at Iwo, Haha, and Chichi Jima.

The period from August 29 to September 28, 1944 was spent steaming in company for Task Force 38 during air strikes on the Palau Islands and initial strikes on the Southern and Central Philippines.

The carrier force continued its rampage, hitting the North and Central Philippines. The first weeks of 1945 took the destroyer to patrol and escort duty in Philippine waters.

On March 11 the destroyer aided in the bombardment of Zamboanga, went on to screen landings at Malabang-Parang-Cotabato areas in Mindanao, and convoyed ships in and out of the Philippine area for the next two months.

In June, the *McCalla* screened landings and shelled beaches at Brunei Bay, Borneo.

It was a red-letter day on the *McCalla's* calendar on July 22, 1945 when she received passengers from the *Detroit* (CL-8) for transportation to the States. On August 9, the battle-worn destroyer docked in

Portland, Oregon.   As the war ended, she was inactivated at Charleston Navy Yard.

The *Farenholt*

When the USS *Farenholt* (DD-491) ran up the VJ flag on August 15, 1945, she displayed 5 planes, 3 ships, 5 shore batteries and 9 shore bombardments in the painted scoreboard high on her director. This destroyer had seen three and one-half years of the toughest war service and although twice pounded by enemy shells, she was in there pitching at the end.

Commissioned April 2, 1942 the 1630-ton tin can headed for the Pacific, where she made her debut with a carrier task force, supplying much-needed air support for the Guadalcanal operations. The "Fighting F" was on hand when the old *Wasp* sank, picking up 143 survivors. Her next action was at the Ellice Islands on October 3, 1942. Then on October 8 the *Farenholt,* along with the *San Francisco, Helena, Salt Lake City, Boise, Buchanan, Laffey* and *Duncan* moved in to intercept the Tokyo Express. The now-famous night battle of Cape Esperance followed and although the *Farenholt* took four 6-inch shell hits, she came through the holocaust to fight again. She lost 3 dead and 25 wounded in this encounter but the Japs lost 2 heavy cruisers, 1 light cruiser, 1 transport and 5 destroyers. Aided by the *Aaron Ward,* the Fighting F finally steamed into Pearl Harbor.

Damage was so heavy that it was February, 1943 before she came back to the Solomons, landing smack in the middle of the huge enemy air raids on shipping in that area. In June, landings commenced on Rendova Island against bitter Jap resistance. The *Farenholt* rang up hits on three planes, two shore batteries and a sub. Meanwhile she was undergoing desperate torpedo attacks from enemy planes and submarines. For almost a month her crew practically lived at battle stations, existing on sandwiches while pounding shells into Rendova. In between these actions she escorted supply ships along the Solomons "slot"—a rugged assignment.

After liberty at Sydney, Australia, in mid-October, she was rushed back to the Solomons for the Treasury Island and Bougainville landings. Next the *Farenholt* joined a carrier task force in a strike at Rabaul, then continued a round of convoy operations and raids in the waters of the Solomons.

Early in February, 1944 she again pounced on Rabaul, bristling Jap fortress on New Britain, in the Bismarcks. This mission started as a suicide run for in addition to minefields the Japs were known to have a number of heavy fleet units based there. But the skill and swiftness of the raiders enabled them to maul the more powerful enemy. The *Farenholt* slammed 214 salvos into troop and supply depots and steamed to the very harbor nets before unleashing a torpedo attack against shipping inside.

From there the destroyer went on to Kavieng, New Ireland, where she sank a Jap merchant ship and pounded shore batteries. (An enemy shell slammed into her fire room but there were no casualties.)

In the spring of 1944 the destroyer returned to the States but in June she was back in the Pacific screening the beach at Guam as the Marines went ashore. Then joining with fast carriers, she was in on persistent air strikes on the Palaus, Yap, Philippines and Morotai Islands. Upon completion of these strikes, the Fighting F retired for repairs, rejoining Task Force 38 just in time for the landings on Leyte. Then the busy can escorted the crippled cruisers *Houston* and *Canberra* back to Ulithi.

The next several months were quiet but in April, 1945, the *Farenholt* was ordered to Okinawa at top speed. The Japs gave her a rough welcome, sending over swarms of suicide planes in the first 24 hours. The rain of Kamikaze planes continued unabated and it was with relief that the destroyer put out to sea with a small carrier force to strike at the Sakishima group. On July 28 she was back in Buckner Bay, scheduled to go out on picket station. That night the ship she was scheduled to relieve was sunk and the next night another destroyer was a Kamikaze victim just outside her anchorage, but the *Farenholt* was still in one piece and afloat when the conflict ended.

The *Claxton*

Destroyer Squadron 23, known as the "Little Beavers" because of its busy and insolent treatment of the Japs, included the USS *Claxton* (DD 571) in its group of six. The *Claxton* was commissioned December, 1942, and after a brief trip as a convoy escort, joined the squadron in the Solomons. Her first real action was in the shore bombardment of Buka and Shortland Islands on October 31 and November 1, 1943.

On a night sweep south of Bougainville on November 2, with Cruiser Division Twelve and Destroyer Division 46, the *Claxton* as a unit of Destroyer Division 45 made a torpedo attack on a large Japanese force which was en route to attack our newly established base in Empress Augusta Bay. As a result of torpedo hits and a subsequent night gun duel, one Jap cruiser and four destroyers were sunk, and two cruisers and two destroyers damaged.

On the return voyage a Japanese air attack of eighty planes was repelled by the gun fire and the combat air patrol of the *Claxton* and her mates.

The *Claxton* participated in a second bombardment of Buka Island on the night of November 17, which did severe damage to enemy installations.

On the night of November 24 the *Claxton,* in company with the *Charles Ausburne, Dyson, Converse* and *Spence,* surprised and made a torpedo attack on six Japanese ships off Cape St. George, New Ireland, north of Buka Island. Three ships were hit—one disintegrated, a second broke in two and a third was left dead in the water. The *Claxton, Ausburne* and *Dyson* engaged another group with gunfire, sinking two and damaging a third which escaped.

During a bombardment of Sarime Plantation, Bougainville, on February 4, 1944, the *Claxton* was hit by two medium-caliber shells, putting the two after guns and the steering gear out of commission. The bombardment was continued with the forward guns and the *Claxton* subsequently returned to Purvis Bay, steering by propellers.

During these Solomons operations (which also included numerous voyages as escort and several night sweeps through the "Slot") the *Claxton* underwent numerous air attacks in which she shot down five enemy planes and probably a sixth, three of them at night.

On returning to the Pacific after repairs, the *Claxton* operated with escort carriers in support of the landings on Peleliu Island.

In October she joined assault forces in the landings on Leyte, bombarding the area north of Telosa.

The *Claxton,* with the destroyers *Cony* and *Thorn,* maintained a screen to westward of the battle line during the Battle of Surigao Strait later in the month and assisted in sinking a damaged Japanese destroyer.

During subsequent operations in Leyte Gulf the *Claxton* was heavily damaged aft by a hit from a suicide plane, which killed and wounded 28 men.

In spite of this damage she assisted the *Abner Read,* which had also been hit, until magazine explosions forced withdrawal, and recovered seven officers and 180 men who survived when the *Read* sank.

After temporary repairs in Manus the *Claxton* returned to the Philippines and acted as escort and fire-support ship in the landings at Lingayen, Nasugbu, Mariveles and Corregidor, Panay, Negros and Mindanao. Although shore batteries were engaged and waters were heavily mined, the ship suffered no subsequent damage.

The *Claxton* then proceeded to Okinawa where she joined the radar picket line which had been losing numerous destroyers to suicide planes.

From May, 1945, until the end of the war she alternated on picket duty, undergoing numerous attacks, sometimes by as many as 12 Kamikaze planes.

During picket duty at Okinawa the *Claxton* shot down three suicide planes and assisted in shooting down a fourth.

Along with the *Charles Ausburne, Dyson, Spence, Converse* and *Stanly,* she received the Presidential Unit Citation for her squadron:

"For extraordinary heroism in action against enemy forces during the Solomons Island Campaign, from November 1, 1943, to February 23, 1944. Boldly penetrating submarine-infested waters during a period when Japanese naval and air power was at its height, Destroyer Squadron Twenty-three operated in daring defiance of repeated attacks by hostile air groups, closing the enemy's strongly fortified shores to carry out sustained bombardments against Japanese coastal defenses and render effective cover and fire support for the major invasion operations in this area."

The *Dyson*

If the Japanese knew all the exploits of the "Little Beaver Squadron," they must have thought it a resourceful little navy in itself. And they couldn't have been far wrong for there was little that warships could do in a war that the "Little Beavers" did not at some time accomplish.

Actually, the Little Beavers were only part of Destroyer Squadron 23, which operated in the South Pacific during 1943 and 1944 under Capt. Arleigh A. Burke, whose shifty, broken field tactics called for such speed that he quickly became known as "31-knot Burke." There were six Beavers in all: The *Charles Ausburne, Converse, Claxton, Stanly, Spence* and *Dyson.* Though they were almost constantly exposed to enemy attack, none succumbed to enemy fire, and only the *Spence* failed to survive the war, having foundered and sunk in a typhoon off Luzon on December 18, 1944.

It is hard to choose among Burke's Beavers but certainly none was more active than the tidy *Dyson* (DD-572). Launched at Orange, Texas in April, 1942 and commissioned that December, the *Dyson* left for the South Pacific in May, 1943. In the next year and a half her crew saw action at New Georgia, New Guinea, Treasury–Bougainville, Bismarck Archipelago, Marianas, Philippines, and Okinawa.

In the Bougainville battles, in the face of fierce enemy fire from aircraft and shore batteries, the *Dyson* helped cover our initial night landings in the Buka-Buin area. Then, in preparation for our landings at Empress Augusta Bay, she made a daylight assault which silenced shore batteries, knocked out other shore installations, and pulverized enemy airfields on the Shortland Islands. These attacks brought out big Japanese surface ships, and in the ensuing battle, the *Dyson* and her Beaver companions helped sink one enemy cruiser and four destroyers.

One action followed another in breathless succession. Having secured the Empress Augusta Bay area, the *Dyson* and her sister raiders then turned to escort our first transport echelons to this hard-won battle—the destroyers and transports were harassed continually from the air, mainly by deadly Jap torpedo bombers.

The Japs retreated before American landings and the Beavers had their work load increased. With Jap positions more and more untenable, the enemy attempted to evacuate key aviation personnel from the Buka-Buin fields. On November 24, 1943 six enemy destroyers were occupied in an operation which soon caught the eye of the *Dyson* and the others. The result was a three-hour torpedo and gun battle in which four enemy destroyers were sunk and the other two damaged, one badly. The Beavers came through unscathed!

In the following months, the Beavers, with the *Dyson* always prominent, continued to harass enemy shore installations, shipping, and troop movements. One of the *Dyson's* particularly daring exploits found her moving up to the beach of Corregidor Island after the US reoccupation in 1945 and breaking up a banzai charge against beleaguered American troops. "When the army counted the enemy the next morning, the soldiers found two hundred and fifty dead," said an official report.

An entirely different kind of operation occupied the *Dyson* and the other Beavers when they were patrolling "up the slot" in the Solomon Sea between Choiseul Island and Kolombangara where we had a Japanese garrison under siege. The mission of the Beavers was to see to it that no Jap reinforcements got to this garrison. Ordinarily this was a tricky but uneventful patrol, but one night, dark and rainy and made to order for a sneak attempt, the *Dyson* suddenly spotted three or four Jap barges trying to make Kolombangara. Apparently the other Beavers had also spotted the quarry, because at 11:20 one of them fired star shells which illuminated the whole area. Immediately the Jap barges were under fire and though they tried to flee, three were sent to the bottom.

If the Beavers went unrecognized by the Japs, they were well recognized at home. For their work, notably in the period November 1,

1943 to February 23, 1944, they received the Presidential Unit Citation which said, in part: "Commanded by forceful leaders and manned by aggressive, fearless crews, the ships of Squadron 23 coordinated as a superb fighting team; they encountered the enemy's fierce aerial bombing attacks and destroyed or routed his planes; they intercepted his surface task forces, sank or damaged his warships by torpedo fire and prevented interference with our transports."

During this period Captain Burke won the Distinguished Service Medal, the Navy Cross and the Legion of Merit. Other officers in the squadron received 6 Navy Crosses, 6 Silver Stars, 39 Bronze Stars and several Letters of Commendation.

What were these awards for? A bare statistical summary of the squadron's achievements in the four months of the citation period will indicate its contribution to victory:

"In 22 separate engagements, the versatile squadron is credited with the destruction of 1 Jap cruiser, 9 destroyers, 1 submarine, 1 auxiliary vessel, 1 coastal destroyer-minelayer, 1 large cargo vessel and 4 barges and numerous aircraft, estimated at possibly 30."

The *Callaghan*

At 8:00 P. M. on July 28, 1945 the destroyer *Callaghan* (DD-792) was cruising southwest of Okinawa under a three-quarter moon when Comdr. Charles M. Bertholf stepped to the ship's public-address system and said:

"Now hear this! The ship has received orders. We will be relieved at 0130, stopping off for fuel at Buckner Bay preparatory to leaving for the West Coast for a Navy Yard overhauling."

The decks and passage ways rang with cheers from hundreds of sailors, for this was the message the crew had been awaiting during 18 months of campaign duty. The *Callaghan* had been off Okinawa alone for 125 consecutive days—days filled with shrieks and crashes and the sound of death.

At 12:30 A. M., just as the ship was completing arrangements for the journey to Buckner Bay, General Quarters sounded as a lone Jap plane approached the patrol group. It was an antiquated biplane and its dive on the *Callaghan* was driven off by heavy fire. But the Jap came skimming back over the water, unobserved in the darkness until just before he reached the destroyer. The Kamikaze hit the *Callaghan* on the starboard side at 12:41 A. M. exploding in a tremendous blast as the plane's ignited gasoline sent up a fearful 150-foot sheet of flame. A bomb had penetrated to the after engine room and exploded four minutes later, blowing holes in the hull that caused immediate flooding. Meanwhile the fire topside was exploding ammunition in all directions.

At 12:30 A .M. the *Callaghan* was abondoned except for a salvage detail. One officer and 47 enlisted men had been killed 49 minutes before the *Callaghan* was scheduled to start back to the States. She sank at 2:34 A. M.

The *Callaghan* was commissioned on November 28, 1943 at Terminal Island, California, entering her first fleet duty, antisubmarine patrol in the Marshall Islands, on March 7, 1944. She was named for Adm. Daniel Callaghan, killed on the *San Francisco*. For the next five months she was with a task group of escort carriers. In June, 1944 she supported carrier strikes at Saipan, Tinian, Rota, and Guam, shooting down three Jap planes in these actions. She then went for more carrier strikes against Palau, Mindanao and Luzon in September, and Okinawa and Formosa in October, when she got three more Jap planes before returning to the Philippines to cover the landings at Leyte. The *Callaghan* was in the task group at Cape Engaño that stopped the Jap forces from upsetting the invasion. Then before the Okinawa campaign she supported more strikes in the China Sea, at Tokyo and Iwo Jima, coming safely through the typhoon of December 17, 1944 in which three destroyers were lost.

Her final assignment was pre-invasion bombardment and Kamikaze picket duty off Okinawa, where she arrived on March 25, 1945.

The Japs will remember the *Callaghan*, for she shot down twelve planes and assisted in splashing twelve more in addition to sinking a midget submarine, a picket boat and destroying or damaging three suicide boats. Commander Bertholf received the Bronze Star medal for "heroic and meritorious achievement."

The *Colhoun*

"Her first engagement was the invasion of Iwo Jima, where she received damage from shore batteries; her second and last was the Okinawa campaign."

There, simply, is the two-month battle record of the unlucky *Colhoun* (DD-801). She entered the war in February, 1945; in April she was at the bottom of the East China Sea. The fact of the *Colhoun's* dying is simple. The manner was heroic.

Her last battle started hours before dawn on April 6, 1945 while she was standing guard on a radar picket station off Okinawa. The Japs no longer had a fighting navy; aircraft gave the only support to their harassed land forces. In the darkness, bomber formation after bomber formation tore at the *Colhoun.* Eleven times they came and eleven times they failed.

But other ships were not so fortunate. That morning the *Colhoun's* radio intercepted a half-finished message from the destroyer *Bush* indicating that she was in trouble. The *Colhoun's* radar showed 20 to 30 enemy aircraft battering the *Bush,* and she sped to give assistance. By doing thirty knots the *Colhoun* found the flaming *Bush* at four that afternoon. Still hovering overhead were three "Zekes." To fight them off, the *Colhoun* radioed for the Combat Air Patrol planes under her direction, but they were already heavily engaged with other Japs to the south.

The fight was not long in coming. At five that afternoon, 12 enemy planes converged on the *Colhoun* and the *Bush.* Three peeled off, and one, strafing as it came, headed for the *Colhoun.* Guns roared, and the Jap splashed into the sea.

Another trio came—two of them flashing at the *Colhoun* from different directions. One 5-inch salvo finished the first; another blast accounted for the second. This made it three up and three down for the destroyer. But the odds soon caught up with her. The third plane of the formation smashed into her 40mm mount, fired the main deck, fell through to the fire room, blew up there and burst gaping holes in the port side below the waterline.

Still more Japs came on, singly and in varying formations; the *Colhoun* shot down more than her share; but others hit all over the ship, disabling the guns, killing gun crews, blowing up engines and plates. The last Jap suicider, flaming and out of control, crashed into the *Colhoun's* bridge. The final score read: of the 12 Jap planes, 6 were shot down, 1 was damaged, 1 fled, and 4 scored hits.

That finished the Jap action for the day; but it also finished the *Bush* (which had sunk after an hour) and the *Colhoun.* The heroic ship didn't go down; but while being towed by the destroyer *Cassin Young* more fires broke out and she was abandoned and sent to the bottom by the *Young's* own guns. For "extraordinary heroism" in this battle, the *Colhoun's* master, Commander George Reiss Wilson, won the Navy Cross.

Earlier, at Iwo, the *Colhoun* had begun her war experience with an unfortunate collision with the USS *Knox* and USS *Libra* while all three were harassing Jap land forces with night bombardments. The accident tore a huge hole in the starboard side, and while anchored off Iwo Jima to repair the damage, the *Colhoun* was the target for enemy shore batteries.   One man was killed and 16 injured, and the destroyer had to limp back to Saipan for extensive repairs.

With remarkable speed she was made ready again for battle; and with remarkable fortitude she took up the fight at Okinawa which ended only as she sank.

The *Janssen*

On a cold, stormy February day in 1944 the destroyer escort *Janssen* rendezvoused with Task Group 21.11 off Cape Henry, Virginia. Flagship of the group was the escort carrier *Bogue* and other ships were the destroyer *Hobson,* and the DEs *Haverfield, Willis* and *Swenning*.   As an antisubmarine "hunter-killer" group it remained almost intact until the end of the war.   The *Janssen* (DE 396) was awarded the Presidential Unit Citation for her combat duty.

On March 9, just as the German sub U-575 was about to fire a torpedo at the *Bogue,* the *Janssen* let go with a 9-charge depth attack. The U-boat crash-dived and escaped, to be sunk four days later by the other DEs.   Nazi survivors told of the carrier's narrow escape.   On June 24, returning from Casablanca, planes from the *Bogue* attacked and sank a submarine which turned out to be the Japanese RO-44, and the *Janssen* swept the area to recover large blocks of crude rubber which the sub was running to Germany.

August 20 found the carrier's planes again attacking and sinking an undersea raider, this time the U-1229, the *Janssen* picking up 42 survivors.   On constant U-boat patrol until April, 1945 the *Janssen* was unable to sink another submarine until two weeks before VE-day.

The *Janssen's* last Atlantic cruise began on April 16, when in company with two carriers and 22 DEs it made up a large force throwing a barrier across the ocean from Iceland to the Carolinas against German subs known to be bound for the US.   The *Janssen* delivered repeated depth-charge attacks on many U-boats, but not until April 24, after the destroyer escort *Frederick C. Davis* had been torpedoed with heavy loss of life, was she able to score a kill.   Ten DEs closed in on the sub which had sunk the *Davis,* the *Flaherty* gaining and losing contact, and the *Janssen* then picking it up.   The *Janssen* attacked three times, dropping forty charges, with other ships making attacks in order.   Just before dusk the German submarine U-546 surfaced, her weary and frightened crew abandoned ship, and she sank.

The European war over in May, the *Janssen* returned to the Norfolk Navy Yard for refitting preparatory to sailing for the Pacific.   She made

Pearl Harbor just about the time the atomic bomb hit Japan, so she became a transport ferrying soldiers back to the States. In October, 1945 she joined the reserve fleet in St. John's River, Florida.

The *Eversole*

The destroyer escort *Eversole* (DE 404) received her baptism of fire in what turned out to be a harmless comedy of errors off Bermuda in April, 1944.

Commissioned on March 21, 1944 the *Eversole* was on convoy duty off Bermuda on the night of April 12 when she was ordered to investigate an unidentified radar contact. Intercepting her target, the *Eversole* fired two rounds of star shells, and after the second round she challenged the unknown ship by flashing light. But the challenge was answered incorrectly and the mystery ship opened fire as the *Eversole* closed in.

More star shells illuminated the target sufficiently to reveal it as a large surface craft and the suspicion that it might be a fast surface raider was strengthened as it let loose a second salvo at the *Eversole*. Attempting to further identify the ship, the DE switched on its 24-inch searchlight, revealing her own position. This brought another round from the "raider" and the *Eversole* changed course and drew abeam at considerable range, firing more star shells. These were answered by three additional rounds from the "enemy's" guns, the shells whistling uncomfortably close over the *Eversole*.

At 11:15 P. M. the DE's Executive Officer reported radio messages indicating that a US ship was being fired upon in a coinciding position. The *Eversole* continued to close the target, challenging by light as she drew near and finally the identity of the "raider" was established. It was a US merchant vessel, the *Esso Springfield*. No one was hurt in the entire action.

After finishing Atlantic convoy duty in May, the *Eversole* was transferred to the Pacific. Early in the morning of October 29, 1944 the DE was steaming out of Leyte Gulf when an enemy submarine got her with a pair of torpedoes. Although her sinking was tragic enough in itself, the enemy sub, operating in true Japanese fashion, returned to bomb and machine-gun surviving personnel as they floated helplessly in the sea. Lt. Comdr. George Marix, the vessel's commanding officer, reported her sinking as follows:

"The Gulf of Leyte was cleared at twenty knots, leaving an air raid about a mile behind. En route to join the task group, the ship picked up a sonar contact. Before I could get to the bridge, the first torpedo struck the ship. I noticed the ship took on a 15-degree list. A second torpedo hit two minutes later.

"No panic was seen in the 'abandon ship' procedure. Three men were frozen to the rail, afraid to move; I beat their fingers until they dropped into the water below. After stepping into the water, I towed a man with a broken leg to a floater net about a hundred yards away. On the way to the net I managed to pick up a life preserver as I had given mine to the injured man.

"There was another floater net about a hundred yards away. I ordered them lashed together so as to concentrate the men. Officers were placed around nets ten yards out to pick up any who might slip off and drift away.

"A sub surfaced near a group of men, and thinking it was a rescue ship, they yelled. The sub opened fire with 20mm and strafed the area. It was so dark and rainy that he couldn't see us and no one was hit. Men were ordered to keep quiet as the sub circled us twice about 150 yards away.

"Twenty minutes later the sub submerged. Five minutes later there was a terrific underwater explosion that killed or wounded everyone in the water. I was seized by a very bad cramp. Unconscious men began drifting from the floater net and injured men helped each other to stay on."

The *Bull* (DE 693) picked up the survivors with the *Whitehurst* (DE 634) covering.

Not a single man aboard the *Eversole* escaped injury, and eighty were reported dead or missing. The Japs had added another black mark to their war records.

The *Rich*

Nine months after her commissioning the destroyer escort *Rich* (DE 695) steamed from Plymouth, England, in the vanguard of a powerful echelon of American ships. It was June 5, 1944—D-day minus one. Three days later the *Rich* sank with heavy loss of life—but not before she had rendered sturdy service in the invasion of Fortress Europa.

By dawn of D-day the *Rich* was leading the battleship *Nevada* into Normandy channel for the bombardment of shore positions.

On June 7 the new destroyer *Meredith* (DD 726) struck a mine close by the *Rich* and was enveloped in a mass of flames. At this point the *Rich* had to decide whether to go alongside the burning ship or remain on station. The *Rich* elected to stay and protect the heavy fire-support ships by laying down a smoke screen. Another destroyer escort steamed in to rescue the *Meredith's* personnel. That evening a message came ordering the *Rich* to speed to the aid of the destroyer *Glennon.*

The *Rich* soon arrived in the *Glennon's* area and was requested to stand by and watch for drifting mines and enemy planes, so she dropped her whaleboat and maneuvered at slow speed. At 9:20 A. M. a heavy explosion shook the ship as a mine detonated fifty yards to starboard. Light and power were temporarily lost, sound-powered telephones went dead and three depth charges were blown from their projectors into the water.

Three minutes elapsed before the second explosion was heard, this one coming aft and directly under the ship. Bridge personnel were thrown from their feet, and when they recovered, saw about fifty feet of the vessel's stern floating away with several crewmen aboard.

Two minutes more had passed when the third and final blast occurred. This one made the destruction complete. The flying bridge vanished in hundreds of pieces and the foremast crashed down across the debris. Witnesses reported that all personnel appeared to be dead or unconscious; many were thrown clear of the ship. The bow began to sag forward.

Several men recovered sufficiently to assist in lifting the wounded into whale boats and life rafts. British tugs and Coast Guard patrol craft stood in to offer assistance. The ship started her final plunge fifteen minutes after the third explosion. Men who had been working to remove personnel stepped from the doomed ship with the last injured man just as the deck went under.

According to the ship's commanding officer, Lt. Comdr. Edward A. Michel, Jr., USN, who wrote his report from a hospital bed, 27 men were known dead, 62 missing, and 73 wounded. Fifty-four other injured men recovered sufficiently to return to duty.

For her first assignment the *Rich* escorted a transport to Argentia, Newfoundland; further convoy duty took the DE to Panama; and by the beginning of 1944 the destroyer escort seemed destined for regular North Atlantic convoy duty, but she was diverted to take part in the invasion.

SUBMARINES

The élite corps of the Navy, US submarine men are all volunteers. They receive, in addition to certain shore privileges, fifty per cent higher pay. Anyone who doubts that these distinctions are well earned is referred to Admiral King's report (below) or the brief outlines of what the *Dace, Tirante, Greenling, Tang,* and *Barb* went through in World War II.

In his Final Official Report on the US Navy at War, Fleet Admiral Ernest J. King reported that US submarines sank *63 per cent of all Japanese merchant shipping of 1,000 or more gross tons.* More powerfully than any other argument, this demonstrates the devastating performance of the US submarine fleet. In addition to these merchant-ship sinkings our submarines also found time to sink one battleship, four carriers, four escort carriers, three heavy cruisers, nine light cruisers, 43 destroyers, 23 submarines and 189 minor combat vessels.

Persistent submarine patrolling, plus air sweeps, were responsible for the strangling of the enemy supply lines along the sea lanes of the East Indies and the coast of Indo-China. During the later stages of the war our submarines were very active in the East China Sea and the Yellow Sea. (The *Barb,* not content with prowling sea lanes, landed a party on the coast of Honshu and successfully blew up a bridge and a speeding train crossing it.)

In addition to such performances, submarines admirably performed such dangerous assignments as sowing mines, mine-sweeping, charting dangerous shoal waters, landing guerrilla parties and commando units, rescuing aviators, and generally plaguing the Japanese.

Submarines were fair game for everyone. Friendly and enemy planes alike dropped bombs and depth charges on any sign of a periscope. What it was like to spend months dodging death in a submarine's closely confined quarters is hard to imagine but one skipper, Lt. Comdr. Edward L. Beach (who commanded the USS *Piper*) gave some indication when at the end of the war he wrote:

Never again the blind groping of the water mole, listening, always listening—and often finding it quite unnecessary to listen—nor the steaming, sweating, drenching heat, the decks and bulkheads solid water, perspiration running down your bare chest and back, soaking the rags and towels you vainly throw around you, soaking your trousers and shoes—while you pay no attention, act unconcerned, keep reliefs going to the planes and steering, keep checking all compartments after each salvo, keep the best soundman on—he's dead tired but you couldn't get rid of him anyway—and you listen, and guess, and maneuver, and wait. . . .

Here, briefly, are the war stories of five US submarines. We lost 52 undersea craft during the war.

The *Barb*

The submarine *Barb* (SS 220) ran up some of the most amazing achievements of any of the Navy's undersea boats. In just seven war patrols she destroyed or damaged a quarter-million tons of enemy shipping, setting a record for American submarines, and managed to emerge with a whole skin. In taking this toll she made assaults from shallow, uncharted harbors; used rockets (the first sub to do so); sought cover behind an iceberg; and fired the most destructive torpedo salvo by a Navy vessel. To top it all off and demonstrate her ingenuity, the *Barb* landed a force on the Japanese mainland which blew up a railroad train!

On July 24, 1943, the *Barb* put into the submarine base at New London, Connecticut, after five war patrols in European waters. The Germans had few surface vessels afloat and the Italian Navy was bottled up in the Mediterranean so the *Barb* did not score a single hit during the five patrols. It was during her seven Pacific patrols that the damage was done.

In October the *Barb* left Pearl Harbor for her first stab at the Japanese. On the night of the 29th, after missing two targets, she encountered a 4-ship convoy with four escorts. The *Barb* maneuvered into position and fired four torpedoes, two hitting on one cargo ship, while one tin fish damaged another. The remainder of the patrol was unfruitful and the *Barb* steamed back to Pearl for overhaul.

On March 2, 1944, the *Barb* was underway for her seventh patrol, and on board was her new prospective commanding officer, Comdr. Eugene B. Fluckey, under whom the *Barb* was to make her mark. For the first three weeks west of the Marianas all was quiet. But on the night of March 28, just before midnight, three torpedoes fired into the *Syowa Maru* sent that Jap Q-boat to the bottom. Raza Island, northwest of the Marianas, was bombarded in joint action with the *Steelhead* (SS 280) on April 17, smashing many industrial installations. The patrol ended late in the month, the *Barb* returning to Midway.

Commander Fluckey was in charge when the submarine headed out for her eighth patrol on May 21. Ten days later the new skipper's first attack resulted in three hits on a merchant ship, which went down in a few minutes. The same night another vessel was the subject of an assault, this ship going down two minutes after being hit. The *Herring* and *Golet,* US subs working with the *Barb,* were both sunk by depth charges loosed by Japanese escorts in the area. Proceeding north into the Kuriles' icefields, the *Barb* sank two trawlers with surface fire on

June 11. The night of July 3 the *Barb* fired her last two torpedoes at an escorted cargo ship, sending it down, but the escort released thirty-eight depth charges which almost meant the end of the submarine. The 50-day patrol ended on July 9.

The ninth war patrol began on August 4 when the *Barb* joined the *Queenfish* and *Tunny* in wolf-pack operations. On the last day of the month the three boats encountered a large convoy. The *Queenfish* and *Tunny* scored hits, but it was not until the following day that the *Barb* sent three tin fish at a freighter and tanker, sinking both. The wolf-pack followed the convoy all day, and that evening the *Barb* broke a Jap warship in two with three torpedoes from the forward tubes. On September 4 a Jap sampan was sunk with surface fire. A few days later, seeking to rescue Australian and British prisoners who had been aboard a Jap transport which had gone down, the *Barb* ran into a convoy which included a 22,500-ton aircraft carrier and an 11,500-ton tanker. Firing six torpedoes from her bow tubes, the *Barb* sank both the enemy carrier and the loaded tanker, for the biggest grand slam of her career. On the 17th fourteen Allied survivors of the sunken transport were picked up and returned to Pearl Harbor.

Heading for the East China Sea, the *Barb* started her tenth patrol on October 27. Thirteen days later she picked up an auxiliary cruiser north of Sasebo and at 3:30 A. M. in the morning attacked. The Jap warship listed but did not sink, so the *Barb* approached within five hundred yards and launched a third torpedo which did the job. As the *Barb* steamed clear of the area enemy patrol boats dropped depth charges. Several cargo vessels and schooners were sunk, and a large carrier damaged, before the *Barb* returned to Midway on November 25.

During the eleventh patrol a transport, freighter, tanker, and ammunition ship were sent to the bottom. And on January 23, 1945, the *Barb* picked up a large group of ships anchored in the lower reaches of Namkwan Harbor. Running into the shallow harbor, the *Barb* launched eight hits in the space of a minute, sinking and damaging thirty-six thousand tons of Jap shipping. Pursued by enemy escort ships, the *Barb* dashed out of the harbor, reaching safety in an hour.

It was on the twelfth patrol that the railroad train was destroyed by a submarine. On June 22, at midnight, off the town of Shari in Hokkaido, the *Barb* unleashed the first rocket attack launched by a submarine, demolishing a 500-yard area in the center of the town. On July 2 a shore bombardment was made on the town of Kaikyo, the *Barb* literally standing on the outskirts—in six fathoms eight hundred yards off—and throwing in salvo after salvo. In the ensuing days

three cargo ships, a frigate, a lugger and a sampan were added to the
Barb's score before the daring feat of landing a saboteur force to plant
a demolition charge was accomplished.

Conditions were right on the night of July 22, dark with heavy
clouds, as men from the *Barb* prepared to shove off in rubber boats for
the shores of Patience Bay, two fathoms of water beneath the sub's
keel. The eight men chosen from among the volunteers were Lt.
William M. Walker, CGM Paul G. Saunders, ES Billy R. Hatfield, SM
Francis N. Sevi, SC Lawrence W. Newland, TM Edward W.
Klingesmith, and CMMM James E. Richard, and John Markuson. At
10:00 P. M. the boats splashed their way into the black night to land
a half hour later. Lieutenant Walker, making his way forward, fell
into a ditch. Suddenly a hundred yards down the tracks a train appeared,
and the entire raiding party hit the ground, to be up in a few moments
to lay the charge. At 1:44 A. M., as the raiding party waited offshore in
their rubber boats, another train swung around the bend and came
roaring down the tracks. A minute later the explosion came, and the
engine, 12 freight cars, 2 passenger cars, and 1 mail car were sent
hurtling off their path.

The rest of the cruise was anti-climactic but rewarding. Shiritori
was hit with rockets on July 24. On the 25th Kashiho was assaulted,
six sampans sunk, and later in the day Chiri was bombarded. Shiritori
was set afire the next day, and a trawler sunk by ramming on the 27th.
The patrol ended soon after.

The twelfth patrol was the *Barb's* last, for the war was over shortly
after the cruise began. Here is a paragraph in Commander Fluckey's
final report:

"What wordy praise can one give such men as these? Men who
offer half a year's pay for the opportunity to land on Jap soil, to blow
up a Jap train with a self-trained demolition team. Men who flinch
not with the fathometer ticking off two fathoms beneath the keel. Men
who shout that the destroyer is running away after we've thrown every
punch we possess and are getting our ears flattened back. Men who
will fight to the last bullet and then want to start throwing the empty
shell cases. These men are submariners."

The *Greenling*

Some enemy ships are too small for a submarine's notice, but none
is too large. While returning from her second war patrol for a refit
at Midway in August, 1942 the *Greenling* (SS 213) met a 50-ton
fishing vessel which she strafed with machine-gun fire, boarded and

sank. But much more to her liking was a 22,000-ton carrier which she took on during her sixth patrol in June, 1943. She didn't sink the carrier, missing with four torpedoes, but she gave it a hot time and evaded the big ship's return fire of shells and depth charges.

All told the *Greenling,* which joined the Navy on January 21, 1942, went out on 12 submarine patrols—occasionally in a wolf pack, but more often alone. She operated mainly in the China Sea, in the area off Truk, in and around the Solomons, and off Bougainville. On her second patrol in the vicinity of Truk she got the 13,000-ton troop carrier *Brazil Maru,* which was identified by a prisoner picked up by the sub when she surfaced. On the same patrol she got another loaded passenger vessel rated at ten thousand tons.

The next time out, in the waters off Honshu, the intrepid *Greenling* got an 11,000-ton freighter and four other ships of varying size; she also tangled with a 22,000 ton converted aircraft carrier and landed two very damaging torpedo hits. On her fourth patrol in the area north of the Bougainville Straits the *Greenling* did even better, smashing a four-ship convoy and getting a 1,500-ton enemy destroyer and other ships.

The *Greenling* went out four times under Lt. Commander Bruton, who in February, 1943, turned the ship over to Lt. Comdr. J. D. Grant. On the latter's first patrol, the sub was the victim of an extremely severe depth-charge attack from two torpedo boats which sent her to Brisbane for repairs.

In the middle of July, 1944 Lt. Comdr. J. D. Gerwick took over the *Greenling* and under him she joined with the subs *Billfish* and *Sailfish* in a wolf pack called "Moseley's Maulers" (in honor of Comdr. S. P. Moseley, Officer in Tactical Command). Commander Gerwick took the *Greenling* out on two more patrols, and on the twelfth patrol, the sub's radar went awry. Operating without it at dawn on January 25, 1945 she spotted a beautiful 9-ship convoy. At the same time, however, four enemy torpedo boats spotted the *Greenling* and lost no time in beginning a relentless 3-hour depth charge attack.

The *Greenling's* hull and operating machinery were severely damaged in this attack and on the night of January 25 she was limping back to Saipan for repairs. The trouble was greater than Saipan could handle and the *Greenling* was ordered to Pearl Harbor where she arrived on February 10. She left there for Mare Island, where it was decided that her fighting days were over and she was made into a training vessel.

All told, the *Greenling* sank 21 enemy ships adding up to 102,500 tons and damaged a large converted carrier and two tankers running to some 42,000 tons.

The *Dace*

On November 4, 1943, the United States submarine *Dace* started her first war patrol, off the coast of southern Japan. She cruised submerged in the daytime, surfaced at night. Her first contact was made the night of November 7—four enemy ships—and the *Dace* (SS 247) let go with two torpedoes at the Japs. One missile scored and black smoke poured out of the target's stack as the sub dropped back to observe results.

A large oiler with two escorts loomed ahead as the *Dace* returned for a second attack, cutting loose with more torpedoes. As the Japs flashed searchlights and dropped depth charges, the *Dace* calmly left the area without submerging.

Early in the evening of November 11 a patrol boat caught the *Dace* on the surface. The sub turned away and tried to open the range as the patrol boat, now revealed as a destroyer, commenced pursuit. When the range closed to six thousand yards the submarine fired a spread of torpedoes in a desperate attempt to halt the Jap but when the destroyer failed to take the final dive, the *Dace* submerged—and fast. The Jap rushed over, dropped four depth charges, but the *Dace* escaped.

On the 19th a tanker and an escort were sighted but the Japs became suspicious and the tanker turned away while the escort located the sub and attacked. The first depth charge was close; light bulbs broke and cork flew off the bulkheads. Within an hour three more patrol boats joined the fun and tried to relocate the *Dace*. Fourteen more depth charges boomed close before the Japs gave up and left. Finally on December 4 the *Dace* was ordered back to Midway for rest and refit. The patrol had lasted 53 days.

Lt. Comdr. J. F. Enright was relieved as commanding officer by Lt. Comdr. B. D. Claggett, and on January 7, 1944 the *Dace* set out on her second war patrol, entering the assigned area between the Bismarck Archipelago and the Caroline Islands on January 18. Contact was established the night of the 26th on a large tanker with two escorts. For three hours the group was tracked, then the *Dace* turned to attack.

One of the escorts complicated the attack by interposing itself between the sub and the main target. Maneuvering skillfully, the *Dace* passed successfully behind the escort and fired torpedoes at the tanker. Seconds later two violent explosions shook the sub, and the *Dace* turned away as a destroyer began chasing her. The destroyer stayed about a mile and a half dead astern for hours, then gave up.

On February 2 the *Dace* arrived in Tulagi for refueling and minor repairs, getting underway again on the 3d, for patrol south of the Caroline Islands, near Truk. After 49 days of cruising the *Dace* returned to Milne Bay, New Guinea. She was ready for sea March 16. After reconnoitering the coast near Hollandia, she surfaced after dark on March 23 and put off five commandos in a rubber boat. A nasty two-bomb straddle from a Jap bomber which dived suddenly out of the clouds on the 31st shook her, but she escaped and on April 6 contacted a task force of three Jap cruisers and four destroyers. Two torpedoes were fired at each cruiser but there were no hits.

The *Dace* received orders April 10 to meet the badly damaged *Scamp* and escort her home, arriving at Seeadler Harbor April 16. On April 19 the *Dace* got underway for patrol once again, ending on May 16 at Brisbane, Australia.

After a 30-day refit, including two weeks' leave in Brisbane and Sydney, the *Dace* was ready for sea. She headed north and cruised submerged close to the Mindanao coast during the day, prowling on the surface at night. On July 9 she made an attack on a large transport with two escorts, scoring at least three hits. A total of 43 depth charges was dropped as the Japs buzzed around, but the *Dace* was lucky and escaped.

Just after dawn on July 26 smoke was seen on the horizon. This contact was chased all day although the *Dace* was forced to submerge eight times to avoid detection by planes. That night after dark contact was reestablished and the *Dace* attacked on the surface. Ten torpedoes were fired into a convoy of three ships and six escorts—one ship was sunk. The *Dace* was forced to submerge to avoid being rammed as 26 depth charges thudded around her.

The afternoon of July 31 a submerged attack was made on a small unescorted freighter. One hit sank it. The next morning the last four torpedoes were fired at a medium-sized freighter with four escorts. The freighter nimbly dodged all torpedoes while the escorts climbed on the *Dace* to the tune of ten close depth charges.

On September 1 the *Dace* left Brisbane in company with the submarine *Darter* and escorts. After an uneventful transit of Banka Passage the patrol area was reached and the *Dace* commenced minesweeping operations. With 20mm gunfire, she sank six drifting mines and exploded one moored mine (part of which became firmly embedded in the deck).

Next she proceeded to Balabac Strait. A 7-ship convoy of tankers and freighters with two destroyers was sighted, and shortly after midnight on the 14th the *Dace* firmly established her position inside a treacherous area of reefs and shoals and proceeded to attack. Torpedo explosions on the targets alerted the destroyers and tracers streaked through the air towards the *Dace* but no enemy shells came close. Results of this attack were one 10,000-ton tanker and one 7,500-ton transport sunk.

Orders were received to return to base, but acting on a hunch the *Dace's* skipper requested to be allowed to stay. Sure enough, an enemy task force of 12 big men-of-war guarded by fast destroyers was spotted. The *Dace* and *Darter* began preparations for a dawn attack.

The *Darter* made the first run; later the *Dace* executed her own assault which cost the Japs their largest heavy cruiser, the *Maya*. An enemy destroyer counter-attack followed which the subs weathered, only to have the *Darter* run aground on Bombay Shoal. When it was found that she could not be freed, her crew was transferred in small rubber boats through heavy surf to the *Dace*. The destruction of the grounded submarine was underway when an enemy plane appeared and began a bomb run. Full on the surface, the subs were caught cold, but luckily the Jap selected the *Darter* as the target and again the *Dace* enjoyed good fortune. With two full crews aboard she sailed for Freemantle, Australia. The patrol had lasted 67 days.

At Freemantle the *Dace* was refitted and Commander Claggett was relieved by Comdr. O. R. Cole, Jr. On December 2, 1944 the *Dace* proceeded along the Singapore–Hong Kong trade route, mining the channel between Pulau Gambir and the mainland. The next assignment was off Camranh Bay. Heavy seas made for a miserable existence and even submerged patrolling proved difficult. On the 19th a convoy of five large ships with three escorts was sighted and an attack started. Just as the first torpedo was sent on its way, a series of four depth charges exploded, shaking the *Dace* violently. More depth charges followed the initial pattern, starting oil leaks. The *Dace* decided to break off the attack and evade. She hit bottom and while resting there anxiously waiting for the Jap escorts to go away, the strong current took charge, carrying her bumping, turning, scraping and clanking along the bay. (How she avoided being detected will probably never be known.) Finally she surfaced and proceeded north after making repairs.

On December 28 another opportunity for attack came, resulting in the sinking of one medium freighter of four thousand tons and the damaging of another of the same size. A periscope contact of two columns of ships was made on December 31, including a Jap escort carrier which sent a plane over to drop depth bombs on the *Dace*. No damage was done and the *Dace* later surfaced to run down the targets, but was forced to dive two minutes later by further air attacks. The next few days were spent in normal patrol and on January 17, 1945 the *Dace* reached Saipan along with the *Skipjack* and *Fulton,* and arrived at Pearl on January 28. The duration of this patrol was 58 days.

From Pearl the sub proceeded to San Francisco for her first navy-yard overhaul and on April 26 she left San Francisco bound for combat again in company with the *Whale.* The seventh war patrol began May 25 as the *Dace* and *Cabezon* left for the cold waters of the Kuriles.

The morning of June 10 a large freighter and a small tanker were sighted about eight miles ahead and the *Dace* went to full speed. At one time the fog cleared up enough to show a large destroyer escort only six miles away. An hour later another escort was observed. In thirty minutes the formation was within range and the *Dace* submerged. The freighter was dead ahead only 380 yards off and coming bow on as the *Dace* fired, hitting the vessel amidships. Other torpedoes were fired at the smaller tanker. Through the periscope one destroyer was seen heading straight for the submarine. Minutes later four depth charges rocked the boat, and in quick succession 19 more explosions were felt. Five minutes passed and 12 more "ash cans" went off overhead as the men in the *Dace* waited grimly.

During the next few hours the *Dace* silently eased away from the searching escorts, one of which had been hit. Late that afternoon, after hours of freezing quiet, the sub came up for a periscope peek; heaters were turned on and the circulation was restored in numb limbs by stamping feet and gulping hot coffee. The lucky *Dace* was safe again!

On June 16 the *Dace* joined the *Cabezon, Apogon,* and *Manta* for a wide patrol sweep up the eastern side of the Kuriles, at the same time searching for the crew of a downed US Army plane. On the 18th the *Dace* sailed down the western side of the Kuriles alone, and contacted a single ship that night. Shortly after midnight, after much maneuvering, the *Dace* was ahead of her target. It was very dark, but the water was illuminated with phosphorescence, and when the *Dace* fired her torpedoes the water was churned into brilliant blue. The target was revealed to be a heavily armed *Mikura*-class frigate, and the sub turned tail full power. Flashes from the Jap frigate's bow, thought to be torpedo hits, were identified as gun fire as shells dropped into the water ahead of the *Dace.* The sub let go with more tin fish, then dived rapidly. During the next three minutes the *Dace* rocked under the explosions of 18 depth charges, then another pattern of 18. Making way slowly at great depth, she got away.

One day a week later, during a heavy overcast, the bridge watch was startled to hear the whine of an approaching airplane. The *Dace* crash-dived, the last man down the hatch seeing the Jap roar by one hundred feet overhead. A half minute later bullets were smacking the sub's hull, and a depth bomb exploded. The *Dace* escaped to surface near the coast at Mayro Wan and drop a few shells into a refinery. June 26 the *Dace* joined other members of the wolf pack and continued a sweep through the Okhotsk Sea and along the lower channels of the Kuriles chain. On July 2 the *Dace* swept Krita Uruppu channel, and on the 6th the *Dace* and *Cabezon* left the area after 47 days at sea. The *Dace* was preparing to leave Midway on August 15 for another war patrol when news of the surrender came. She returned to New London after seven war patrols had accounted for 73,000 tons of Jap shipping.

The *Tang*

The submarine *Tang* was one of the marvels of the war. In a short but brilliant career which began in January and ended in October, 1944 she sank 227,793 tons of Jap shipping, rescued 22 naval aviators, and won two Presidential Unit Citations. She suffered a tragic finish when she was sent down by one of her own torpedoes during a smashing attack in the Leyte Gulf campaign. After every one of her five war patrols she received the highest commendation of the Commander of Submarine Forces, Pacific Fleet. Her history in Navy files is titled *A Story of a Death-Dealing Devil of the Deep.*

The *Tang* (SS 306) was commissioned at Mare Island, Calif., on October 15, 1943. She arrived at Pearl Harbor in January, 1944, her skipper Lt. Comdr. Richard Hetherington O'Kane, the former executive officer of the famous sub *Wahoo.* Navy Secretary Frank Knox's letter of instructions to Commander O'Kane just before the *Tang* left on her first patrol said:

"Your future Fleet, force, and unit commanders must rely on the USS *Tang* as an effective fighting unit from the hour when she reports to them for duty. It is your task to justify their confidence."

The *Tang* and her men never wavered.

On January 22 she shoved off, bound for the deep water between the Carolines and the Marianas. Early on the morning of February 17 she saw her first action, a brush with two freighters convoyed by a destroyer and five smaller warships. The *Tang* tracked, then went in for the attack. At seven thousand yards the *Tang* was detected and forced down with a depth-charge barrage; she eluded the Jap escort and in 15 minutes was again closing in on the formation. The range shortened to fifteen hundred yards and the *Tang* cut loose with a salvo of four torpedoes. Three hit solidly and the freighter went down by the stern in the midst of milling enemy vessels.

Five days later the *Tang* drew second blood. A convoy was sighted and tracked on the night of February 22, and the *Tang* maneuvered into position on the port bow of one of the freighters. At 1500 yards, the sub dead in the water, she poured four tin fish into the unsuspecting Jap ship, which disintegrated and sank before the *Tang* had time to turn around. She zipped away, then returned for another attack. An escort on the port bow of a Jap sub tender in the convoy was lax and moved out of position in the formation. The *Tang* sneaked in and took the escort's position, then fired four torpedoes into the tender which blew up almost immediately. The concussion on the *Tang's* crew was tremendous. Two nights later a freighter and a tanker were spotted in convoy, and the freighter destroyed with three accurate hits. The *Tang* maintained contact with the enemy and at dawn sent four torpedoes at the tanker, three of which connected. The tanker exploded with a mighty roar and sank in four minutes as depth charges began pouring down on the *Tang* from angry Jap destroyers.

The *Tang* returned to Midway for a refit and on March 16 set out on her second combat patrol around Truk, Palau and the Philippines. This was the cruise on which the submarine rescued 22 downed aviators of the large carrier task force operating in the western Pacific. To accomplish this the *Tang* had to operate within range of shore batteries, and on one occasion when passing Ollan Island, bombarded Jap gun emplacements there. No enemy shipping was sunk, and on May 15 she returned to Pearl for refit, leaving there June 8 for the East China and Yellow Sea areas.

June 24 was unlucky for the enemy ships sighted by the *Tang*. Spotting six large ships with 16 escorts, the *Tang* bravely tore into them on the surface with six torpedoes. Three hit a 7500-ton freighter and three blasted a 10,000-ton tanker. Both went down and the *Tang* scooted to safety.

Five days later the *Tang* scored again on an unescorted freighter. The daring sub had to surface to make enough speed to get into firing position, and after four hours running submerged to fire. The torpedoes missed and the freighter made a depth charge attack. The *Tang*, after lying low, surfaced and gave chase again. This time she connected at

750 yards and the Jap vessel broke in two. Another morning a medium freighter and an escort freighter crossed the *Tang's* path while the sub was surfaced. The *Tang* went down to periscope depth for an attack and sank the escort ship in two minutes and twenty seconds. Trailing the other ship submerged until dusk, one torpedo at five hundred yards resulted in a terrific explosion. The Jap had been carrying munitions.

July 4 was celebrated with real fireworks. A 16,000-ton seaplane tender was unfortunate enough to sail into the *Tang's* area, and was polished off with two tin fish. The sub surfaced to clear a shoal and found herself in the midst of 34 fishing boats rescuing fifty survivors of the tender. The same afternoon a merchant ship was torpedoed and sunk, one unwilling survivor being picked up at the point of a machine gun. The following night under a full moon the *Tang* sent down her eighth victim of the patrol, a medium freighter. She made Midway on the 14th.

When the *Tang* returned from her first patrol, the Commander of Submarine Forces had said:

"The first war patrol of the *Tang* can only be classified as outstanding. Of the six attacks made, five were made on consecutive days. Five of the attacks resulted in destruction of the target and tremendous damage was inflicted on the enemy."

Now he wrote that the third patrol of the *Tang* "was an outstanding example of judgment, expert area analysis, bulldog tenacity, and severe damage to the enemy. In a period of twelve days the *Tang* made nine torpedo attacks, sinking eight vessels. Each attack was carefully planned and brilliantly executed. This patrol sets a record for submarines operating in the Central Pacific Area as to the most damage inflicted upon the enemy."

She was awarded her first Presidential Unit Citation for the three war patrols.

The *Tang* sailed right up to the coast of Japan on her fourth patrol. For her first kill she sank a freighter and damaged a second off Honshu, suffering a severe depth charge attack in retaliation. Next she attacked a patrol yacht on the surface, scoring eight hits, demolishing the deck house, and smashing the hull with her 4-inch gun. One black night she found at anchor a patrol vessel which had previously attacked her, and had revenge by sending it down with a well aimed torpedo. On August 23 a loaded transport, screened by four warships, was hit twice at eight hundred yards and went down, and a few days later a diesel tanker steaming close inshore was finished off. With all torpedoes expended, the *Tang* went back to Pearl for overhaul.

The submarine's last patrol began on September 27, and of it has been said:

"The Force Commander considers the fifth patrol of the *Tang* to be one of the great submarine cruises of all time. The fight was relentlessly carried to the enemy throughout, and in four precisely executed attacks, a total of thirteen enemy ships were destroyed. The first two were unopposed attacks against single ships, but the last two were stirring action of the *Tang,* unsupported, against large, well-armed and heavily escorted convoys."

On October 11 the sub sank two big freighters. On October 23 she encountered a formation of three tankers, a troop transport, a freighter, and escorting destroyers. The *Tang* sailed into the center of the group, delivering a torpedo attack on all tankers, and then firing at the freighter. The angry transport bore down on the *Tang,* intent on ramming, but emergency speed and hard left rudder saved the situation. The *Tang* was now boxed in by three blazing tankers on one side, and the freighter, transport and destroyers on the other. Despite the hail of gunfire, Commander O'Kane launched another torpedo attack which blew the freighter and transport out of the water, and broke through the escorts to escape. In ten minutes the *Tang* had sent to the bottom 45,000 tons of Jap shipping.

The next day contact was made with another big convoy loaded with planes and troops to support the Leyte campaign. Again the *Tang* rushed in fearlessly and launched four torpedoes, a transport and tanker being hit at a thousand yards. The burning ships were off the bow, another transport and tanker were astern, and destroyers were charging in from both sides. The *Tang* fired three torpedoes and all found their marks, one smashing into a destroyer. With two tin fish left, both were sent at the crippled transport ahead. The first ran true to the target, but the other circled after leaving the tube and in twenty seconds crashed into the *Tang's* own stern. Commander O'Kane and several crew members were blown from the bridge and the *Tang* sank immediately with a heavy loss of life. Only nine men were captured by the enemy, to be liberated after the war.

On her last patrol the *Tang* destroyed 107,324 tons of enemy shipping, and for her fourth and fifth war cruises received her second Presidential Unit Citation.

The *Tirante*

Early in the spring of 1945, the submarine *Tirante* (SS 420) was reconnoitering heavily guarded Quelpart Island, off the coast of Korea.

This, according to the Presidential Unit Citation awarded for the action, was what happened:

Leaving the ten fathom curve far behind, she penetrated the mine and shoal obstructed waters of the restricted harbor despite numerous patroling vessels, and in defiance of five shore-based radar stations and menacing aircraft. Prepared to fight her way out on the surface if attacked, she went into action, sending two torpedoes with deadly accuracy into a large Japanese ammunition ship and exploding the target in a mountainous and blinding glare of white flame. Instantly spotted by the enemy as she stood out plainly in the flare of light, she quickly fired her last two torpedoes, to disintegrate in quick succession the leading frigate and a similar flanking vessel. With emergency full speed ahead, the *Tirante* cleared the gutted harbor and slipped undetected along the shoreline diving deep as a pursuing patrol dropped a pattern of depth charges at the point of submergence.

This was the *Tirante's* closest call but she engaged in other daring actions while bagging enemy freighters, tankers and troopships in the seas around the Japanese home islands. She also had some less dangerous experiences.

On the way back to Midway from Quelpart Island, the *Tirante* met three Japanese flyers afloat on some wreckage. They seemed very reluctant to be rescued and when the *Tirante* closed in on them, they swam away in three directions. One of them committed suicide by drowning. A second was brought aboard by main force as two members of the *Tirante's* crew went over the side to get him. The third, seeing no harm come to his captured colleague, gave himself up.

On her first patrol, the *Tirante* operated in company with the *Spadefish*. On her second patrol she was placed in command of a nine-ship wolf pack named "Street's Sweepers," for the *Tirante's* skipper, Lt. Comdr. George L. Street. The wolf pack operated on information relayed to it by airplane scouts; they sank a small freighter, and, after a daring raid, a 2,300-ton collier.

Then, shifting operations to the Yellow Sea, south of Dairen, the Sweepers found a small target. After surfacing and preparing the guns, someone shouted "Don't shoot; don't shoot." The *Tirante* held her fire and sent out a boarding party which returned with the skipper of a four-masted schooner. He reported that the American blockade of the Japanese islands was quite thorough and that the Japanese had little food and little shipping.

The Sweepers were ordered to rout the junk shuttle service with which the Japs tried to open their sea lanes. With the *Tirante* leading, the wolf pack closed in on the junks as they appeared. The system was to stop the junk, send over a boarding party, take the skipper prisoner, put the crew in life boats and fire the junk. Each attack took no more than twenty minutes. One member of the wolf pack bagged sixteen junks; the *Tirante* herself got a dozen.

The *Tirante* was completed at Portsmouth Navy Yard in November, 1944, and did not start her first war patrol until March 3, 1945. Her third patrol had barely started when the war ended. Even so she had a distinguished record. Despite the scarcity of targets so late in the war, the *Tirante* and her "wolf pack" accounted for 8 merchant-men, a transport, 2 frigates, and an undetermined number of junks and other ships.

Besides the Presidential Unit Citation, the *Tirante* and her crew won many other awards. Lieutenant Commander Street received the Con-gressional Medal of Honor and the Navy Cross. Awarded to others were the Gold Star, 2 Silver Star Medals, 3 Bronze Star Medals, and many Letters of Commendation.

PATROL VESSELS

Perhaps a "good little man" can't beat a "good big man," but the history of patrol vessels in World War II proved that many "good little ships" were more than a match for the "good big ship." Some of the most heroic engagements are bound up in the tales of the torpedo boats, frigates, corvettes, gunboats, and subchasers manned by the Navy and Coast Guard.

Over twelve hundred patrol craft were on duty at the end of the war, hundreds more had been built in the United States for our Allies. From 63-foot PT boats to 328-foot gunboats, these small vessels pro-tected coasts and harbors, followed the fleets around the world, and carried the war to the enemy in every theater. They hunted and killed submarines, fought enemy aircraft, supported amphibious operations, prowled rivers and shallow waters, convoyed merchant ships, did rescue work, and gathered weather and other information. The sea services could not have done without them.

Life aboard them wasn't easy . . . cramped quarters, water rationing, monotonous chow, tossing in rough weather. But their crews stuck it out and didn't complain. Many were sunk, but the final score was in favor of "the little guys."

FRIGATES

Frigates are just under destroyer escorts in size, about 300-feet long, and carry about 180 men. They are of about 1,000 tons, have an 18-knot speed, and mount 3-inch guns. They are particularly valuable in antisubmarine patrol, bombardment of minor positions, and rescue operations. The Navy built about one hundred frigates, of which about twenty went to the British. The Coast Guard manned all frigates operating with the US Navy.

The *El Paso*

This frigate (FF 41) left the States early in 1944 and took part in antisubmarine warfare and nearly a dozen strikes against the enemy in the Pacific. In May, at Maffin Bay, New Guinea, her guns raked Jap installations heavily enough to permit Allied troops to break through a native village. At Wakde Island, New Guinea, with two destroyers, she accomplished a similar mission. In June she was called off antisubmarine duty for night bombardment of Aitape, another New Guinea area.

The *El Paso* once furnished support to cover a rescue party landed on a Pacific beach by PT boats. The rescuers ran into considerable Jap ground opposition, but after the frigate's gun smashed at enemy positions, every one of the party got back safely. Later, at Morotai, the *El Paso* was part of an escort screen that led forty Liberty ships, LSTs and LCIs into the harbor against Jap air opposition. She participated in the invasion of Leyte, returned to New Guinea for bombardment duty, and once again sailed for Leyte on patrol. She was being overhauled in a rear-area Navy yard when the war ended.

CORVETTES AND GUNBOATS

Temptress class corvettes were British and Canadian designed and built, and were acquired by the Navy when the U-boat menace was at its height in the Atlantic. They were about 200 feet long, about 900 tons, made 16 knots, carried 120 men, and mounted one 3-inch and one 4-inch gun. They were used mainly in antisubmarine duty off the Atlantic coast.

The gunboats *Charleston* and *Erie* were the Navy's largest patrol vessels, 328 feet long and 2,000 tons. They made 20 knots, mounted four 6-inch guns, and had a crew of 200. The *Erie* was sunk by a German sub off Curaçao in November, 1942. The *Charleston* served in the Aleutians as a patrol and escort ship, and as a guardship for air-sea rescue operations. During the occupation of Attu by US forces in May, 1943, the *Charleston* gave fire support against Jap shore installations. She was engaged in 130 escort missions, convoying 253 ships.

The gunboats *Vixen, Williamsburg* and *Dauntless* served as flagships of the various fleets, the *Dauntless* flying the flag of Fleet Admiral Ernest E. King, wartime Chief of Naval Operations.

CONVERTED YACHTS

Yachts offered to the Navy during the war were stripped of their luxury fittings and coverted into weather stations, coastal convoy ships, and boarding ships. The Navy had about thirty of these vessels.

SUBMARINE CHASERS

In addition to subchasers, there were submarine-chaser escorts (PCE) and submarine-chaser sweepers (PCS). They range from 135 to 185 feet in length, from 250 to 800 tons, make from 14-20 knots, and carry 40-80 men. Older subchasers are wood hulled, newer vessels have steel hulls. They are armed with depth charges and light guns, and the PCS type is equipped with minesweeping gear.

The PC 1588, formerly the minesweeper *Annoy,* saw action from the Aleutians to Iwo Jima. In the north, PC 1588 was on anti-submarine patrol and did escort, training and surveying duty. Later she escorted transports to the Marshalls and Gilberts, and in February, 1945 was part of a formation supporting the invasion of Iwo Jima. She was under frequent enemy air attack during the landings, her gunners repulsing several Jap planes. She stayed on the picket line until the island was occupied, and then turned to air-sea rescue work and antisub patrol.

MOTOR TORPEDO BOATS

As practically everyone knows, these hard-hitting little boats struck the first American offensive blows of the war at Bataan and Corregidor. Lt. John D. Bulkeley's story and the saga of the famed "mosquito fleet" in the early days of the conflict have been well told by war correspondent W. L. White in *They Were Expendable.* The PT work of torpedoing, escorting and rescuing remained as effective as ever during the period from Bataan to Okinawa, from Casablanca to Normandy.

Sleek midgets, resembling speed boats and cabin cruisers, these ply-wood warships make 40 knots or more, are 80 feet long and carry four torpedoes, two twin-50s, 20mm, 37mm and 40mm guns, auto-matic rifles, sub-machine guns, and depth charges. They sank and damaged thousands of tons of enemy shipping, shot down hundreds of enemy planes.

In the Mediterranean two PTs took on two German destroyers, luring them away from a convoy. The PTs moved in close, fired their tin fish and scooted. When the destroyers gave chase, the PTs threw up a smoke screen and darted back in to unleash more torpedoes. The unprotected German convoy was wiped out by other Allied warships.

At Surigao Strait the PTs helped rout a great Jap task force of battleships, cruisers and destroyers. The PTs, 39 of them, knocked the Japs off balance and exposed their position to larger US fleet units, which moved in for the kill. During the Normandy invasion the motor-torpedo-boat squadrons smashed the German E-boats trying to sneak in among the Allied transports. At Mindoro the PTs were commended by the Secretary of the Navy for stopping the Jap counteroffensive from Luzon and Panay.

In March, 1946 all PT boats were retired, not because the Navy no longer believed in them, but because of their rapid individual obsolescence. In event of emergency they can be produced rapidly.

FLEET AUXILIARIES

The term "naval might" is chiefly associated with the glamorous ships of the line . . . battlewagons, cruisers, carriers, destroyers, submarines—and the patrol and mine vessels which got the headlines and glory. But without the auxiliaries, the Service Force vessels which keep the fleet fit and ready, our fighting ships could not long function in extended areas. With the Navy fighting on every ocean in World War II, more new auxiliary types were built than ever before.

Ships of the fleet train—oilers, ammunition and hospital ships, tenders and transports—the Navy has had for long. But with amphibious war came the amphibious force flagship, the attack cargo and attack transport, the aircraft ferry, the floating dry dock and the water-distilling ship. It was these vessels that enabled the fleet to sustain itself in the far reaches of the Pacific and to support the great invasions of Europe. Many auxiliaries won the Presidential Unit Citation or the Navy Unit Commendation, many others were sunk or damaged in action.

CRANE SHIP

There was just one of these vessels, fitted with a 250-ton capacity crane built on the hull of the old battleship *Kearsarge*. Weighing 8,725 tons, she was 375 feet long, had a 92-foot beam.

DESTROYER TENDERS

Destroyer tenders are assigned to destroyer and destroyer-escort squadrons and divisions as mother ships. They are from 417 to 530 feet long, make from 8 to 18 knots, and are usually armed with 20mm and 40mm and 3-inch guns. They have mobile base and repair facilities, carry fuel, ammunition and other stores. Besides the *Melville*, *Black Hawk*, *Cascade* and *Alcor*, there are the *Dobbin*, *Altair*, *Dixie* and *Hamul* classes of destroyer tenders.

The *Melville*

Few ships in American naval history can match the wartime duty of the *Melville* (AD-2). (This tender was at Queenstown, Ireland, servicing US destroyers in World War I.) Shortly after Pearl Harbor she was again in Ireland, this time at our newly established escort base at Londonderry. Then she sailed to Iceland, going from there to the mouth of the Amazon, which was swarming with German subs. As Force Flagship at Recife, she served as repair ship for cruisers, destroyers, auxiliaries, gunboats, subchasers, minesweepers, British corvettes, Brazilian submarines, merchant vessels and even a battleship. No wonder she was called on for the invasion of France!

Two months before the invasion the *Melville* was rearming LSTs in Scotland, going from there to Southern England to join the invasion armada. Versatile *Melville* men repaired hair clippers, potato peelers, and washing machines, in addition to their regular jobs.

But her big task was in repairing LSTs after the invasion. The extensive destruction of enemy ports and the speed of the Allied advance through France made it necessary to continue to use landing craft, which meant enormous maintenance and repair problems. After VE-day, homebound LSTs and other ships tied up alongside the *Melville* to secure their cargoes for the long sea trip, so the tender was one of the last ships to reach the States.

AMMUNITION SHIPS

Some ammunition ships were built by the Navy on modified C2 hulls, most are converted Maritime hulls. They carry from 3,000 to 8,000 tons of ammunition. They have cooling plants to maintain temperature in storage spaces, make from 10 to 16 knots and are armed with 20mm, 40mm and 5-inch guns. They sometimes carry mail and personnel.

There were nineteen ammunition ships. In addition to the *Sangay*, there were the *Pyro, Lassen* and *Wrangel* classes. The *Mount Hood* (AE-11) was sunk at Manus, Admiralty Islands, on November 10, 1944.

The *Pyro* (AE-1) was commissioned in 1921. She was at Pearl Harbor on December 7, 1941, and carried ammunition from the west coast to Hawaii until late 1942, when she took a load of mines to Alaska. In 1943 she was at Espíritu Santo in the New Hebrides, then sailed to Australia and New Guinea replenishing combat ships. In 1944 she was in on the Hollandia landings, and in December of that year was at Leyte Gulf, at general quarters most of the time because of air attacks. She left Subic Bay as the war ended.

TRANSPORTS

The troop transports, converted from passenger liner or Maritime Commission hulls, were of all lengths, sizes and capacities. The Navy had about ninety at the end of the war. Others had been turned over to the Army, or converted into attack-transports and hospital ships.

As they traveled alone a good part of the time, most transports had to be speedy, although they were armed.

And they had to fight many times.

It was on the transports that the soldiers came closest to Navy life, seeing the sailor in action, listening to the strange Navy jargon as the "word is passed" over the ship's announcing system, preceded by the shrill boatswain's pipes.

One soldier on a transport, reacting to such sea lingo as *Now hear this! The smoking lamp is lighted! Ease out and lash up! Clean sweep down fore and aft!* said, "I don't know what they're saying. Half the time they don't know themselves. Hell, they call floors 'decks' and walls 'bulkheads' and stairs 'ladders'."

Compared to the number who went over, not many men were lost at sea, although some transports went down. Among them were the *George F. Elliot,* lost off Guadalcanal in 1942; *Edward Rutledge,* off Morocco; the *Leedstown,* off Algiers; the *Tasker H. Bliss, Hugh L. Scott, Susan B. Anthony* and others.

The *West Point*

Perhaps the best known of all Navy transports is the *West Point* (AP-23), the former SS *America,* largest passenger ship ever built in the United States. She carried more than 250,000 men and women during the war, traveling more than 14 times around the world; always unescorted because of her 22-knot speed. Her routes were from Bombay to Marseille, Capetown to Guadalcanal, Canal Zone to Liverpool, Noumea to Mers–el–Kebir. In continuous service from the outbreak of the war, she crossed the Atlantic 24 times in one year. The *West Point* is big—723 feet long and 93 feet at the beam. In addition to a crew of 800 she can carry more than 7,700 passengers.

The *West Point* weathered many hot spots. At the fall of Singapore she was the target of Japanese artillery from the hills and bombs from enemy planes overhead. Her sister transport, the *Wakefield*, was set afire at that time. Off Rio de Janeiro a torpedo from a Nazi sub streaked across the *West Point's* bow. At Milne Bay her gunners repelled a Jap air raid and in the Red Sea and at Suez her men were at battle stations against German torpedo planes. Storms have damaged her, but she never lost a passenger.

In addition to transporting troops, the *West Point* carried Axis prisoners back to the States, and after VE-day acted as a hospital ship for a time.

NET-LAYING SHIPS

These are horn-bowed ships, from 500 to 1000 tons. Antisubmarine nets are laid and kept in repair by these vessels, which also do much miscellaneous work. The *Teak* (AN-35) received the Navy Unit Commendation. The *Ailanthus* (AN-38) was sunk in the Aleutians on February 26, 1944.

The *Catclaw*

This net layer (AN-60) was commissioned at Rockland, Maine, on January 14, 1944. Her first task was to assist in refloating the submarine *Razorback*, aground off New London. On June 23 she sailed with a convoy to Belfast, then was ordered to Cherbourg. With the harbor of Brest closed and supplies badly needed in France, the *Catclaw* and other vessels laid Liberty ship moorings at Morlaix Roads, Bretagne, enabling sufficient freight to be handled there. In September the *Catclaw* was the second ship to enter Le Havre, working on clearance and salvage operation. The large inner harbor at Le Havre could not be used until the *Catclaw*, working with the *Chinaberry* (AN-61), lifted the lock gates.

In December the *Catclaw* was en route to the States in a convoy of crippled ships, when the LST-359 and the *Fogg* (DE-37) were torpedoed west of the Azores. After overhaul, the *Catclaw* reached the Pacific in June, 1945, operating at Okinawa until war's end.

NET CARGO SHIPS

These ships work with net-laying ships and net-tending tugs, transporting and laying antisubmarine nets before fleet anchorages and harbor entrances. There were five AKNs: the *Indus, Sagittarius, Tuscana, Keokuk,* and *Zebra.*

GENERAL STORES—ISSUE SHIPS

These were special cargo ships used as advance supply bases where there were no shore facilities. They were converted Liberty ships, LSTs, and C2 hulls. The *Pollux* (AKS 2) foundered off Newfoundland on February 19, 1942.

CARGO SHIP—AIRCRAFT FERRY

These were aviation supply ships, transporting aircraft and aviation stores to forward areas. They also brought back damaged planes from the combat zones. The two ships in this class were the *Kitty Hawk* and the *Hammondsport.*

HIGH-SPEED TRANSPORTS

Flush-deck destroyers and destroyer escorts were converted into high-speed transports to carry landing craft which could be lowered into the water for invasions. Many earned Presidential Unit Citations before and after being converted, many others were sunk in combat.

The *Barry*

This high-speed transport (APD 29), Presidential Unit Citation winner in the Battle of the Atlantic, lost the last fight of her 25-year career to a Japanese suicide plane off Okinawa—then literally rose from her grave to knock out one more Kamikaze.

As a flush-deck destroyer, the *Barry* had been a member of that heroic task group of the escort carrier *Card* in the Atlantic, along with the *Borie* and the *Goff.* Vintage 1920, this four-stacker saw duty in the North and South Atlantic, the Caribbean, and the Mediterranean, when she took part in the invasion of Southern France. Early in 1945 she went to the Pacific.

On May 25 the *Barry* was patrolling 35 miles northwest of Okinawa when suicide planes attacked. Gun crews shot down one, but a second crashed into her at the waterline and 28 men were wounded. The ship caught fire, and finding that the magazines could not be flooded, commanding officer Lieutenant Hand and a skeleton crew, with parties from the *Sims* and *Roper,* went back aboard for a survey at this point. The flooded ship was again attacked by suicide planes, and although only a few hands were on board, they brought down a Jap.

Days later the *Barry,* stripped of all useful gear, was taken in tow to be sunk. A few miles out of Kerama Retto a Kamikaze pilot, not realizing the damaged condition of the ship, roared in to destroy himself in the sinking hulk. It was a fighting end for the gallant *Barry.*

Another suicide plane crashed and sank the *Barry's* escort, the LSM-59.

The *Sims*

Soon after the destroyer *Sims* (DD 409) was sunk by Jap planes in the Coral Sea on May 7, 1942, her successor was speeding down the ways at Norfolk Navy Yard. The war record of this rugged little ship is typical of the fine performance of her type during the war.

First of her class, the *Sims* (then DE 154) got off to an impressive start soon after her fitting-out, when Secretary of the Navy Knox, Admirals King and Leahy and other high ranking Allied officers inspected her at the Washington Navy Yard. After a shakedown cruise to Bermuda she joined Task Group 21.6 during the summer of 1943, escorting tankers across the Atlantic. During 20 Atlantic crossings the *Sims* lost only one tanker to the swarming U-boats.

On September 23, 1944 the *Sims* was sent to the Boston Navy Yard for conversion to a high-speed transport. That completed, she proceeded to Norfolk in December, 1944, and served as a training ship until January 24, 1945.

On that date the *Sims* (now APD 50) sailed from Norfolk and proceeded to the Pacific via San Diego, joining Task Unit 51 for the Okinawa invasion late in March, 1945.

From then until the end of the war, the *Sims* had a hectic time. After a quick run to Ulithi early in April with a convoy, she was back on the picket line off Okinawa on April 11. On April 16 a Jap suicide plane crashed close alongside.

After another escort trip to Ulithi, the *Sims* was back off Ie Shima on May 18 when two Kamikazes dove in simultaneously. Repeatedly hit by gunfire, they exploded close enough to the ship to damage it slightly, but after temporary repairs the *Sims* was back in the line on the night of May 25, in time to receive another suicide attack. This time the Japs came even closer, wounding an officer and four men. At this point the *Barry* (APD 29) was set afire by a suicide-plane hit and the *Sims* went alongside to fight the flames. After the *Barry* had been abandoned because of danger of exploding ammunition, a volunteer party from the *Sims* stayed alongside and fought the fires despite heavy enemy air attacks.

When the *Sims* left for Leyte late in May her scoreboard showed four Jap planes downed. Following the Jap surrender the *Sims* returned a group of British Marines to the Yokosuka Naval base and several days later landed US Marines for the occupation of the Tokuyama naval air station. Following her return to the States in December, 1945, the *Sims* was placed on inactive service.

ATTACK CARGO SHIPS

These ships are converted Maritime Commission hulls; 426 feet long, 6,800 tons fully loaded, with 16½-knot speeds. The Navy had 108 of these attack cargo ships in service during the war. With attack transports and large landing craft, the AKSs were the nucleus of the Amphibious Forces. The attack cargo ships carried small landing craft, troops and cargo. Their job was to operate inshore at the beachheads, discharge their men and supplies and provide covering firepower at the same time.

The *Alchiba*

The *Alchiba* (AKA 6), is the only attack cargo ship to receive the Presidential Unit Citation. Even before Pearl Harbor she had steamed through the dangerous Atlantic, eluding submarines and fighting storms. On one trip she carried troops and supplies to Iceland, on another she picked up copper from Chile.

When the Pacific war began, the *Alchiba* was ordered to New Zealand, where she loaded cargo for Noumea. In August, 1942 she took part in the first land offensive of the Pacific at Guadalcanal, bringing up supplies and reinforcements from Samoa. Time after time the *Alchiba* shuttled from Pago-Pago to Tulagi and Guadalcanal, chancing enemy ships and air raids on every trip. Finally her luck ran out, for as she was unloading cargo one day, a Jap sub spotted her and sent a torpedo into her port side. Gasoline and ammunition on board exploded, but her quick-thinking skipper, Comdr. J. S. Freeman, flooded her compartments and ran her on the beach. He saved not only the *Alchiba* but her sorely needed cargo as well.

The *Alchiba's* crew performed heroically during their 104-hour fight against the fires started by the torpedo. BM Edward B. Cutting was awarded the Silver Star for entering a blazing hold and removing ammunition which would have blown up the ship. CMMM F. O. Ulrich, who got the Silver Star and Purple Heart, was wounded while rescuing a shipmate from a flooded engine room. There were other awards, too many to mention here.

The *Alchiba's* troubles were far from over. While temporary repairs were being made, a Jap midget sub surfaced and sent another tin fish into the damaged ship, killing and wounding many men and flooding the engine room and No. 4 hold. The damage was so great that the Navy believed the *Alchiba* was beyond repair and listed her "lost in action." But her crew was determined to keep her afloat, and temporary repairs were again started. As a result, she was able to limp into Mare Island, California, and eight months later she was back in the Pacific war.

During the initial landings at Bougainville her gunners shot down two attacking Jap planes and helped splash three more. In June, 1944 she went back to the States for further repairs, ending her war career with service trips to Ulithi, Guam and the Philippines.

CARGO SHIPS

During the war the Navy had about 175 cargo ships of all types, some of them converted Victory and Liberty ships, some Maritime Commission conversions, and others converted from former Axis and neutral cargo vessels. Cargo ships carried mainly guns, tanks, aircraft and mechanical equipment to the fighting fronts in Europe and the Pacific. Five were sunk.

The *Arided*

The *Arided* (AK 73) was commissioned in November, 1942 after having been converted from a Liberty ship. She is 441 feet long, has a loaded displacement of 12,000 tons, makes 12 knots, and carries 12 officers and 154 men. She served 35 continuous months in the Pacific, steamed 77,000 miles, and carried 80,000 tons of cargo and 780 passengers. She was typical of the Navy's cargo ships.

She worked out of Samoa, the New Hebrides, New Zealand and other south Pacific ports, and was in part of the Guadalcanal show, where she was attacked by shore-based bombers. Places like Bougainville, Milne Bay, Palau and Okinawa were familiar to the *Arided's* crew, for they loaded and unloaded at those harbors for all the long, weary months sweating out the war, the heat and the storms.

SUBMARINE RESCUE VESSELS

These craft were converted minesweepers, built as tugs and converted. They are about 250 feet long, 2000 tons, and make 16 knots.

They can bring men up from disabled submarines by means of a rescue chamber. There were about 15 of them. Two ships of this type, the *Pigeon* and *Macaw,* were sunk.

The *Pigeon*

The *Pigeon* (ASR 6) received two Presidential Unit Citations for actions in December, 1941 before she went down at Corregidor May 3, 1942, from Japanese air attack.

Before the little 180-foot submarine rescue vessel was finished her crew shot down several enemy planes. She was in the thick of the battle from Cavite to Corregidor, repairing other vessels, towing them, running supplies, and fighting back all the time. In the end an enemy dive bomber, after attacking the *Pigeon* for ten hours, dropped a bomb on her starboard quarter. She went down in 16 minutes.

Her first citation:

"For the outstanding and courageous performance of duty of the officers and men attached to the USS *Pigeon* on the occasion of the Japanese aerial attack on the Navy Yard, Cavite, P. I., on December 10, 1941, when that vessel, despite the severe bombing attacks by enemy Japanese aircraft at the time and without the use of regular steering equipment, towed to safety the USS *Seadragon* and assisted generally in clearing the docks of that Navy Yard, then a roaring inferno, of naval vessels and yard craft secured thereto."

Her second:

"For displaying excellent fighting ability when the personnel of the USS *Pigeon* on two occasions, during the month of December, 1941 shot down several attacking enemy Japanese aircraft; this despite the fact that the primary mission of the ship was the rescue and salvage of submarines."

STORE SHIPS

The Navy had 48 provision store ships, generally known in the fleet as "beef boats." They have large refrigerator spaces, carry from 3,000 to 8,000 tons of provisions, and vary considerably as to speed and size. The *Mizar* was a former United Fruit ship; the *Tarazed* belonged to the United Mail Line; the *Uranus* and *Roamer* were former Danish vessels; the *Cygnus* was a Munson liner and the *Aldebaran* and *Polaris* were converted Maritime Commission cargo ships.

MOTOR TORPEDO BOAT TENDERS

These ships carry spare parts, engines, fuel and supplies for torpedo boat squadrons. There were twenty of them,—converted from yachts, cargo ships, and sea-plane tenders. The *Niagara,* which was sunk in the Solomons in May, 1943, served with Squadron 3, the first operational PT squadron.

SURVEYING SHIPS

These ships chart tides, currents, and depths for the Hydrographic Office. There were seven of them, mostly former minesweepers, gunboats and subchasers.

HOSPITAL SHIPS

These vessels, the "Great White Ships" of the fleet, are noncombatant in the strictest sense. Operating under the Hague and Geneva conventions, they evacuate wounded men from combat areas. They are painted white, have red crosses on stacks and sides, and a green band around the hull. Brightly illuminated at night, they travel alone, answering every challenge. They all bear "peaceful" names such as *Comfort, Mercy, Hope, Benevolence, Consolation* and *Tranquility.*

Most hospital ships are about 400 feet long, 6,000 to 8,000 tons, with speeds of 15 to 18 knots. They are fully equipped as modern hospitals, with complete staffs of physicians, dentists, nurses and hospital corpsmen. Such ships have evacuated casualties from beachheads all over the world, operating under the fire of shore batteries. Some have actually been attacked by the enemy in violation of the treaties protecting them.

The *Solace*

The first hospital ship *Solace* transported sick and wounded men in both the Spanish-American War and World War I. The second *Solace* was built in 1927 as the passenger liner *Iroquois,* and converted by the Navy in 1941. She was at Pearl Harbor when the Japs came over, and her work here was recognized by a letter of citation by Admiral Nimitz. Later she was awarded the Navy Unit Commendation.

For a time in 1942 she was the only hospital ship operating in the Pacific. She evacuated many of the Navy wounded at the Battle of the Coral Sea, and many of the Marines from Guadalcanal. Later she was ordered directly into the battle areas at Tarawa, Kwajalein and Eniwetok to take the injured aboard. In the Saipan invasion she evacuated 1,335 casualties to base hospitals in the Solomons, and in the occupation of Guam more than a thousand patients were shuttled back to Kwajalein and Pearl. Later the *Solace* was at Angaur and Peleliu, where another thousand wounded were taken off. She was at Iwo Jima on D plus 4 and handled over 2,000 patients, 400 of them in one day.

The Okinawa campaign was next, and here, with the Japs throwing their last, desperate punch, the *Solace* was attacked by enemy bombers. Another hospital ship, the *Comfort,* was hit by a Kamikaze plane. Consequently the hospital ships blacked out at night and were furnished with destroyer escorts. Over four thousand casualties were evacuated by the *Solace* in seven trips from Okinawa. Her medical staff administered 1,800 units of whole blood, 1,200 units of plasma, 136,000 sulfa doses, and 2½ billion units of penicillin.

During the war the *Solace* treated more battle casualties than any other hospital ship, and steamed 170,000 miles without a major overhaul.

FLOATING DOCKS

Although not strictly ships, these vessels made an important contribution to the war in both oceans by enabling damaged ships to be overhauled and repaired without returning to major yards. Beginning with the floating dry dock (ARD 1) in 1943, which was able to handle destroyers, the design and construction of floating docks advanced to the huge ABSDs which accommodate battleships and the largest carriers. In addition to ARDs, other types are ARDC, concrete repair docks; ABD, advance base docks; AFD, mobile floating dry docks, and ABSD, advance base sectional dock. Some docks are towed, others are self-propelled.

SEAPLANE TENDERS

Seaplane tenders "mother" patrol squadrons of flying boats, providing repairs, ammunition, supplies and fuel for the big planes and occasionally quarters for their crews. They also serve as forward radio and weather stations and rescue ships. (The old *Langley,* the first aircraft carrier, was converted to a seaplane tender and lost off Java in February, 1942.)

The *Curtiss* (AV 4), was the first ship built as a seaplane tender. She was 527 feet long, 11,000 tons loaded, and could make 18 knots. The *Curtiss* and *Albemarle* (AV 5) had two stacks, while the newer ships of the *Currituck* class (AV 7) had only one stack, were 540 feet in length, and carried four 5-inch guns. Some destroyers were converted to seaplane tenders and classified AVD. One of them, the *McFarland,* won the Presidential Unit Citation. Another, the *Thornton,* was sunk on April 5, 1945.

Small seaplane tenders, some converted from minesweepers, are about one thousand seven hundred tons. The *Heron* (AVP 2) received the Presidential Unit Citation; the *Gannett* (AVP 8) went down off Bermuda on June 7, 1942.

The *Orca*

This little ship (AVP 49), about the size of a destroyer, had an action-filled career in the Pacific from May, 1944, until hostilities ceased. Three of the PBY squadrons based with her at Hollandia were awarded the Presidential Unit Citation. After Hollandia, the *Orca* ran air-sea rescue missions for Army Air Force strikes at Halmahera, Celebes and Borneo.

In November the *Orca* moved into Leyte Gulf, shooting down a Jap suicide plane diving on the *Oyster Bay* (AVP 28), and bringing down another in flames as it dived on the *Orca* itself. The same afternoon *Orca* gunners helped splash another Kamikaze pilot. Early in January, 1945, after Comdr. Everett O. Rigsbee had relieved Commander Fleming, the *Orca,* part of a large convoy heading for Lingayen, was the target of a three-plane suicide attack. The lead Jap was hit squarely at 1000 yards, plane number two was hit at 500 and the third Kamikaze was picked off at 300 yards. Six men in the *Orca* gun crews were wounded.

The day following the Lingayen invasion the *Orca* began air-sea rescue operations in the face of desperate attacks from Japanese suicide boats. In addition to picking up Army and Navy personnel, she took several Jap prisoners, usually after a struggle. (One Navy pilot rescued was Comdr. McPherson B. Williams, who had been skipper Rigsbee's roommate at Annapolis.) Only a mile off Jap-held Bataan the *Orca* rescued the crew of an Army C-47 and the pilot of a P-51. After the occupation of the Philippines was completed, the *Orca* was overhauled at Manus. She was at sea again on VJ-day.

BARRACKS SHIPS

Unpowered barracks ships (APL) were houseboats used as floating barracks. They were unmanned. Those fitted with diesel engines are classified (APB) and have names such as *Benewah, Colleton, Echelos, Marlbore* and *Mercer.*

REPAIR SHIPS

Repair ships (AR) are somewhat similar to destroyer tenders. Fitted with machine shops and foundries, they overhaul and replace gear, from small instruments to heavy machinery. They have saved many heavily damaged vessels. The Navy had about twenty, including the *Vulcan, Medusa, Vestal, Ajax* and *Hector.*

Battle damage repair ships (ARB) make temporary repairs to damaged ships in forward areas. Some of them were the *Oceanus, Zeus, Midas,* and *Nestor.*

Other repair ships (ARG) are small, mobile machine shops for servicing gasoline and diesel engines at advanced bases. The *Oglala,* salvaged at Pearl Harbor, became ARG 1. Others were the *Luzon, Cebu, Samar,* and *Hooper Island.*

Heavy hull repair ships are classified ARH. Aircraft repair ships, the *Chourre, Webster, Adventinus* and *Chloris,* are designated ARV.

The *Amycus*

The *Amycus* (ARL 2) originally LST 489, is a landing craft repair ship, commissioned in July, 1943. She is fitted with a heavy hoist and equipped with numerous machine shops.

The log of the *Amycus* indicates the hectic nature of her war duty. At Buna, from December 6 through December 31, she serviced 46 LCTs, 3 LCIs, a high-speed transport, 3 minesweepers, a minelayer, 4 LSTs, 3 subchaser sweepers, 9 coastal transports, 8 subchasers, and 9 other US and Australian ships for a total of 364 jobs!

In April, 1944, the *Amycus* took part in the landing at Hollandia, and helped install the first Navy water supply there. In December she joined a convoy headed for Lingayen Gulf, acting as the command ship of a salvage unit. After D-day her job was to repair the LCIs and LSTs damaged by Jap suicide-boat attacks; her excellent work here won a citation. After months at Lingayen she sailed for Luzon. She was there when the war ended.

MISCELLANEOUS AUXILIARIES

These ships (AG) usually have definitely assigned tasks, in contrast with unclassified vessels, which perform many different tasks. Target ships, weather ships, and mobile training ships are rated in this classification. The *R. L. Barnes* (AG 27) and the *Muskegat* (AB 48) were sunk. The *Dupont* (AG 80) earned three battle stars and was awarded the Presidential Unit Citation. The Navy had 86 AGs.

The *Dupont*

The *Dupont* was a four-stack destroyer converted to a miscellaneous auxiliary. First commissioned in 1919, she saw peace-time service in every sea and before Pearl Harbor was on neutrality patrol in the Atlantic.

After Pearl the *Dupont* went on convoy duty to North Africa and the Mediterranean, then joined the escort carriers *Card, Block Island* and *Bogue* in antisub patrol. In April, 1944 the *Dupont* and *Goff* were assigned as escorts to the seaplane tender *Albemarle* (AV 5), ferrying personnel and aircraft parts to the European Theater and bringing home wounded men. In September, 1944 the *Dupont* was severely damaged in the great hurricane which struck the Atlantic coast, and after repairs she was converted to an AG as a target and control ship for Navy torpedo bombers.

AMPHIBIOUS FORCE FLAGSHIPS

These ships were originally known as Combined Operations–Communications–Headquarters Ships. They have the latest in radio and radar gear, and carry fleet or ground force commanders and staffs on amphibious operations. Most of them were converted from C2 hulls.

The *Appalachian*

This vessel, Joint Task Force One Flagship at the Bikini atomic bomb test in July, 1946, was the first AGC. Commissioned on October 2, 1943 with Capt. James S. Fernald as commanding officer, she saw combat from Kwajalein to the occupation of Japan.

The "Big Apple" (as she became known), took aboard Rear Adm. R. L. Conolly, Commander Amphibious Group Three, and headed for the islands of Roi and Namur for the landing by the Fourth Marine Division in February, 1944. Maj. Gen. Harry Schmidt, commander of the ground forces, was also aboard.

In June the Big Apple headed for Guam, carrying Marine Maj. Gen. Roy Geiger, in command of the Third Amphibious Corps and the 77th Army Division. The force was to hit Guam two days after the Saipan landings, but 52 miles out of Saipan it ran into a Jap fleet and withdrew, postponing the invasion.

Admiral Spruance's fleet worked on the Japs for a week, and the Guam attack was finally made on July 14, with officers aboard the *Appalachian* supervising the pre-assault bombardment. Her own 5-inch gun pounded Orote airfield as she joined the battleships *Colorado* and *Idaho* in smashing shore installations. The *Pennsylvania* and *New Mexico* arrived, then came fire-support cruisers, dive bombers and underwater demolition teams to soften the Jap stronghold. The troops went in on the 21st, and when the island was secure the Big Apple's ensign flew over Guam. On July 30 Capt. Charles R. Jeffs relieved Captain Fernald.

Maj. Gen. A. V. Arnold of the Army's 7th Division was aboard when the *Appalachian* went in for the assault on Leyte in October, 1944. Adm. T. C. Kinkaid was on the *Wasatch* (AGC 9) and Gen. Douglas MacArthur was on the cruiser *Nashville,* in column behind the Big Apple. Landings were made on October 20 and the *Appalachian* shoved off before the big sea battle at Leyte Gulf. In January, 1945 she was back at Lingayen Gulf, part of the reinforcement group carrying the 25th Army Division for the Luzon invasion. Her mission completed, the *Appalachian* set course for San Francisco and yard overhaul, getting back to the Philippines in July, 1945, where Capt. Joseph B. Renn became the new skipper.

The Big Apple ended the war by carrying the staff of the IX Army Corps into Japan for the occupation.

OILERS

These ships need little description as to function. They carry oil or gasoline in their tanks, and replenish ·ships at sea and supply advanced bases. Some were modified to carry aircraft, tanks, or landing craft in addition to regular cargo. The Navy and Maritime Commission jointly designed some oilers, others were Navy-built, and a few were converted from Liberty ships. Oilers of the *Cimarron* class carried more than six million gallons of fuel and displace 25,000 tons.

The *Cimarron*

This ship (AO 22) was the first of a new line of Navy oilers, and at the time of commissioning in March, 1939 was the largest and fastest tanker in the United States. In September, 1941, under Capt. H. J. Redfield, she joined Task Force 15 engaged in transporting Army troops to Iceland. In November she was part of a convoy that included the *Ranger, West Point, Wakefield,* and *Mt. Vernon,* bound for Singapore. She was two days out of Capetown when Pearl Harbor was attacked. The *Cimarron* was ordered to Norfolk where Comdr. R. M. Ihrig took command, and then steamed alone for Iceland again, using her speed to escape two German submarines on the way.

When Jimmy Doolittle's Army fliers struck Tokyo in April, 1942 from the carrier *Hornet,* the *Cimarron* was in the task force, fueling the ships in force before and after the Tokyo raid. She just missed the Coral Sea action in May but was in on the Battle of Midway, staying in the area refueling the task units for 15 days. There was no rest for this ship. In August she joined Task Force 11 for the Guadalcanal operation, fueling the *Enterprise, Saratoga, Quincy, Vincennes,* and *Astoria.* She was dispatched to the Fiji Islands for reloading, and late in the month was back at Guadalcanal where for thirty days she serviced the fleet.

In October she was at Samoa, and was ordered to leave there with two destroyers (one of them the *O'Brien*) as escorts. The *O'Brien* had been damaged by Japanese bombs and two hours out of Samoa she began to break up in the heavy seas. The *Cimarron* rescued all the *O'Brien* crew and took them back to San Francisco. While there she was refitted with heavier armament and better radar and in January, 1943, was again in the New Caledonia area. While steaming with 16 escorts one day, a Jap sub surfaced five hundred yards astern of the *Cimarron* but was quickly destroyed. The sturdy oiler participated in the occupation of New Georgia in June with Task Force 36, and in November was with Task Unit 16.20.2 in the Gilbert Islands operation.

The *Cimarron* was with the fleet in the drive up through the Central Pacific, hitting the Marshalls, Eniwetok, Kwajalein, Saipan, Guam and Tinian. She was never far from the fighting ships, always within range of enemy aircraft. Early in 1945 the *Cimarron* found herself in the China Sea, Tokyo and Iwo Jima engagements. (She was one of the few Navy ships to be in both the 1942 and 1945 strikes on Tokyo.) From the time she left Ulithi on March 26 until April 16, she supported the Okinawa invasion continuously. From June until August she gave continuous support to the strikes against the Empire. She anchored in Tokyo Bay on September 10, 1945.

According to an official statement, "the *Cimarron* fueled more ships than any other oiler in the Navy . . . participated in every major operation in the Pacific since the beginning of the war."

GASOLINE TANKERS

Tankers (AOG) are similar to oilers, except they are generally smaller and carry high-test fuel for aircraft and PT boats, diesel oil, and occasionally, freight. Some were built under Navy contracts, some by the Maritime Commission. The *Genesee* (AOG 8) is 310 feet long, weighs about 5,000 tons. She operated in the Pacific, was under attack at Okinawa, and was the first cargo ship to enter Naha harbor there. During the war she steamed 39,000 miles, delivered 20 million gallons of gasoline and oil and 6,000 tons of freight.

ATTACK TRANSPORTS

These ships (APA) were combat-loaded transports which carried vehicles, troops and landing craft. They were mostly modified Victory ships, converted Maritime Commission hulls and old passenger liners. The Navy had about 250 attack transports operating in all theaters.

The *Fuller*

The *Fuller* (APA 7) was the former Baltimore Mail Lines' ship, SS *City of Newport News*. In July, 1941 she landed Marines in Iceland, and in March, 1942 was making the run to Ireland. After that it was the Pacific, and the *Fuller* debarked Marines at Guadalcanal and Tulagi, shooting down several enemy planes during the invasion. After the battle off Savo Island the *Fuller* picked up survivors of the Australian cruiser *Canberra*. Until April, 1943 she made runs between Noumea and Guadalcanal and in November took part in the invasion of Bougainville, putting troops ashore in Empress Augusta Bay. During this action she was hit by a Jap bomb which killed and wounded 37 men.

After an overhaul in the States, the *Fuller* returned to the Pacific for the Saipan landings in June, 1944. The Tinian show was next, then the invasion of the Philippines in October. In April, 1945 the *Fuller* hit the bloody beaches of Okinawa with a Marine Air Group aboard, bringing down several Jap planes during the action. After being withdrawn again for overhaul, she stood out once more for the battle zone, and was underway from Ulithi for Leyte when the war ended.

SALVAGE VESSELS

Most salvage vessels (ARS) are converted minesweepers or tugs, a few were constructed as salvage craft. Wooden-hulled ships of this type are about 185 feet long and about 800 tons. The steel-hulled vessels are about 215 feet in length and 1,400 tons. They are fitted with cranes, diving gear, and other machinery for harbor salvage work. Salvage craft tenders, designated ARS (T), were converted LSTs.

The *Cable*

This salvage vessel (ARS 19) won the Navy Unit Commendation for her combat service in the Pacific. Even on her shakedown cruise in March, 1944 the *Cable* saw salvage duty taking in tow a distilling ship which had been disabled in the Gulf of Mexico. And on her initial trip to Pearl in May she had two lighters in tow. From Pearl she made Kwajalein, where she was put to work recovering barges and setting buoys.

Sent to the aid of the grounded SS *Chief Joseph* off Cape Nelson, New Guinea, in July, the *Cable* made the trip in vain as the merchant ship freed herself before the arrival of the Navy vessel, but she did do a propeller repair job on the SS *Hanyank*. The next day the *Cable* was ordered to the assistance of the grounded transport *Monterey* and with the aid of four LCIs succeeded in floating the ship. In September, after sailing to the Admiralty Islands and Australia, the *Cable* was ordered to embark fire-fighting and salvage teams and proceed to northwestern New Guinea. From there she went to 'Alexishafen, then Hollandia, recovering buoys, moving drydocks and taking floating repair shops in tow.

In October the *Cable,* in company with other service force units, headed for Leyte to offer logistic support for the invasion of a few days earlier. On the way she took in tow a barge carrying gasoline and was separated from the convoy. As the *Cable* entered San Pedro Bay, Leyte, a straggler towing high-test fuel, she was subject to three Jap air raids. On the first attack she was straddled with two 100-pound bombs. At noon and again in the late afternoon the Japs came over, only to be beaten back by the AA fire of the plucky little repair ship and other fleet units.

The destroyer *Grant,* which had been hit nineteen times in the Battle of Surigao Strait, limped into the bay and shortly began sinking. The *Cable* and the fleet tug *Chickasaw* put their pumps to work and in two days the *Grant* was seaworthy. Another *Cable* job was extinguishing the fire aboard the merchant ship *Benjamin Wheeler* which had been crashed by a Kamikaze. After patching up the *Wheeler,* the salvage vessel freed the SS *Cape Cumberland* from a reef and repaired the SS *David Field.*

In November the Japs began making special targets of the US destroyer screen in Leyte Gulf, and the *Claxton* and the *Killen* were early victims. The *Cable* repaired both, and a week later put out fires on the repair ship *Achilles,* hit by a suicide plane. On Thanksgiving Day the SS *Gus Darnell* was hit by a torpedo and it took the *Cable* 16 hours to subdue the flames, assisted by the fleet tugs *Hidatsa* and *Quapaw.* During the fire-fighting a Jap bomber came over but was damaged and set afire by *Cable* gunners. Until the middle of December the *Cable* was busy repairing destroyers and subchasers, and floating and raising beached and sunken landing craft.

In January, 1945 the *Cable* joined the force heading for the invasion of Luzon, and on the 9th moved into Lingayen Gulf, brushing off a few Jap air raids. From then until mid-February the *Cable* did salvage work off Luzon, moving next to Subic Bay and then Manila Bay, where she cleared the outer harbor of some sixty Japanese ships which had been sunk. In May the *Cable* sailed for Halmahera to salvage amphibious craft, and then to Borneo for the invasion of Balikpapan, the great oil depot. On July 10 divers from the *Cable* were able to make available two pierheads for the mooring of large ships.

Ordered again to the Philippines, the *Cable* ended the war as she had begun it, towing a drydock and a barge into Subic Bay.

The citation to the Ship Salvage, Fire-Fighting and Rescue Unit, Service Force, Seventh Fleet, of which the *Cable* was a part, reads:

"For extremely meritorious service in support of military operations in the Philippine Islands Area from October 17, 1944 to June 10, 1945. Accompanying the preliminary bombardment groups, Ship Salvage, Fire-Fighting and Rescue Unit operated under continuous enemy attack throughout the assault phase of nine major landings, including Leyte, Ormoc and Lingayen invasions, and rendered invaluable service in fighting and extinguishing fires in combatant ships. Within a period of three months, this gallant unit completed the emergency clearing of Manila Harbor, raising, removing or disposing of over 350 vessels together with large quantities of Japanese underwater ordnance to open the port fully to Allied use. The skilled teamwork and the personal heroism of the officers and men of Ship Salvage, Fire-Fighting and Rescue Unit during the fulfillment of a difficult and hazardous mission contributed essentially to the successful liberation of the Philippine Islands and reflect the highest credit upon the United States Naval Service."

SUBMARINE TENDERS

Submarine tenders (AS) "mother" submarine squadrons, usually tending 16 to 18 boats. They carry everything essential a submarine might need, such as spare parts, diesel oil, torpedoes, and general supplies. Some tenders were converted, some built as tenders on C3 hulls. They vary in length from 350 to 550 feet, carry from 400 to 1,200 men, make up to 18 knots, and are generally well armed.

The *Fulton*

The *Fulton* (AS 11) was commissioned at Mare Island in September, 1941 and was on her shakedown cruise two days out of Panama when the Japs struck Pearl Harbor. The Navy needed seaplane bases in the Caribbean, and despite the fact that the *Fulton* was a submarine tender, she was ordered to build and outfit two seaplane bases, tasks she completed by February, 1942.

In March the *Fulton* arrived at the submarine base, Pearl Harbor, and immediately began refitting the submarine *Drum*. In June, while the Battle of Midway was in progress, the *Fulton* left on a special mission to pick up survivors of the carrier *Yorktown*, sunk in that battle. Midway Island secured by the Navy and Marines, the *Fulton* was ordered to establish a submarine base there, which she did in July. After Midway she shoved off for Brisbane, Australia, and while there did much refitting and repair work on many other vessels besides submarines. At Milne Bay, New Guinea, in October, 1943, eighty per cent of the *Fulton's* work load was on vessels other than subs.

In July, 1944, the *Fulton* was back at Midway after an overhaul in the States, operated at Saipan in September, and at Guam in April, 1945. In September she was back in Seattle. During the war she had made repairs and overhauls to 332 vessels.

OCEAN TUGS

There are four types of ocean tugs—auxiliary (ATA), fleet (ATF), old (ATO), and rescue (ATR). They range from small, wooden-hulled ships to large, steel-hulled vessels, and vary from 300 to 1,300 tons. The Navy had approximately three hundred tugs in service during the war. Ten were sunk and 13 were awarded the Navy Unit Commendation, second highest award to United States ships.

Tugs are familiar to every Navy man, and probably to most soldiers and marines who saw overseas duty. The powerful little ships are on hand puffing and pushing every time a large ship makes port or gets underway, they tow disabled vessels in mid-ocean, and are pressed into service for every odd job in the Navy, particularly rescue work. Some even patrolled convoy lanes. They have seen their share of attack and defense against raiding submarines and enemy planes.

The *Chowanoc*

"Disaster, wrought by either man or weather, was the *Chowanoc's* (ATF 100) calling card to duty," the Navy has said of this doughty fleet tug which spent twenty months in the forward areas of the Pacific. The *Chowanoc's* jobs ranged from raising sunken ships to shooting down raiding Jap planes. She won the Navy Unit Commendation.

On April 12, 1944 the *Chowanoc* left Jacksonville, Florida, with a floating drydock in tow, bound for the Pacific. On June 26 the 9,000-mile tow job ended when the drydock was secured to a buoy at Kwajalein. The *Chowanoc* proceeded to Eniwetok for around-the-clock duty as a harbor tug, pushing barges loaded with ammunition, water, and freight from supply ships to fleet units.

The tug's first salvage work came on July 21 when the SS *Sea Flyer,* en route to the Guam invasion, ran aground. It took the *Chowanoc* three days to free the vessel. After shuttling back and forth between Eniwetok and Kwajalein, the tug shoved off in convoy on October 1 for Manus, Admiralty Islands, then joined a larger convoy for the invasion of Leyte. When the *Chowanoc* made Leyte her first task was to lay a smoke screen around the crippled cruiser *Honolulu* while she repaired torpedo damages.

Repair work on the *Honolulu* was interrupted by raiding Jap planes, and the *Chowanoc's* crew laid down their tools long enough to shoot down a bomber, and then spent the entire next day at General Quarters. Eleven enemy planes came over; one was damaged by *Chowanoc* gunners and another crashed after being hit. A few hours later, while the tug was salvaging a capsized Navy patrol plane, it was again attacked by three Japs, and one of the raiders was splashed 350 yards to port. At night one Jap plane which strafed the ship and dropped a bomb fifty yards off was brought down, although the *Chowanoc* crew suffered casualties.

Next day, to prove she was still a tug and not a fighting ship, the *Chowanoc* pulled a seaplane tender off a reef and then went to the aid of a burning Liberty ship loaded with aviation gasoline. During the next two days she pumped out the damaged destroyer *Ross.*

A typhoon whipped up on October 29 and the busy tug was sent in search of a foundering LST loaded with Army radar gear. The landing craft, her bow opened, had to be towed stern first. Back at Leyte, the *Chowanoc* raised the SS *Augustus Thomas,* and then after another typhoon struck, cleared the area of beached pontoons.

The *Chowanoc* refitted at Manus for the Lingayen invasion, then sailed December 31 as part of a troop transport group. En route the crew of a disabled repair ship was rescued. After going in at Lingayen, the tug was ordered to clear the invasion beach of landing craft. A near miss on January 11, 1945 rocked the *Chowanoc,* and she got underway immediately, just as more enemy planes came over and scored several other near misses which almost capsized the tug.

In February the *Chowanoc* sailed for Ulithi and the Kamikaze belt, but did not come under direct attack. Until the end of the war, she was kept on the go as a salvage and repair ship, putting into Guam in September for overhaul.

The *Ontario*

This tug (ATO 13) was the oldest, largest and most powerful in the Navy, and saw duty in two wars. Commissioned in 1912, she was equipped with minesweeping gear and cleared mines from British and European waters in World War I. From 1920 until 1941 she served in Samoa.

She was in Pearl for an overhaul when the Japs came over on December 7, and even though she was armed with but two .50-caliber machine guns, the *Ontario* shot down one enemy plane. In 1942 and 1943 she took part in many Pacific engagements, particularly in the Gilbert and Marshall Islands. During most of 1944 she serviced the Fleet at Ulithi and set buoys at Peleliu. On December 21, 1945 she towed two patrol vessels to San Diego for her first visit to the States in 25 years.

The *Apache*

This fleet tug (ATF 67) shot down four Japanese planes and won the Navy Unit Commendation for her fighting and work under fire. At Guam she dislodged a beached landing craft while being bombarded by heavy artillery and mortars.

As part of a salvage group headed for Lingayen Gulf in the Philippines, she was attacked by eight planes. One, coming in astern, was splashed by 20mm and .50-caliber fire. Another off the port quarter was smashed with 3-inch shells and blew up, and a third off the starboard bow was hit and crashed into the water. A fourth was damaged and set afire, continued on to attack an LCI, and then went down. All the action was packed into nine minutes.

DISTILLING SHIPS

These ships, modified Liberty tankers and oilers, distilled and carried fresh water to ships and shore stations for boiler feed and drinking. They were the *Stag, Wildcat, Pasig,* and *Abatan.*

UNCLASSIFIED VESSELS

In this classification (IX) are about two hundred ships of various types and functions. Among them are the training ships *Prairie State,*

Wheeling, and *Dover;* the naval relics *Constitution* and *Constellation;* the receiving ships *Reina Mercedes, Seattle,* and *Camden;* the training carriers *Wolverine* and *Sable;* hulks *Cumberland* and *Antelope;* yachts *America* and *Freedom;* the tug *Favorite;* ketch *Araner;* schooners *Blue Dolphin, Migrant,* and *Puritan;* yawl *Congaree;* barge *Silica;* ferry *Mariveles,* and assorted cargo vessels, tankers, minesweepers and old LSTs. The schooner *Ronaki,* storage tanker *Porcupine,* and barge *Asphalt* were lost in combat.

A sub-type of unclassified vessels was the oil storage tanker, a converted Liberty or Maritime Commission hull. Their job was to deliver diesel fuel, lubrication oil and gasoline to Navy and Army ships in the forward areas. They were not armored, had few guns, yet had to stay pretty much in the thick of it to service combatant and auxiliary ships with fuel and high octane gasoline. Whether underway or at anchor they were constantly subject to air attack. A bomb or mine hit or Kamikaze crash on a storage tanker usually meant an instantaneous explosion of the entire ship with not much chance of the crew's survival. Duty on ships such as this went unnoticed and unapplauded, but the men who sweated out the war aboard them were among the real heroes.

The *Panda*

The guns of the oil storage tanker *Panda* (IX 25) were almost as busy as her pumps during her year and a half in the Pacific war. Converted from a Liberty ship, she was commissioned at New Orleans on January 6, 1944 and reported to the Seventh Fleet two months later.

During the Philippines invasion the *Panda,* standing off four separate attacks, sent five enemy planes down in flames. Before the Battle for Leyte Gulf the *Panda* saw much service in the Southwest Pacific, longest at Hollandia.

The mobile tanker shot down her first plane on October 26, 1944 when a lone Jap dive bomber, coming in low with great speed, was dropped short of its mark with a heavy barrage from the *Panda's* gunners. A second successful scrape with enemy planes came on November 12. Three dive bombers tore in, one heading for the *Panda.* Guns roared and chattered, and the damaged plane missed the *Panda* and crashed into the landing craft repair ship *Achilles* (ARL 41).

Two more planes were shot down in a third attack on November 27. One appeared out of the heavy overcast, and after being riddled by gunfire from the *Panda,* plunged into a nearby auxiliary repair dock (ARD 19). Ten minutes later a second torpedo bomber swept in and raked the *Panda* with machine-gun fire, wounding six men. The ship's guns caught the Jap plane going away and splashed it. A fifth plane, brought down in a dusk attack on December 20, was a twin-engine bomber which burst into flames after being hit by 20mm fire.

Following the Leyte Gulf operation the *Panda* shifted to the Manila–Subic Bay area, remaining there until the end of the war.

MINE VESSELS

This class is composed of minelayers and minesweepers, both divided into numerous sub-types such as converted, coastal, light and auxiliary minelayers, and high-speed, fleet, coastal and motor minesweepers. At the end of the war the Navy had about 750 mine vessels. One submarine classed as a minelayer was lost, and numerous other minelayers and minesweepers were sunk in the Atlantic and Pacific.

Minelayers sow their explosives in enemy waters, particularly near ports and harbors, where moored mines are used. They have special stowage space for mines, special gear and deck tracks for dropping the mines into the water. Minelayers are converted destroyers and merchant ships, a few were built for the purpose. They are from 230 to 450 feet long, from 1,700 to 8,000 tons, and do from 10 to 33 knots.

Minesweepers are smaller vessels, many of them also converted, which sweep up the mines laid by enemies. They operate with convoys and fleet units, and are especially valuable in sweeping landing areas for the amphibious forces. They have special gear aft that sweeps for the mines and cuts mine mooring cables. They range from 170 to 2,000 tons.

Mine vessels often had assignments not connected with minelaying or minesweeping, such as escorting, patrolling, fire support and picket duty. It was all rough and dirty work.

The *J. William Ditter*

This 2,200-ton minelayer, converted destroyer, had a brief but effective combat career and was knocked out of action in the closing phase of the Okinawa operation. The *Ditter* (DM 31) was commissioned in October, 1944 and reached the Pacific early in 1945.

Six days before the invasion of Okinawa, in March, 1945, the *Ditter* acted as a fire-support ship for minesweepers clearing mines for the amphibious landings. She was credited with the probable destruction of an enemy submarine, and the sinking of two Jap suicide boats. In addition she destroyed several floating mines.

On April 2, the day after the invasion, the *Ditter* was escorting a convoy which was suddenly attacked by enemy aircraft. The gun crews of the minelayer bagged two bombers in one minute, and assisted in destroying a third. On April 13 *Ditter* gunners shot down another bomber.

At the height of Jap Kamikaze attacks off Okinawa the *Ditter* was pressed into service as a picket vessel, to be stationed alone far out on the flanks of Fleet units in order to give early warning of enemy air attacks. She was frequently the target of suicide planes and was missed by only thirty feet by a Kamikaze on April 28. But she continued to splash Jap raiders and by May 28 her score was 8 downed and assists on 3 others.

Early in June while the "J. Willy" was on patrol with another mine-layer, eight Jap planes attacked the two ships. In short order the *Ditter* knocked down four of the enemy and the other vessel accounted for three. The eighth plane, however, had the *Ditter's* number and crashed into her, killing 10 and wounding 27. After temporary repairs the damaged minelayer sailed back to the States, where she was decommissioned on September 28, 1945 and stricken from the Navy list on October 11.

The *Heed*

The minesweeper *Heed* (AM 100) was commissioned in 1942 and was in action throughout most of the war. Her first combat duty was escorting convoys in the invasion of the Aleutians, where, according to a member of the crew, "a thirty-degree roll was commonplace and the fog grudgingly allowed the sun through a couple times a week—maybe."

During the invasion of the Marshalls the *Heed* went in ahead of the landing force to sweep for mines. Under bombardment from Jap shore batteries, the *Heed* and a sister ship made contact with four mines but could find only three to explode. The fourth mine showed up when it exploded fifty feet off the *Heed's* stern.

During the fighting at Saipan the *Heed* patrolled between Saipan and Tinian within the range of Jap guns. Despite close shaves there and at other places in the Marianas, the *Heed* survived. Many of her sister ships, including the *Skylark, Portent, Sentinel* and *Skill,* went down.

The *Ellyson*

This destroyer minesweeper (DMS 19) saw tough, exciting duty in both oceans before the curtain fell on World War II. Commissioned as a destroyer (DD 454) just ten days before Pearl Harbor, the *Ellyson* spent her first six months on antisub patrol along the Atlantic coast, in the days when German submarines were sinking our vessels within sight of the beaches. On June 15, 1942 the *Ellyson* became the flagship of Destroyer Squadron Ten, the famous Atlantic sharpshooting squadron of tin cans such as the *Emmons, Rodman, Hobson, Corry, Hambleton, Macomb, Forrest* and *Fitch*. The *Ellyson* was to remain a flagship even after becoming a minesweeper.

In July she convoyed a cargo of planes to Africa, and on D-day at Casablanca was screening our carriers in the invasion. At Fedala she just missed being hit by a torpedo which smashed into the *Hambleton*. In February, 1943 she was patrolling off Newfoundland, and in May she joined the British Home Fleet with the *South Dakota,* protecting convoys on the Murmansk run. In October President Roosevelt set out for the Teheran conference aboard the battleship *Iowa* with the *Ellyson* as escort. Before returning to the States the *Ellyson* saw duty around the Azores, Dakar and Bermuda.

The *Ellyson* and Destroyer Squadron Ten were in the Mediterranean in May, 1944, where they sunk the German submarine U-616 after a 72-hour struggle. After putting into Plymouth, England, to prepare for the Normandy invasion, the *Ellyson* was off Pointe de la Hoe, France, on D-day, bombarding German positions. During the engagement the *Corry* struck a mine and went down. On June 25 the *Ellyson* knocked out two Nazi guns at Cherbourg and laid smokescreens for the large ships. Later, in the invasion of Southern France, the *Ellyson* led the Destroyer Fire-Support Group, smashing troop concentrations, shore batteries and tanks. In November she returned to the States to be converted to a minesweeper.

The *Ellyson* crew did not take to minesweeper conversion easily. They had thought of themselves as part of the "destroyer Navy," and no sailors are more fiercely loyal to their ships than men of the tin-can fleets. But when the refitting period was over and the *Ellyson* emerged as a Pacific-bound minesweeper, the men who had been in action at Casablanca, Normandy and Cherbourg discovered they were interested in seeing another theater of war.

Mine Squadron Twenty, with the *Ellyson* in the lead as flagship and with the *Butler, Jeffers, Harding* and *Gherardi* in addition to other converted minesweepers of old Destroyer Squadron Ten, were the first ships into Okinawa waters in March, 1945. The group remained for the entire operation—ninety days of continuous action. Only one ship of the squadron, the *Gherardi,* escaped damage. The *Emmons* was sunk. Casualties in the squadron were 100 killed and 200 wounded.

During pre-invasion days the *Ellyson* cleared the waters ahead of battleships and cruisers of Task Force 58, stood picket duty, and supported the smaller minesweepers. After the landing the *Ellyson* spent most of her time on picket stations, helping screen the huge fleet concentration off Okinawa. The *Emmons* went down when it was attacked by fifty suicide planes, five of them crashing into the ship. The *Emmons* shot down six. The *Ellyson* sunk the burning hulk of the *Emmons* after the crew abandoned ship.

The *Ellyson* splashed three Kamikaze planes, but one, which dived for the ship and missed by twenty feet, caused damage and seven casualties.

During July the *Ellyson* was flagship of a task group which swept 7,900 miles of the East China Sea, the largest minesweeping operation in naval records. Following the China Sea operation the *Ellyson* was with the Third Fleet off Tokyo, and on August 28 became the first major warship to enter Tokyo Bay as she swept the waters there for the *San Diego* and *Missouri.*

The *Aaron Ward*

"We all admire a ship that can't be licked. Congratulations on your magnificent performance." With this terse message Fleet Admiral Chester Nimitz expressed the Navy's pride in the third *Aaron Ward,* a ship which survived although six Kamikazes crashed into her on May 3, 1945.

The first *Ward* was launched in 1919 and was one of the fifty destroyers transferred to Great Britain in exchange for bases in the Atlantic. The second *Aaron Ward* was a destroyer (DD 483) sunk near Guadalcanal in April, 1943.

The third *Aaron Ward* (DM 34) a fast minelayer, reported for duty at Pearl Harbor in February, 1945. Before the May 3 attack she had undergone frequent air raids while on mine-destroying duty in the Okinawa area. Her men had seen plenty of suicide crashes, had watched an ammunition ship explode into bits after she was "Kamikazed." But the *Ward's* gunners, who had knocked down three enemy planes in one night, were far from ready to say "uncle" to the Japs.

"We were plenty cocky," said one of her officers. "We were aching for Japs even after we had seen what Kamikazes had done to the other ships."

They got all the planes they had dreamed of on May 3. The *Aaron Ward* was on radar picket station that afternoon some eighty miles west of Okinawa. Suddenly, from 10 to 12 Jap suicide planes appeared and a savage and coordinated attack began with one Jap remaining out of range to act as a suicide director for the other planes—a traffic cop of winged death.

The first plane to dive on the *Ward* was driven off its course by antiaircraft fire, tipped over and plummeted into the sea about a hundred yards away. Parts of the engine and wing were thrown upon the deck of the ship.

A second Kamikaze was shot down. A third, armed with a large bomb, came in despite withering antiaircraft fire. The bomb penetrated the hull to explode in the after engine room. The plane disintegrated against the superstructure, covering the area with flaming gasoline, severely damaging a gun mount and jamming the rudder. With steering control locked, the *Ward* began circling.

Another formation of enemy planes headed for the minelayer in the midst of fire-fighting and rescue efforts. Two planes which began runs on the *Ward* were shot down jointly by the combat air patrol and the ship's guns. A third plane stayed on its course through intense AA fire. As it neared the bridge it pulled up from the dive and swerved away, clipping the signal halyards and lines to the steam whistle and siren and finally plunging into the sea. Damage to the ship was minor, but escaping steam lessened visibility and the screaming whistle hampered communications.

Smoking from fires and lurching erratically due to flooding and steering difficulties, the *Ward* met the seventh attacking plane. Gunners accurately plugged the plane, but could not force it off course. The Jap plowed into the stricken ship, opening another fire room to the sea and robbing the ship of all power of propulsion. In the midst of the inferno, suicider No. 8 dived into the ship four seconds later.

All but one of the major engineering spaces were flooded by damage from No. 8's hit. Fires were raging in topside ammunition magazines, and control or rescue measures were practically impossible due to loss of power and the rapidity of the attacks.

The *Aaron Ward* was practically dead in the water. One Diesel generator was started which provided limited power to forward stations. The wounded and dying, in desperate need of medical care, made the situation acute.

Obscured by smoke, suicide plane No. 9 approached at high speed and blew itself apart on the ship. This crash set off new fires and more ammunition exploded. The *Ward* was settling rapidly, her decks and superstructure a shambles, fires out of control, ammunition exploding all over the after part of the ship and a major portion of her vital below-deck spaces flooded.

Yet when Kamikaze No. 10 peeled off to finish the stubborn little minelayer he was riddled with bullets from her determined gunners. Though hit, the plane smacked into what was left of the superstructure and fell to the deck, a mass of burning, twisted wreckage. The after stack had been toppled over, taking guns and men in its path.

With gaping holes in her side and maindeck, her deckhouse cluttered with wreckage, enemy planes, and bodies, and with fires burning in her ammunition spaces and engine rooms, the crew of the *Aaron Ward* worked furiously to stay afloat and administer to the needs of the wounded and dying. The battle to keep the ship afloat lasted far into the night. Enemy planes were still in the area. Below decks the "black gang" sweated to get up steam and water.

Two nearby landing craft support ships, the LCS(L) 83 and LCS(L) 14, came to the aid of the minelayer, taking off some of the casualties and helping to bring fires under control. An hour after the final attack all fires were extinguished.

Another minelayer, the *Shannon,* towed the helpless *Ward* to an island base where the remainder of her casualties was removed. There an auxiliary ship, the *Zaniah,* pumped out water and made emergency repairs to keep the *Ward* from sinking. What the *Ward* looked like when the *Shannon* arrived is told by the *Shannon's* Frank Madden, CBM:

Arriving at the scene this ship steamed cautiously through the oil-covered water. A number of small craft, PCs and LCI gunboats, were already busily engaging in searching for survivors. Drawing abeam, the water could be heard slushing back and forth as the seas washed through two gaping holes in her side. The *Shannon's* crew marvelled at the vessel's ability to "take it" and still remain afloat.

The port side aft was a mass of rubble. One stack was gone and jagged pieces of metal was all that remained of her after 40-millimeters. In darkness the ship resembled a scrap metal pile.

The racing motors of the portable pump, the "handy-billy," rose above the sounds of rasping metal and muffled orders as they worked to save the ship and trapped personnel. The only light visible on the black hulk of the ship was a beam of a hand lantern, flickering on and off, revealing men in silhouette, through a hole aft, working laboriously.

Occasionally a searchlight from one of the guardian craft would sweep close to the stricken ship and a number of high-pitched voices, close to hysteria, would scream, "Put out that light." Muttered cursing would follow.

Once a voice pierced the quiet, shouting, "There's a man off our port bow!" then pleading, "Please pick him up."

Another survivor was talking to his rescuers from the water. His legs were badly mangled but the sailor showed no evidence of pain. A body floated by face-down amidst debris.

The *Ward* returned to the United States July 8, and was routed to the Brooklyn Navy Yard for permanent repairs and general overhaul.

LANDING CRAFT

Various types of landing craft, under experiment for years, came into prominence with our invasions in the Pacific, Africa and Europe. Prior to this, the British had developed some, and others had been tested by the Navy and Marine Corps. There are about 25 types in all, making up about 85,000 landing craft, divided into ocean-going and ship type, small craft transported by other vessels, and tracked and wheeled amphibious land vehicles.

With the exception of LSDs (landing ship, dock) and LSVs (landing ship, vehicle), all landing craft open their bows to unload. (LSDs and LSVs carry small landing craft, hoisting them over the side or floating them off the after end.) LSTs (landing ship, tank) unload through bow ramps, as do LSMs (landing ship, medium).

LCIs (landing craft, infantry) carry about two hundred troops loaded from transports. LCTs carry tanks or cargo. LCMs (landing craft, mechanized) carry troops, cargo or tanks, and are carried aboard attack cargo and transport ships. LCVPs (landing craft, vehicles, personnel) and LCPs (landing craft, personnel) carry 36 men or small cargoes. Landing vehicles, generally known as "amtracs," are designed to negotiate reefs, swamps and streams.

Many landing craft received high awards and citations, among them LCI(L) 1, LCS(L) 31, 51 and 57; LCT(S) 30 and 540, and LST 464. About 150 were sunk in the invasions.

LCS(L) 31

This craft, commissioned on September 20, 1944 was part of the gunfire support force in the landing on Iwo Jima. LCS(L) 31 laid down two rocket barrages ahead of the initial assault waves and then gave close fire support to the advancing troops. It also conducted night harassing fire, served as an artillery observation post, and was used in close photographic reconnaissance.

LCS(L) 31 later took part in the Okinawa invasion, then went on radar picket support and anti-suicide boat patrol. In three actions the ship shot down eight Jap planes. Six were splashed on May 4, 1945 when she was attacked by suicide planes. In this engagement, for which she was awarded the Presidential Unit Citation, LCS(L) 31 was severely damaged, suffered many casualties. But this little giant came back strong, and in September, 1945 she supported the landings of occupation troops in the Osaka-Kobe area of Japan.

THE MERCHANT MARINE

No story of fighting ships in World War II would be complete without a tribute to the US Merchant Marine. Vice Adm. Emory S. Land said in his report to the President:

"Transport was the jugular vein of the United Nations' war effort. The Nazis paid our merchant fleet the unwelcome tribute of unrestricted submarine warfare . . . the Japanese selected our merchant ships as targets for their Kamikaze planes."

Said Fleet Admiral Ernest J. King:

"During the past three and a half years, the Navy has been dependent upon the Merchant Marine to supply our far-flung fleet and bases. Without this support, the Navy could not have accomplished its mission."

General Eisenhower knew about the Merchant Marine, too:

"When final victory is ours," he said, "there is no organization that will share its credit more deservedly than the Merchant Marine."

At the time we entered the war, the Merchant Marine fleet included some 900 dry-cargo vessels and about 440 tankers. At VJ-day this had swollen to 4,421 vessels, with an actual carrying capacity of 44,940,000 tons.

In 1942 the Axis sank 39% of ships' tonnage built that year. In 1943 this dropped to 11%; 1944 to 8% and in 1945 losses were down to 4% of new ship construction for the year.

Although there were about thirty main types of vessels, about 75% of the fleet was Liberty ships. This packhorse of the war had only 11 knots speed, carried 10,800 deadweight tons. Victory ships carried about the same tonnage as Liberties, but could kick along at 15 to 17 knots. The 55,000 seamen constituting our Merchant Marine in 1941 grew to a sea-going force of over 250,000 by war's end.

Like the Army and Navy, the Merchant Marine awarded medals for outstanding conduct. Highest award is the Merchant Marine Distinguished Service Medal, won by 141. Next comes the Meritorious Service Medal, and there were 362 to receive this honor. Finally, there is the Mariner's Medal, similar to the Purple Heart, of which 5,099 were awarded, many posthumously.

In addition to these individual medals, the Merchant Marine gave a "Gallant Ship" citation, similar to the Presidential or Navy Unit award.

We lost, in all, over one thousand five hundred merchant ships from September, 1939 to August 15, 1945. The bulk of the tonnage lost was accounted for by the sinking of 733 vessels of over 1,000 tons by direct war causes.   Over 5,600 seamen lost their lives, with thousands more wounded.

But the Merchant Marine delivered the goods.

The SS *Adoniram Judson*

Loaded with three thousand barrels of high-octane gasoline and carrying sorely needed steel airfield mats, this Liberty ship fought her way into Taclobán harbor the day after that city was captured. On October 22, 1944 the *Adoniram Judson* steamed into San Pedro Bay with her highly-explosive cargo, and despite continuous Jap bombing attacks, she dropped anchor at Tacloban.

During the next 72 hours the ship was subjected to 56 bombing and strafing runs but her Navy armed guard and merchant crew fought off the attackers and successfully unloaded the cargo. The ship brought down six Jap planes; seven of her crew were wounded. Any kind of hit on her high-octane gasoline would have blown her sky-high. Said her Citation: "The stark courage of her stalwart crew against over-powering odds caused her name to be perpetuated as a Gallant Ship."

The SS *Cedar Mills*

First tanker and second merchant vessel to win the Gallant Ship Award, the *Cedar Mills* won her laurels in a hurricane. On Thanks-giving Day, 1943 she sailed from Freemantle, Australia, bound for Karachi, India. The French destroyer *Le Triomphant* accompanied her for protection.

Halfway to Karachi the destroyer ran out of oil and in the refueling operations the oil hose snapped, and the ships were slammed together by mounting seas. Taken under tow, the destroyer tried refueling again but the hose snapped a second time. Just about this time the cyclone struck in full force, severing the towing line as the two ships pitched and tossed. Unable to raise steam, *Le Triomphant's* plight became desperate as she sprang a leak and began to settle under the terrific pounding of mountainous waves.

Meanwhile the *Cedar Mills* stood by, pouring oil on the water around the destroyer in an effort to lessen the surging seas. When it appeared that the destroyer was certain to sink, volunteers manned two *Cedar Mills* lifeboats and plunged into the foaming seas. The boats could not maneuver close enough to *Le Triomphant* and her men had to jump over the side. Merchant seamen and Navy armed guard in the lifeboats dove in to help exhausted Frenchmen. Then water fouled the motor of one lifeboat and it had to be rowed.

Darkness fell as barracudas swarmed hungrily about the struggling men, to be driven off by incessant rifle barrages. Finally, despite her 45 degree list, the captain of *Le Triomphant* decided he might still save her, and as rescue operations continued through the night, the destroyer was again taken in tow. Her sailors, treated for wounds and exhaustion, returned to their ship and food and fresh water were sent over on a line.

The next day daring members of the destroyer crew dived under her keel and improvised patches were placed on the leaking hull. The *Cedar Mills* resumed tow and the battered ships finally made port.

The SS *Henry Bacon*

The men who made the Murmansk run are creatures set apart from their fellows, for they knew they had taken the toughest merchant run of the war and had come through. Even Vice Admiral Land said, "Our merchant ships ran innumerable gauntlets of air, surface and submarine attack . . . but none of these combined all elements of danger from man and nature alike, as did the Murmansk run." Forced to plod slowly through iceberg-filled waters, close to the coasts of Nazi-occupied Norway, with its swarming U-boat docks and airfields, the proudest boast of any Merchant Marine seaman is—"I made the Murmansk run!"

Many gave their lives in this effort to bring supplies to our Russian ally. Here is the story of the *Henry Bacon,* en route back to the States after carrying 7,500 tons of war matériel to Murmansk:

Carrying 19 Norwegian refugees, the Liberty ship lost contact with her convoy in heavy weather off Norway. Suddenly a plane burst out of the overcast and circled like a huge vulture. Then they came . . . over a score of Nazi bombers, piling in on the lone freighter. Her guns blazing, the *Henry Bacon* took violent evasive action, and five enemy planes plummeted into the sea as her gunners refused to concede defeat. But there were too many bombs whistling down now, and at last one plunged into her hold. The stricken freighter began settling at once, her guns still banging defiantly back at the Nazis.

The order to abandon ship was finally given but with one lifeboat already smashed by the heavy seas, another was lost in lowering, leaving only two to be launched. Capt. Alfred Carini and all senior officers went down with the ship. Crown Prince Olav wrote the War Shipping Administrator:

"I am in receipt of a communication from the Norwegian High Command commending . . . the *Henry Bacon* . . . During a storm the

Henry Bacon . . . came into a life-and-death fight with the enemy. After having downed five enemy planes the vessel was sunk. The *Henry Bacon* carried 19 evacués . . . all 19 were saved.

". . . I find it incumbent upon me to express to you my appreciation and admiration of the outstanding discipline and self-sacrifice displayed by the officers and crew of the *Henry Bacon,* in pact with the finest tradition of American sailors."

The *Esso Bolivar*

There is no limit to the ironies of war. Those who cannot forget that many Jap bombs were made from American scrap metal may be comforted to know that the fates also sometimes worked the other way. Consider, for example, the Panamanian flag tanker *Esso Bolivar.* Built in Germany in 1937, and sailed to the U.S. on her maiden voyage by a German crew, this vessel was the target for one of the most gruelling Nazi submarine attacks. Here is her story:

On February 26, 1942, the *Esso Bolivar* left New York bound for Aruba, Netherlands West Indies. Manned by a crew of forty-four, and a Navy gun crew of six, the tanker was armed with a four-inch stern gun and four caliber .30 machine guns. The trip down the coast was uneventful, but the *Bolivar's* crew had seen the wreckage of sister ships lining the Florida reefs and the air was heavy with apprehension.

At 2:30 A. M. on the morning of March 7 the tanker was about thirty miles southeast of Guantanamo, Cuba. The night was clear and warm, a bright moon silhouetted the ship clearly as she moved along. Suddenly the silence was broken by the sharp and unmistakable crack of gunfire. Seconds later the first shell screamed past, throwing up a geyser of water dead ahead. The war was on with a vengeance and as the general alarm sounded, the surfaced Nazi sub, lying low on the horizon, continued to pump shells at the *Bolivar.*

As is so often the case, the element of surprise decided the day. Even as the gun crew raced for their stations, German gunners found the target with deadly precision. A burst of shrapnel put the radio out of commission, but not before the alert operator had flashed an SOS. As the *Bolivar* went to full speed and commenced evasive action, other shells burst on the after deck. The third shell, by unhappy chance, started a fire in the galley which blazed upward like a torch, driving the gun crew from the four-inch gun. Ablaze and silhouetted in the moonlight with no protective heavy gun, the ordeal of the *Bolivar* now began.

The same incendiary shell that set the galley on fire also cut the feed line leading to the deck fuel oil. Flames shot through ventilators and hatches and bulkheads caved in under the intense heat. Shells crashed into the stern, putting the steering gear out of commission. Cylinders of acetylene gas in the deck cargo blazed fiercely and the wounded tanker circled out of control as shells continued to pump in with clock-tick regularity. Life rafts and the four lifeboats were damaged or shot away. In the midst of this carnage the *Bolivar's* men and officers went calmly about their assigned duties, fighting to get the ship under control while they dropped under the hail of gunfire.

When the "abandon ship" order came, only one lifeboat could be launched. Captain James Stewart, commander of the *Bolivar,* was killed by a shell as he led a group to the starboard side, facing defiantly toward the unseen enemy as the others fell to the deck. Many of the others were wounded, and Chief Mate Fudske, who assumed command, died as he attempted to lower the lone remaining lifeboat. Despite his wounds he persisted in trying to clear the falls for the other men. Six survivors who finally got the boat clear were machine-gunned without effect, jumping into the sea to escape the harassing fire.

The sub continued to shell the crippled tanker for two hours, circling and playing a searchlight on it. Shortly before daybreak the Nazis fired a torpedo which blasted a huge hole amidships. Still the *Esso Bolivar* refused to sink. Cries from wounded and drowning crew members filled the quiet night—cries filled with increasing terror as sharks closed in on those in the water. Able Seaman Charles Richardson, along with Chief Engineer Thomas McTaggart, Fireman-Watertender Arthur Lauman and Chief Mate Fudske received Presidential Citations for bravery. Here is Richardson's citation:

For heroism above and beyond the call of duty.
On duty with the Navy gun crew while his ship was under heavy submarine shell fire, he undertook the rescue of two wounded Navy members of the crew when the abandon ship order was given. Although himself wounded in the back by a shell fragment, he got both men in the water, placed one on his back and had the other grasp him about the neck. In this manner he was swimming toward a lifeboat when sharks attacked and he was obliged to defend himself and his companions by slashing out with a knife. A shark pulled the wounded man off his back and this man was lost, but he succeeded in getting the second wounded man and himself into the lifeboat. He suffered hand lacerations while fighting off the sharks . . .

Meanwhile the sub, angered by the stubborn refusal of the *Esso Bolivar* to go under, continued to circle the burning vessel. She was finally frightened off by an approaching Navy vessel. One man, Wiper

Matthew Carlo, was aboard all during the action. Receiving a head wound, he was unconscious when the ship was abandoned and had to endure the hail of enemy shell until rescued. The minesweeper USS *Endurance* and the destroyer *Stringham* reached the survivors shortly before noon. The wounded were rushed to a naval hospital at Guantanamo. But the story of the *Esso Bolivar* was far from finished.

On March 8, a group of the survivors, led by Chief Engineer McTaggart, requested permission to attempt to save the stricken ship. When naval air reconnaissance photos were checked, the *Bolivar* was shown listing heavily to starboard and still ablaze. Nevertheless, McTaggart & Co. convinced the Navy that she could be saved and back to sea they went, aboard the net tender USS *Mulberry*. At 9:00 A. M. they reached the still-burning *Bolivar*. By noon the worst fires were out and the ship restored to even keel. By 2:00 P. M. the main engine was started and a few minutes later the *Bolivar* was under way. Despite thirty shell holes and a torpedo hole 50 feet long and 35 feet deep, she moved along at eight knots to the utter amazement of spectators at the rescue scene.

After temporary repairs at Guantanamo, the *Esso Bolivar* went to Mobile, where permanent repairs were completed on July 24, 1942. She went on to make thirty-five voyages before the end of the war, carrying over 3,600,000 barrels of oil from the vital Aruba refinery to the Allied war machine.

The *Allan Jackson*

The *Allan Jackson,* voyaging alone and unarmed, was the first Esso tanker to be destroyed by an enemy submarine. On the night of January 17, 1942, while running up the Atlantic Coast off North Carolina, she was hit by two torpedoes. The ship broke in two forward of amidships and flames immediately swept her decks, blazing oil covering the water in a few minutes.

Only one lifeboat could be launched and many of the men were forced to jump overboard. The burning vessel sank within ten minutes. Of the crew of 35, 22 lost their lives; of the 13 survivors, eight were injured, five seriously.

The *Allan Jackson,* commanded by Captain Felix W. Kretchmer, had departed from Cartagena, Colombia, with 72,870 barrels of crude oil on January 11, bound for New York. In the early morning hours of Sunday, January 18, she was off Cape Hatteras.

Here is Captain Kretchmer's account:

"I was in bed when at 1:35 A. M. the ship was struck without warning by two torpedoes amidships on the starboard side. The second explosion was very severe and broke the vessel apart and set her on fire. The oil on the water spread over an area about one-half mile around and was aflame."

Third Mate Boris Voronsoff reported that he and some others tried to launch No. 2 lifeboat but the flames came so close they had to leap into the sea.

Captain Kretchmer continued:

"Flames were coming through the portholes and doors and my only means of escape was the porthole in the bathroom. Seeing no sign of the crew, I started up the ladder leading to the bridge. The decks and ladders were breaking up and the sea was rushing aboard. As the vessel sank amidships, the suction carried me away from the bridge ladder. After a short struggle I came to the surface, on which oil was afire a short distance away. I never saw any member of the crew or any lifeboat afloat at any time, but later I distinctly saw a large submarine emerge.

"With the help of a couple of small boards I was able to keep afloat until I was picked up, about seven hours later, by the destroyer USS *Roe*. I was almost completely exhausted and hardly regained consciousness until I was landed at Norfolk and placed in the Marine Hospital, where I remained until January 31."

Boatswain Rolf Clausen had this to say:

"When the torpedoes struck I was in the messroom on the port side aft playing cards. We rushed out on deck and made for the nearest lifeboat, No. 4, but we couldn't launch it because the wind was carrying the flames in that direction. With men who joined us, we all went over to the starboard lifeboat, No. 3, which we immediately started to launch. I jumped into the boat with seven other men, including the chief engineer.

"When the boat was in the water and held in position by the painter we were three to four feet from the ship's side. Around us, within a short distance, were the flames of crude oil burning on the surface of the sea.

"What saved us was the strong discharge from the condenser pump. The outlet happened to be just ahead of the lifeboat. The force of the stream of water, combined with the motion of the ship, pushed the burning oil away to a few yards outboard of the boat.

"I unhooked the falls and cut the painter. At that time, the broken-off bow of the *Allan Jackson* was listing to port and the main part of the vessel was listing to starboard, over our lifeboat. After cutting the painter I found that in the excitement no one had unlashed the oars. By the time I cut the lashings and the oars were manned, the boat was being sucked toward the propeller. The propeller blades hit the boat a number of times before we succeeded in clearing it by shoving with oars against the ship.

"Again we were saved from the surrounding fire because by that time we were in the backwash of the propeller, which made a clear lane through the flames. Not a man in that boat would have lived except for two elements of luck—the condenser discharge and the propeller backwash.

"We did all we could to find survivors. In the darkness we heard several calls and about fifteen minutes after leaving the ship we picked up the radio operator, Stephen Verbonich. Then we saw a white light, low over the sea, which was undoubtedly on a submarine. Putting up sails, we steered for shore in a westerly direction.

"About two and a half hours after being torpedoed, we sighted a bluish searchlight east of us. I started using my flashlight as a signal, turning it on the sail and beginning a message in Morse code. None of us knew until later how important the brief use of the flashlight had been, for the glow turned on and off the sail had by chance been picked up by an American naval vessel.

"Shortly before daylight we could see the silhouette of a destroyer's superstructure [USS *Roe*] and we sent up two distress signal flares. They were acknowledged by blinker signals asking questions, to which I replied by again signaling with my flashlight on the sail."

The *Roe* asked the name of the torpedoed ship and the names of three of the men in the boat, which Clausen flashed back. The *Roe* had picked up others of the *Allan Jackson*. As Clausen explained, the commanding officer of the *Roe* had been an observer on British escorts before the war and had been on two ships sunk by the craftiness of Nazi U-boats.

"In reply to my answers," Clausen continued, "we got a blinker signal meaning 'Wait.' Then the *Roe* circled and stopped and picked us up. After that the destroyer picked up a body and then succeeded in rescuing Captain Kretchmer. Finally three more bodies were found, and after six hours more search the *Roe* gave up."

The *M. F. Elliott*

The Esso tanker *M. F. Elliott,* chartered to the War Shipping Administration, was torpedoed without warning on the afternoon of June 3, 1942, about 150 miles northwest of Trinidad. Of the ship's total complement of 45, including a seven-man Navy gun crew, 13 merchant seamen were lost. Two of the 32 survivors, Able Seaman Raymond Smithson and Ordinary Seaman Cornelius F. O'Connor, were rescued by the German submarine which sank the *Elliott.* The U-boat later set them adrift in a small dinghy from which they were rescued a second time by the Brazilian tanker *Santa Maria* after five days.

The *Elliott,* a single-screw vessel of 10,450 deadweight tons capacity, was built in 1921 at Oakland, California. From the outbreak of the war she sailed dangerous coastwise and Caribbean routes carrying oil until that June day when her number came up in the savage submarine warfare.

Captain Harold I. Cook was in command of the *Elliott* when she left Newport News on May 19, 1942 to join a convoy near Cape Henry, Virginia. The *Elliott's* destination was Carapito, Venezuela. Off the Florida Keys she left the convoy.

Sailing along at about ten knots on a choppy sea under a blue sky, her Navy gunners manning a 4-inch gun and two .50-caliber machine guns aft, and two .30-calibers on the bridge, a terrific explosion occurred at 3:58 P. M. on the starboard side aft. None of the lookouts had spotted either a periscope or the torpedo, and the impact of the Nazi tin fish was a complete surprise. The *Elliott* began to settle rapidly by the stern, taking a starboard list at the same time, and Captain Cook saw almost at once that the ship would go down. He ordered an SOS sent and all lifeboats lowered. One boat had been wrecked so that only three could be used, but when all hands were aboard, the three boats were capsized when the *Elliott* went down in six minutes. Thirteen of the men were drowned but twenty-seven of them were able to reach the ship's four life rafts which had been launched. Three others, who could not make the rafts, floated all night in their life belts. Early in the evening a plane appeared and signaled that help was coming. About 6:00 A. M. on June 4 the destroyer USS *Tarbell* picked up the thirty men and landed them at Trinidad.

Smithson and O'Connor were knocked into the water from No. 2 boat when it capsized and were sucked under when the *Elliott* took her last plunge, but both miraculously got back to the surface. They lashed together a mast, sail and spar from a lifeboat and a plank from the ship, and floundered around until nightfall, when they were ready to give up. Suddenly a big, black shape loomed up—the German submarine, and the two men were thrown a line and pulled aboard.

The U-boat commander spoke perfect English and agreed to take the two American seamen to the rafts, but a plane appeared overhead and the submarine made a crash dive. Smithson and O'Connor sat on the deck in the control room while the German crew fed them hot tea and bread and cheese, and gave them rags to wipe off the oil. The sub surfaced for a few minutes, dived again, and then the two were told by the enemy captain:

"We are going to give you our lifeboat and water and bread. Row six miles south and you should find your comrades. If you do not, keep heading south and you will reach land. This is war, and it is all that I can do."

Smithson and O'Connor rowed for what seemed six miles, saw a flare shot from the rafts, but could not make the rafts because of a heavy sea. For the next two days a plane circled overhead but the pilot failed to spot the boat, and the wind and current carried the small boat away from the rafts. A large plane and then a cargo vessel passed, but the survivors were not sighted. After five days of rowing and being swamped in the blazing sun, the two *Elliott* crewmen collapsed in the bottom of the boat, too weak to do any more. About noon of the fifth day they spotted a ship, and after beating the water cans with the oarlocks, whistling and waving, the vessel turned toward them. It was the *Santa Maria,* bound for Santos, Brazil, where Smithson and O'Connor were landed on July 1.

The *Beaconhill*

This tanker of the Panama Transport Company was in the "Forgotten Convoy" which sailed from New York in January, 1943, and was "lost" for eight months in northern Russian ports. On that trip the *Beaconhill* became known as the "Murmansk Ferry."

When the ship left New York on January 4 the Allied invasion of North Africa was just two months old. When the *Beaconhill* returned to the United States in December, Italy had surrendered, the Russians were in Kiev, and the Marines had taken Tarawa.

Before the trip to Russia the *Beaconhill* had carried gasoline, benzine and kerosene to India, Africa and Great Britain to supply Allied troops. Now she was to take the long Arctic run with aviation gasoline components on board—fuel with which Soviet planes could fight off Nazi bombers.

The *Beaconhill* was one of a convoy of six ships bound for Murmansk and Archangel. Heavy head winds and severe weather resulted in a 24-day crossing to Scotland, and the tanker missed the convoy she had expected to join for the sailing north. On February 15 the *Beaconhill* put to sea in a formation of twenty-five vessels, two others of which were tankers. The Beaconhill carried a merchant crew of 42 officers and men and the Navy armed guard numbered 30. She was armed with a 3-inch high-altitude dual-purpose gun forward, a 5-inch gun aft, and eight 20-millimeters. The convoy was under the protection of a powerful British escort force—a cruiser and 25 corvettes and minesweepers.

Near Iceland the weather was freezing cold, and head winds and rough seas delayed the ships. Soon German observation planes appeared and circled the convoy, and the next day the Nazi raiders attacked, without hitting any of the vessels. For two more days the attacks continued, but the return antiaircraft fire was so intense and well-directed that the Germans were kept at a distance. Snow squalls and poor visibility prevented further bombing raids.

On February 26 the convoy divided, and the *Beaconhill* went with the group proceeding to Archangel. They were met by ice-breakers, and it took five days to sail 150 miles through the ice. During that time there was one air attack. The *Beaconhill* arrived at Molotovsk on March 2, and left on March 20 for Murmansk, arriving three days later. Until April 11, when the *Beaconhill* returned to Molotovsk, she was subjected to constant air attacks, but was not hit, although other ships were. The *Beaconhill* was then ordered to shuttle between Murmansk and Molotovsk carrying fuel oil, and made five such trips, earning the name, "Murmansk Ferry."

All this time the *Beaconhill* and other ships had been waiting for an escort in order to return to Scotland, but for some reason none appeared. The United States naval attaché, with the approval of the American Embassy, issued to each crew member of the American ships a certificate of membership in the "Society of the Forgotten Convoy of North Russia." The Germans knew that the convoy was still in Russia and boasted on their radio that the Lost Convoy would never return.

Finally an escort arrived and on November 1 the *Beaconhill* departed from Archangel, to arrive in Scotland on November 14, where the crew was greeted with stores of fresh meat and food. December 3 the tanker was back in New York, eleven months after leaving. A few weeks later the German battle cruiser *Scharnhorst* was sunk by the British while the German ship attempted to attack another Murmansk convoy.

On its Russian voyage the *Beaconhill* had been commanded by Captain Kenneth Wing. A later skipper, Captain Christian Quist, was commended by Admiral Emory S. Land, War Shipping Administrator, for efficiency in connection with a convoy in the South Atlantic.

The *Hanseat*

The motor ship *Hanseat,* a tanker specially designed to carry lubricating oils, was torpedoed, shelled and sunk by a German submarine at the northern entrance to the Windward Passage on March 9, 1942. On October 14, 1939 the *Hanseat* had been at Scapa Flow when a U-boat penetrated British defenses in the dramatic sinking of the battleship *Royal Oak,* and a few days later, on the 17th, the *Hanseat* was an unwilling witness of a fierce Nazi air raid on Scapa Flow.

The *Hanseat* had loaded her first wartime cargo at New York and was en route to Copenhagen in September, 1939, when she was intercepted by a British cruiser and ordered into Scapa Flow for examination. She arrived there October 8, and six nights later the Germans slipped in to launch four torpedoes at the *Royal Oak,* sink her, and escape. The air raid on the 17th found many neutral vessels in the anchorage, the crews of all desperately wishing they were somewhere else as Nazi bombs thundered around them seeking hits on British ships.

The *Hanseat* received clearance on the 22d, discharged her cargo at Copenhagen, and reached New York on November 15. Le Havre, Rouen, and Furt in France, and Casablanca in North Africa were other ports of call for the motor ship during 1940. Later she was assigned to the U.S. coastwise and South American service, and while in the Caribbean in 1942 was sent to the bottom.

The *Hanseat* had left New York on March 1 bound for Carapito, Venezuela. The coast of Cuba was raised early on the morning of March 9, and at 5:30 A. M. she ceased her zigzag course to make all possible speed. When the *Hanseat* was about ten miles northeast of Cape Maysi, Cuba, about half an hour later, two torpedoes struck the starboard side almost simultaneously. The ship settled by the stern immediately, the account of the skipper (Captain Einar Brandt) said, and at 6:10 A. M. lifeboats were lowered and all hands got aboard.

With the lifeboats in the water and the *Hanseat* slowly settling, the German submarine began to circle the scene submerged, her periscope protruding. The U-boat surfaced several hours later and then ran off a mile and a half, from where she began shelling the hapless tanker. The shelling continued for three hours, more than 200 shots being poured into the *Hanseat* before the port side was set ablaze. In the meantime one of the lifeboats with an outboard motor had made Cape Maysi, where a motor launch was sent in search of the other boats, which were rowing towards shore. About seven miles distant from the *Hanseat*, now just a column of smoke, the men were able to warn the tanker *Phoebus*, which they encountered, of the presence of an enemy submarine.

In mid-afternoon the motor launch from Maysi arrived and towed the remaining lifeboats to shore, from where the *Hanseat* survivors, none of whom were injured, were able to get to Havana.

APPENDIX

PRESIDENTIAL UNIT CITATION

Highest Award to United States Ships

Alchiba	Cargo
Atlanta	Light Cruiser
Barb	Submarine
Barry	High Speed Transport
Batfish	Submarine
Belknap	High Speed Transport
Belleau Wood	Light Carrier
Bernadou	Destroyer
Bogue	Escort Carrier
Borie	Destroyer
Bowfin	Submarine
Buchanan	Destroyer
Bunker Hill	Carrier
Cabot	Light Carrier
Card	Escort Carrier
Charles Ausburne	Destroyer
Chatelain	Destroyer Escort
Claxton	Destroyer
Clemson	High Speed Transport
Cole	Destroyer
Converse	Destroyer
Dallas	Destroyer
Dennis	Destroyer Escort
Dupont	Miscellaneous Auxiliary
Dyson	Destroyer
England	High Speed Transport
Enterprise	Carrier
Essex	Carrier
Fanshaw Bay	Escort Carrier
Flaherty	Destroyer Escort
Flasher	Submarine
Francis M. Robinson	Destroyer Escort
Gambier Bay	Escort Carrier
George E. Badger	High Speed Transport
Goff	Destroyer
Greene	High Speed Transport
Greenling	Submarine
Guadalcanal	Escort Carrier

Guardfish	Submarine
Gudgeon	Submarine
Haddock	Submarine
Harder	Submarine
Haverfield	Destroyer Escort
Heermann	Destroyer
Hobson	High Speed Minesweeper
Hoel	Destroyer
Hornet	Carrier
Houston	Heavy Cruiser
Jack	Submarine
Janssen	Destroyer Escort
Jenes	Destroyer
John C. Butler	Destroyer Escort
Johnston	Destroyer
Kalinin Bay	Escort Carrier
Kitkun Bay	Escort Carrier
Laffey	Destroyer
LCI(L) 1	Landing Craft, Infantry
LCS(L) 31	Landing Craft, Support
LCS 51	Landing Craft, Support
LCS 57	Landing Craft, Support
LCT(S) 30	Landing Craft, Tank
LCT 540	Landing Craft, Tank
Lea	Destroyer
Lexington	Carrier
McFarland	Destroyer
Maury	Destroyer

Motor Torpedo Boats
145, 146, 150, 151, 190, 191, 192, 193, 194, 195, 196
(Attached to Squadron 12)
Motor Torpedo Boats
320, 321, 322, 323, 324, 325, 326, 327, 328, 329, 330, 331
(Attached to Squadron 21)

Nautilus	Submarine
Nicholas	Destroyer
O'Bannon	Destroyer
Osmond Ingram	High Speed Transport
Parche	Submarine
Pigeon	Submarine Rescue Vessel

Pillsbury	Destroyer Escort
Pintado	Submarine
Pope	Destroyer Escort
Queenfish	Submarine
Radford	Destroyer
Rasher	Submarine
Raymond	Destroyer Escort
Sailfish	Submarine
St. Lô	Escort Carrier
Salmon	Submarine
Samuel B. Roberts	Destroyer Escort
Sand Lance	Submarine
San Francisco	Heavy Cruiser
San Jacinto	Light Carrier
Seahorse	Submarine
Sealion	Submarine
Silversides	Submarine
Smith	Destroyer
Spadefish	Submarine
Spence	Destroyer
Stanly	Destroyer
Swenning	Destroyer Escort
Tang	Submarine
Tinosa	Submarine
Tirante	Submarine
Trigger	Submarine
Trout	Submarine
Wahoo	Submarine
White Plains	Escort Carrier
Wilhoite	Destroyer Escort
Willis	Destroyer Escort
Yorktown	Carrier
Wasp	Carrier

NAVY UNIT COMMENDATION

Second Highest Award to United States Ships

Apache	Ocean Tug
Amycus	Repair Ship, Landing Craft
Arikara	Ocean Tug
ATR 2	Rescue Tug
ATR 31	Rescue Tug
ATR 61	Rescue Tug
Bonefish	Submarine
Cable	Salvage Vessel
Chanticleer	Submarine Rescue Vessel
Chickasaw	Ocean Tug
Chowanoc	Ocean Tug
Columbia	Light Cruiser
Cowpens	Light Carrier
Crevalle	Submarine
Dace	Submarine
Darter	Submarine
Egeria	Repair Ship, Landing Craft
Grapple	Salvage Vessel
Grasp	Salvage Vessel
Grayback	Submarine
Gurnard	Submarine
Haddo	Submarine
Hammerhead	Submarine
Hancock	Carrier
Hawkbill	Submarine
Helena	Light Cruiser
Heron	Seaplane Tender
Hidatsa	Ocean Tug
Hopkins	High Speed Minesweeper
Langley	Light Carrier
Lapon	Submarine
LCS 63	Landing Craft, Infantry
LCI 333	Landing Craft, Infantry
LCI 335	Landing Craft, Infantry
LCI(M)	Landing Craft, Infantry
LCI 390	Landing Craft, Infantry
LCI 616	Landing Craft, Infantry
LCI 688	Landing Craft, Infantry

LCI 690	Landing Craft, Infantry
LCI 776	Landing Craft, Infantry
LCI 777	Landing Craft, Infantry
LCI 985	Landing Craft, Infantry
LCI 986	Landing Craft, Infantry
LCI 987	Landing Craft, Infantry
LCI 1033	Landing Craft, Infantry
LCS(L) 21	Landing Craft, Ship
LCS(L) 83	Landing Craft, Support
LCS(L) 84	Landing Craft, Support
LCT 1260	Landing Craft, Tank
LCT 1239	Landing Craft, Tank
LCT 1240	Landing Craft, Tank
LST 464	Landing Craft, Tank

Motor Torpedo Boats 73, 74, 75, 76, 77, 78, 79, 80, 81, 82, 83, 84, 220, 221, 222, 223, 224, 227, 230, 297, 298, 299, 300
(Attached to Squadrons of Task Unit 70.1.4)

Motor Torpedo Boats
127, 128, 129, 130, 131, 132, 133, 134, 135, 137, 138
(Attached to Squadron 7)

Motor Torpedo Boat 375

PC 113	Submarine Chaser
PCE (R) 852	Escort Patrol Vessel
Pennsylvania	Battleship
Permit	Submarine
Picuda	Submarine
Pinto	Ocean Tug
Portland	Heavy Cruiser
Potowatomi	Ocean Tug
Puffer	Submarine
Quapaw	Ocean Tug
Rail	Ocean Tug
Raton	Submarine
Ray	Submarine
Santa Fe	Light Cruiser
Sea Devil	Submarine
Seawolf	Submarine
Solace	Hospital Ship
Sonoma	Ocean Tug

Tabberer	Destroyer Escort
Tautog	Submarine
Teak	Net Layer
Tennessee	Battleship
Thresher	Submarine
Trepang	Submarine
YMS 325	Motor Mine Sweeper
YP 421	Patrol Vessel

UNITED STATES NAVAL VESSELS LOST
DURING THE WAR

Name of Ship	Location	Date
BATTLESHIPS		
Arizona	Pearl Harbor	7 Dec 1941
Oklahoma	Pearl Harbor	7 Dec 1941
AIRCRAFT CARRIERS		
Hornet (CV 8)	Santa Cruz	26 Oct 1942
Lexington (CV 2)	Coral Sea	8 May 1942
Princeton (CVL 23)	Leyte	24 Oct 1944
Wasp (CV 7)	Solomons	15 Sep 1942
Yorktown (CV 5)	Midway	7 Jun 1942
AIRCRAFT CARRIERS, ESCORT		
Bismarck Sea	Iwo Jima	21 Feb 1945
Block Island (CVE 21)	Atlantic	29 May 1944
Gambier Bay	Leyte	25 Oct 1944
Liscome Bay	Tarawa	24 Nov 1943
Ommaney Bay (CVE 79)	Philippines	4 Jan 1945
St. Lô	Leyte	25 Oct 1944
HEAVY CRUISERS		
Astoria (CA 34)	Savo Island	9 Aug 1942
Chicago (CA 29)	Rennell Island	30 Jan 1943
Houston (CA 30)	Java Sea	1 Mar 1942
Indianapolis	NE of Leyte	29 Jul 1945
Northampton (CA 26)	Savo Island	30 Nov 1942
Quincy (CA 39)	Savo Island	9 Aug 1942
Vincennes (CA 44)	Savo Island	9 Aug 1942
LIGHT CRUISERS		
Atlanta (CL 51)	Guadalcanal	13 Nov 1942
Helena (CL 50)	Kula Gulf	6 Jul 1943
Juneau (CL 52)	Guadalcanal	13 Nov 1942
DESTROYERS		
Aaron Ward (DD 483)	Guadalcanal	7 Apr 1943
Abner Read (DD 526)	Philippines	1 Nov 1944
Barton	Guadalcanal	13 Nov 1942

Name of Ship	Location	Date
Beatty (DD 640)	Mediterranean	6 Nov 1943
Benham (DD 397)	Savo Island	15 Nov 1942
Blue (DD 387)	Guadalcanal	22 Aug 1942
Borie (DD 215)	North of Azores	1 Nov 1943
Bristol (DD 453)	Mediterranean	13 Oct 1943
Brownson (DD 518)	New Britain	26 Dec 1943
Buck (DD 420)	Salerno	9 Oct 1943
Bush	Okinawa	6 Apr 1945
Callaghan	Okinawa	28 Jul 1945
Chevalier (DD 451)	Vella Lavella	6 Oct 1943
Colhoun	Okinawa	6 Apr 1945
Cooper	Ormoc Bay	3 Dec 1944
Corry (DD 463)	Normandy	6 Jun 1944
Cushing (DD 376)	Savo Island	13 Nov 1942
De Haven (DD 469)	Savo Island	1 Feb 1943
Drexler	Okinawa	28 May 1945
Duncan (DD 485)	Savo Island	12 Oct 1942
Edsall	South of Java	1 Mar 1942
Glennon (DD 620)	Normandy	8 Jun 1944
Gwin (DD 433)	Kolombangara	13 Jul 1943
Halligan	Okinawa	26 Mar 1945
Hammann (DD 412)	Midway	6 Jun 1942
Henley (DD 391)	South Pacific	3 Oct 1943
Hoel (DD 533)	Leyte	25 Oct 1944
Hull	Luzon	17 Dec 1944
Ingraham (DD 444)	Atlantic	22 Aug 1942
Jacob Jones	Atlantic	28 Feb 1942
Jarvis (DD 393)	Guadalcanal	9 Aug 1942
Johnston (DD 557)	Leyte	25 Oct 1944
Laffey (DD 459)	Savo Island	12 Nov 1942
Lansdale (DD 426)	Mediterranean	20 Apr 1944
Leary (DD 158)	Atlantic	24 Dec 1943
Little	Okinawa	3 May 1945
Longshaw	Okinawa	18 May 1945
Luce	Okinawa	4 May 1945
Maddox (DD 622)	Sicily	10 Jul 1943
Mahan	Ormoc Bay	7 Dec 1944
Mannert L. Abele	Okinawa	12 Apr 1945
Meredith (DD 434)	Solomons	15 Oct 1942
Meredith (DD 726)	Normandy	8 Jun 1944

Name of Ship	Location	Date
Monaghan	Luzon	17 Dec 1944
Monssen	Guadalcanal	13 Nov 1942
Morrison	Okinawa	4 May 1945
O'Brien (DD 415)	Solomons	15 Sep 1942
Parrott	Norfolk—collision	2 May 1944
Peary	Australia	19 Feb 1942
Perkins (DD 377)	New Guinea	29 Nov 1943
Pillsbury (DD 227)	Bali Strait	1 Mar 1942
Pope (DD 225)	Java Sea	1 Mar 1942
Porter (DD 356)	Santa Cruz	26 Oct 1942
Preston	Savo Island	15 Nov 1942
Pringle	Okinawa	16 Apr 1945
Reid	Ormoc Bay	11 Dec 1944
Reuben James (DD 245)	Atlantic	31 Oct 1941
Rowan (DD 405)	Italy	11 Sep 1943
Sims (DD 409)	Coral Sea	7 May 1942
Spence	Luzon	17 Dec 1944
Stewart (DD 224)	Java	2 Mar 1942
Strong (DD 457)	Kula Gulf	5 Jul 1943
Sturtevant (DD 240)	Key West	26 Apr 1942
Truxtun (DD 229)	Newfoundland	18 Feb 1942
Tucker	Espíritu Santo	4 Aug 1942
Turner (DD 648)	Ambrose Light, NY	3 Jan 1944
Twiggs	Okinawa	16 Jun 1945
Walke (DD 416)	Savo Island	15 Nov 1942
Warrington (DD 383)	Atlantic	13 Sep 1944
William D. Porter	Okinawa	10 Jun 1945
Worden	Aleutians	12 Jan 1943

DESTROYER ESCORT VESSELS

Eversole (DE 404)	Philippines	28 Oct 1944
Fechteler (DE 157)	Mediterranean	4 May 1944
Fiske	Atlantic	2 Aug 1944
Frederick C. Davis	Atlantic	24 Apr 1945
Holder (DE 401)	Mediterranean	11 Apr 1944
Leopold	Atlantic	9 Mar 1944
Oberrender	Okinawa	9 May 1945
Rich (DE 695)	Normandy	8 Jun 1944
Samuel B. Roberts (DE 413)	Philippines	25 Oct 1944

Name of Ship	Location	Date
Shelton (DE 407)	New Guinea	3 Oct 1944
Underhill	Philippines	24 Jul 1945

SUBMARINES

Albacore	Japanese waters	Nov 1944
Amberjack (SS 219)	New Britain	Feb 1943
Argonaut (APS 1)	New Britain	10 Jan 1943
Barbel	Borneo	Feb 1945
Bonefish	Japanese waters	May 1945
Bullhead	Java Sea	Aug 1945
Capelin	Celebes Sea	Dec 1943
Cisco	South Pacific	Oct 1943
Corvina	Marshalls Archipelago	Nov 1943
Darter	Palawan Passage	24 Oct 1944
Dorado	Canal Zone, Panama	Oct 1943
Escolar	Japanese waters	Oct 1944
Flier	Borneo	Aug 1944
Golet	Japanese waters	Jun 1944
Grampus (SS 207)	New Britain	Feb 1943
Grayback	Ryukyu Archipelago	Feb 1944
Grayling (SS 209)	Philippines	Aug 1943
Grenadier (SS 210)	Malaya	Apr 1943
Growler	Philippines	Nov 1944
Grunion	Aleutians	Jul 1942
Gudgeon	Marianas Archipelago	May 1944
Harder	Philippines	Aug 1944
Herring	Kurile Archipelago	May 1944
Kete	Ryukyu Archipelago	Mar 1945
Lagarto	South China Sea	Jun 1945
Perch (SS 176)	Java Sea	3 Mar 1942
Pickerel (SS 177)	Japanese waters	May 1943
Pompano (SS 181)	Japanese waters	Sep 1943
R-12	Key West	12 Jun 1943
Robalo	Borneo	Jul 1944
Runner (SS 275)	Japanese waters	Jun 1943
S-26	Gulf of Panama	24 Jan 1942
S-27	Aleutians	19 Jun 1942
S-28	Hawaii	4 Jul 1944
S-36	Straits of Makassar	20 Jan 1942

Name of Ship	Location	Date
S-39	Rossel Island	14 Aug 1942
S-44	Kurile Archipelago	Oct 1943
Scamp	Japanese waters	Nov 1944
Scorpion	East China Sea	Jan 1944
Sculpin (SS 191)	Gilbert Archipelago	Dec 1943
Sealion (SS 195)	Philippines	10 Dec 1941
Seawolf	Morotai Island	Oct 1944
Shark (SS 174)	Molucca Sea	Feb 1942
Shark (SS 314)	Hongkong	Oct 1944
Snook	Hainan Island	Apr 1945
Swordfish	Ryukyu Archipelago	Jan 1945
Tang	Formosa Strait	Oct 1944
Trigger	Ryukyu Archipelago	Mar 1945
Triton	Admiralty Archipelago	Mar 1943
Trout	Ryukyu Archipelago	Feb 1944
Tullibee	Palau Island	Apr 1944
Wahoo (SS 238)	Japanese waters	Oct 1943

MINELAYERS

Gamble	Iwo Jima	18 Feb 1945
Miantonomah	Le Havre	25 Sep 1944
Montgomery	South Pacific	17 Oct 1944

MINESWEEPERS

Bittern	Philippines	10 Dec 1941
Bunting	San Francisco Bay	3 Jun 1942
Crow	Puget Sound	3 Sep 1943
Emmons	Okinawa	6 Apr 1945
Finch	Corregidor	10 Apr 1945
Hornbill	San Francisco Bay	30 Jun 1942
Hovey	Philippines	6 Jan 1945
Long	Lingayen	6 Jan 1945
Osprey	English Channel	5 Jun 1944
Palmer	Philippines	7 Jan 1945
Penguin	Guam	8 Dec 1941
Perry	Palau Island	13 Sep 1944
Portent	Mediterranean	12 Jan 1944
Quail	Corregidor	5 May 1942
Salute	Borneo	8 Jun 1945
Sentinel	Sicily	12 Jul 1943

Name of Ship	Location	Date
Skill	Salerno	25 Sep 1943
Skylark	Okinawa	28 Mar 1945
Swallow	Okinawa	22 Apr 1945
Swerve	Anzio	9 Jul 1944
Tanager	Corregidor	4 May 1942
Tide	Normandy	7 Jun 1944
Valor	Nantucket	29 Jun 1944
Wasmuth	Aleutians	29 Dec 1942

SUBMARINE CHASERS

PC 496	37° 23″ N, 9° 52″ W	4 Jun 1943
PC 558	38° 41″ N, 13° 43″ E	9 May 1944
PC 1129	Luzon	31 Jan 1945
PC 1261	France	6 Jun 1944
PC 1603	26° 25″ N, 127° 56″ E	21 May 1945
SC 521	11° 03″ S, 164° 50″ E	10 Jul 1945
SC 694	Palermo	23 Aug 1943
SC 696	Palermo	23 Aug 1943
SC 700	Vella Lavella	10 Mar 1944
SC 709	Cape Breton	21 Jan 1943
SC 740	15° 32″ S, 147° 06″ E	17 Jun 1943
SC 744	Philippines	27 Nov 1944
SC 751	21° 56″ S, 113° 53″ E	22 Jun 1943
SC 984	New Hebrides	9 Apr 1944
SC 1019	22° 28″ N, 84° 30″ W	22 Apr 1945
SC 1024	35° 12″ N, 74° 57″ W	2 Mar 1943
SC 1059	Bahama Islands	12 Dec 1944
SC 1067	Aleutians	19 Nov 1943

GUNBOATS

PGM 7	Bismarck Sea	18 Jul 1944
PGM 17	Okinawa	4 May 1945
PGM 18	26° 13″ N, 127° 54″ E	8 Apr 1945
Asheville	Java	3 Mar 1942
Erie	12° 03″ N, 68° 58″ W	12 Nov 1942
Luzon	Corregidor	5 May 1942
Mindanao	Corregidor	2 May 1942
Oahu	Corregidor	4 May 1942
Plymouth	37° 22″ N, 74° 25″ W	5 Aug 1943
St. Augustine	38° 00″ N, 75° 05″ W	6 Jan 1944

Name of *Ship*	Location	Date
Wake	Shanghai	8 Dec 1941
PE 56	Portland, Maine	23 Apr 1945

Coast Guard Vessels

CG 58012	41° 53″ N, 70° 30″ W	2 May 1943
CG 83415	France	21 Jun 1944
CG 83421	26° 14″ N, 79° 05″ W	30 Jun 1943
CG 83471	France	21 Jun 1944
Acacia	Caribbean Sea	15 Mar 1942
Alexander Hamilton	Iceland	29 Jan 1942
Bedloe	Cape Hatteras	14 Sep 1944
Bodega	Gulf of Mexico	20 Dec 1943
Catamount	Ambrose Light, NY	27 Mar 1943
Dow	Caribbean Sea	15 Oct 1943
Escanaba	60° 50″ N, 52° 00″ W	13 Jun 1943
Jackson	North Atlantic	14 Sep 1944
Natsek	Belle Island Strait	17 Dec 1942
Vineyard Sound	Vineyard Sound	14 Sep 1944
Wilcox	Cape Hatteras	30 Sep 1943

Seaplane Tenders

Gannet	Bermuda	7 Jun 1942
Langley	Java	27 Feb 1942
Thornton	Ryukyus	5 Apr 1945

Motor Torpedo Boats

PT 22	North Pacific	11 Jun 1943
PT 28	Alaska	12 Jan 1943
PT 31	Philippines	20 Jan 1942
PT 32	Sulu Sea	13 Mar 1942
PT 33	Pt. Santiago	15 Dec 1941
PT 34	Cauit Island	9 Apr 1942
PT 35	Philippines	12 Apr 1942
PT 37	Guadalcanal	1 Feb 1943
PT 41	Mindanao	15 Apr 1942
PT 43	Guadalcanal	10 Jan 1943
PT 44	South Pacific	12 Dec 1942
PT 63	New Ireland	18 Jun 1944
PT 67	New Guinea	17 Mar 1943
PT 68	New Guinea	1 Oct 1943

Name of Ship	Location	Date
PT 73	Philippines	16 Jan 1945
PT 77	Luzon	1 Feb 1945
PT 79	Luzon	1 Feb 1945
PT 107	New Ireland	18 Jun 1944
PT 109	Blackett Straits	2 Aug 1943
PT 110	New Guinea	26 Jan 1944
PT 111	Guadalcanal	1 Feb 1943
PT 112	Guadalcanal	10 Jan 1943
PT 113	New Guinea	8 Aug 1943
PT 117	Rendova Harbor	1 Aug 1943
PT 118	Vella Lavella	7 Sep 1943
PT 119	New Guinea	17 Mar 1943
PT 121	5° S, 151° E	27 Mar 1944
PT 123	Guadalcanal	1 Feb 1943
PT 133	New Guinea	15 Jul 1944
PT 135	5° 29″ S, 152° 09″ E	12 Apr 1944
PT 136	New Guinea	17 Sep 1943
PT 145	New Guinea	4 Jan 1944
PT 147	New Guinea	19 Nov 1943
PT 153	Solomons	4 Jul 1943
PT 158	Solomons	5 Jul 1943
PT 164	Solomons	1 Aug 1943
PT 165	23° 45″ S, 166° 30″ E	23 May 1943
PT 166	Solomons	20 Jul 1943
PT 172	Vella Lavella	7 Sep 1943
PT 173	23° 45″ S, 166° 30″ E	23 May 1943
PT 193	00° 55″ S, 134° 52″ E	25 Jun 1944
PT 200	41° N, 71° W	22 Feb 1944
PT 202	43° 23″ N, 6° 43″ E	16 Aug 1944
PT 218	43° 23″ N, 6° 43″ E	16 Aug 1944
PT 219	Aleutians	Sep 1943
PT 239	Solomons	14 Dec 1943
PT 247	6° 38″ S, 156° 01″ E	5 May 1944
PT 251	Bougainville	26 Feb 1944
PT 279	Bougainville	11 Feb 1944
PT 283	Bougainville	17 Mar 1944
PT 300	Philippines	18 Dec 1944
PT 301	New Guinea	7 Nov 1944
PT 311	43° N, 9° E	18 Nov 1944
PT 320	Leyte	5 Nov 1944

Name of Ship	Location	Date
PT 321	Philippines	11 Nov 1944
PT 322	New Guinea	23 Nov 1943
PT 323	10° 33″ N, 125° 14″ E	10 Dec 1944
PT 337	New Guinea	7 Mar 1944
PT 338	12° 06″ N, 121° 23″ E	28 Jan 1945
PT 339	New Guinea	27 May 1944
PT 346	New Britain	29 Apr 1944
PT 347	New Britain	29 Apr 1944
PT 353	5° S, 151° E	27 Mar 1944
PT 363	Halmahera	25 Nov 1944
PT 368	Halmahera	11 Oct 1944
PT 371	2° 05″ N, 127° 51″ E	19 Sep 1944
PT 493	Philippines	25 Oct 1944
PT 509	English Channel	9 Aug 1944
PT 555	Mediterranean	23 Aug 1944

TANK LANDING SHIPS

LST 6	Seine River	18 Nov 1944
LST 43	Pearl Harbor	21 May 1944
LST 69	Pearl Harbor	21 May 1944
LST 129	Palau	2 Oct 1944
LST 158	Sicily	11 July 1943
LST 167	Vella Lavella	25 Sep 1943
LST 179	Pearl Harbor	21 May 1944
LST 203	Union Islands	1 Oct 1943
LST 228	Azores	20 Jan 1944
LST 282	France	15 Aug 1944
LST 313	Sicily	10 Jul 1943
LST 314	49° 43″ N, 00° 52″ W	9 Jun 1944
LST 318	Sicily	9 Aug 1943
LST 333	37° 59″ N, 4° 1″ E	22 Jun 1943
LST 342	9° 3″ S, 158° 11″ E	18 Jul 1943
LST 348	40° 57″ N, 13° 14″ E	19 Feb 1944
LST 349	Italy	26 Feb 1944
LST 353	Pearl Harbor	21 May 1944
LST 359	42° N 19° W	21 May 1944
LST 376	France	9 Jun 1944
LST 396	8° 18″ S, 156° 55″ E	18 Aug 1943
LST 447	26° 9″ N, 127° 18″ E	6 Apr 1945

Name of Ship	Location	Date
LST 448	Vella Lavella	1 Oct 1943
LST 460	11° 10″ N, 121° 11″ E	21 Dec 1944
LST 472	Philippines	15 Dec 1944
LST 480	Pearl Harbor	21 May 1944
LST 493	50° 20″ N, 4° 9″ W	12 Apr 1945
LST 496	France	11 Jun 1944
LST 499	France	8 Jun 1944
LST 507	50° 29″ N, 2° 52″ W	28 Apr 1944
LST 523	France	19 Jun 1944
LST 531	50° 29″ N, 2° 52″ W	28 Apr 1944
LST 563	Mexico	22 Dec 1944
LST 577	8° 1″ N, 130° 22″ E	11 Feb 1945
LST 675	Okinawa	4 Apr 1945
LST 738	Philippines	15 Dec 1944
LST 749	11° 10″ N, 121° 11″ E	21 Dec 1944
LST 750	Philippines	28 Dec 1944
LST 808	Ie Shima	20 May 1945
LST 906	Italy	18 Oct 1944
LST 921	English Channel	14 Aug 1944

MEDIUM LANDING SHIP

LSM 12	Okinawa	4 Apr 1945
LSM 20	10° 12″ N, 125° 19″ E	5 Dec 1944
LSM 59	Okinawa	21 Jun 1945
LSM 135	Okinawa	25 May 1945
LSM 149	Philippines	5 Dec 1944
LSM 190	26° 35″ N, 127° 10″ E	4 May 1945
LSM 194	Okinawa	4 May 1945
LSM 195	Okinawa	3 May 1945
LSM 318	10° 56″ N, 124° 38″ E	7 Dec 1944

TANK LANDING CRAFT

LCT 19	Salerno	14 Jul 1943
LCT 21	Oran	1 Jan 1943
LCT 23	Algiers	3 May 1943
LCT 25	France	6 Jun 1944
LCT 26	41° 4″ N, 13° 30″ E	25 Feb 1944
LCT 27	France	6 Jun 1944
LCT 28	Mediterranean	30 May 1943
LCT 30	France	6 Jun 1944

Name of Ship	Location	Date
LCT 35	Anzio	15 Feb 1944
LCT 36	Naples	26 Feb 1944
LCT 71	53° 38″ N, 146° 5″ W	11 Sep 1943
LCT 147	France	Jun 1944
LCT 154	37° 8″ N, 10° 58″ E	31 Aug 1943
LCT 175	4° 27″ N, 133° 40″ E	21 Feb 1945
LCT 182	Solomons	7 Aug 1944
LCT 185	Bizerte	24 Jan 1944
LCT 196	Salerno	27 Sep 1943
LCT 197	France	6 Jun 1944
LCT 200	France	Jun 1944
LCT 208	Algeria	20 Jun 1943
LCT 209	France	10 Jun 1944
LCT 215	Salerno	1943
LCT 220	Anzio	13 Feb 1944
LCT 241	Salerno	15 Sep 1943
LST 242	Naples	2 Dec 1943
LCT 244	France	Jun 1944
LCT 253	Tarawa	21 Jan 1945
LCT 293	English Channel	11 Oct 1944
LCT 294	France	6 Jun 1944
LCT 305	France	6 Jun 1944
LCT 311	Bizerte	9 Aug 1943
LCT 315	Eniwetok Atoll	23 Mar 1944
LCT 319	Kiska	27 Aug 1943
LCT 332	France	6 Jun 1944
LCT 340	36° 49″ N, 11° 55″ E	20 Feb 1944
LCT 342	Salerno	29 Sep 1943
LCT 362	France	6 Jun1944
LCT 364	France	6 Jun1944
LCT 366	53° 1″ N, 152° W	9 Sep 1943
LCT 413	France	Jun 1944
LCT 458	France	7 Jun 1944
LCT 459	France	9 Oct 1944
LCT 486	France	7 Jun 1944
LCT 496	English Channel	Nov 1943
LCT 548	Portsmouth, Eng.	Nov 1944
LCT 555	France	6 Jun 1944
LCT 572	France	Jun 1944
LCT 579	Palau	4 Oct 1944

Name of Ship	Location	Date
LCT 582	Azores	22 Jan 1944
LCT 593	France	5 Jun 1944
LCT 597	France	6 Jun1944
LCT 612	France	6 Jun1944
LCT 703	France	6 Jun1944
LCT 713	France	Jun 1944
LCT 714	France	Jun 1944
LCT 777	France	6 Jun 1944
LCT 823	Palau	27 Sep 1944
LCT 961	Pearl Harbor	21 May 1944
LCT 963	Pearl Harbor	21 May 1944
LCT 983	Pearl Harbor	21 May 1944
LCT 984	20° N, 157° W	15 May 1944
LCT 988	20° N, 157° W	15 May 1944
LCT 1029	Iwo Jima	2 Mar 1945
LCT 1075	Leyte	10 Dec 1944
LCT 1090	Luzon	26 Mar 1945
LCT 1151	1° N, 138° 36" E	26 Jan 1945
LCT 1358	California	4 May 1945

INFANTRY LANDING CRAFT

Name of Ship	Location	Date
LCI 1	Bizerte	17 Aug 1943
LCI 20	Anzio	22 Jan 1944
LCI 32	Anzio	26 Jan 1944
LCI 82	Okinawa	4 Apr 1945
LCI 85	France	6 Jun 1944
LCI 91	France	6 Jun 1944
LCI 92	France	6 Jun 1944
LCI 93	France	6 Jun 1944
LCI 219	France	11 Jun 1944
LCI 232	France	6 Jun 1944
LCI 339	New Guinea	4 Sep 1943
LCI 365	Luzon	10 Jan 1945
LCI 396	7° 15" N, 134° 28" E	18 Jan 1945
LCI 416	France	9 Jun 1944
LCI 456	Palau	12 Sep 1944
LCI 457	Iwo Jima	17 Feb 1945
LCI 459	Palau	19 Sep 1944
LCI 468	13° 28" N, 148° 18" E	17 Jun 1944
LCI 474	Iwo Jima	17 Feb 1945

Name of Ship	Location	Date
LCI 497	France	6 Jun 1944
LCI 553	France	6 Jun 1944
LCI 600	Ulithi	12 Jan 1945
LCI 684	Pacific	1945
LCI 974	16° 6" N, 120° 14" E	10 Jan 1945
LCI 1065	Leyte	24 Oct 1944

SUPPORT LANDING CRAFT

LCS 7	Luzon	16 Feb 1945
LCS 15	27° 20" N, 127° 10" E	22 Apr 1945
LCS 26	Luzon	14 Feb 1945
LCS 33	Okinawa	12 Apr 1945
LCS 49	Luzon	14 Feb 1945
LCS 127	California	5 Mar 1945

TUGS

ATR 15	49° N, 00° 26" W	19 Jun 1944
ATR 98	44° 05" N, 24° 08" W	12 Apr 1944
Genesee	Corregidor	5 May 1942
Grebe	South Pacific	2 Jan 1943
Napa	Bataan	8 Apr 1942
Nauset	Mediterranean	9 Sep 1943
Navajo	New Hebrides	11 Sep 1943
Partridge	France	11 Jun 1944
Seminole	Solomons	25 Oct 1942
Sonoma	Leyte	24 Oct 1944

TANKERS

Kanawha	Guadalcanal	7 Apr 1943
Mississinewa	Ulithi	20 Nov 1944
Neches	Hawaii	23 Jan 1942
Neosho	Coral Sea	7 May 1942
Pecos	Java	1 Mar 1942
Sheepscot	Iwo Jima	6 Jun 1945

TROOP TRANSPORTS

APC 21	New Britain	17 Dec 1943
APC 35	Solomons	22 Sep 1943
Barry	Okinawa	25 May 1945
Bates	Okinawa	25 May 1945
Colhoun	9° 24" S, 160° 1" E	30 Aug 1942

Name of Ship	Location	Date
Dickerson	Okinawa	2 Apr 1945
Edward Rutledge	Morocco	12 Nov 1942
George F. Elliott	Guadalcanal	8 Aug 1942
Gregory	Guadalcanal	5 Sep 1942
Hugh L. Scott	Morocco	12 Nov 1942
John Penn	Guadalcanal	13 Aug 1943
Joseph Hewes	Morocco	11 Nov 1942
Leedstown	Algiers	9 Nov 1942
Little	Solomons	5 Sep 1942
McCawley	Rendova	30 Jun 1943
McKean	6° 31″ S, 154° 52″ E	17 Nov 1943
Noa	7° 1″ N, 134° 30″ E	12 Sep 1944
Susan B. Anthony	France	7 Jun 1944
Tasker H. Bliss	Morocco	12 Nov 1942
Thomas Stone	Spain	7 Nov 1942
Ward	10° 51″ N, 124° 32″ E	7 Dec 1944

DISTRICT PATROL CRAFT

YP 16	Philippines	Dec 1941
YP 17	Philippines	Dec 1941
YP 26	Canal Zone	19 Nov 1942
YP 47	Staten Island	26 Apr 1943
YP 72	Aleutians	22 Feb 1943
YP 73	Alaska	15 Jan 1945
YP 74	54° 23″ N, 164° 10″ W	6 Sep 1942
YP 77	Atlantic Coast	28 Apr 1942
YP 88	Aleutians	28 Oct 1943
YP 94	56° 32″ N, 154° 22″ W	18 Feb 1945
YP 95	Aleutians	1 May 1944
YP 97	Philippines	Mar 1942
YP 128	Monterey, Calif.	30 Jun 1942
YP 183	Hawaii	12 Jan 1943
YP 205	18° 30″ N, 65° 00″ W	1 Nov 1942
YP 235	Mexico	1 Apr 1943
YP 270	25° 30″ N, 112° 06″ W	30 Jun 1942
YP 277	Hawaii	23 May 1942
YP 279	Australia	5 Sep 1943
YP 281	16° 53″ N, 177° 18 ″ W	9 Jan 1944
YP 284	Guadalcanal	25 Oct 1942
YP 331	24° 56″ N, 81° 58″ W	23 Mar 1944

Name of Ship	*Location*	*Date*
YP 336	Delaware River	23 Feb 1943
YP 345	Midway	31 Oct 1942
YP 346	Pacific	9 Sep 1942
YP 383	8° 22″ N, 79° 29″ W	24 Nov 1944
YP 387	39° N, 75° W	20 May 1942
YP 389	Cape Hatteras	19 Jun 1942
YP 405	Caribbean Sea	20 Nov 1942
YP 422	New Caledonia	23 Apr 1943
YP 426	31° 59″ N, 80° 48″ W	16 Dec 1943
YP 438	Port Everglades	20 Mar 1943
YP 453	Bahamas	15 Apr 1943
YP 481	Charleston, S. C.	25 Apr 1943
YP 492	Florida	8 Jan 1943
YP 577	Great Lakes	23 Jan 1943

MISCELLANEOUS DISTRICT CRAFT

YA 52	Philippines	1942
YA 59	Philippines	1942
YA 65	Philippines	1942
YAG 2	Philippines	1942
YAG 3	Philippines	1942
YAG 4	Philippines	1942
YAG 17	36° 57″ N, 76° 13″ W	14 Sep 1944
YC 178	Philippines	1942
YC 181	Philippines	1942
YC 523	Portsmouth, N. H.	24 Feb 1944
YC 537	Philippines	1942
YC 643	Philippines	1942
YC 644	Philippines	1942
YC 646	Philippines	1942
YC 647	Philippines	1942
YC 648	Philippines	1942
YC 649	Philippines	1942
YC 652	Philippines	1942
YC 653	Philippines	1942
YC 654	Philippines	1942
YC 664	Guam	1942
YC 665	Guam	1942
YC 666	Guam	1942
YC 667	Guam	1942

Name of Ship	Location	Date
YC 668	Guam	1942
YC 669	Philippines	1942
YC 670	Guam	1942
YC 671	Guam	1942
YC 672	Guam	1942
YC 673	Guam	1942
YC 674	Guam	1942
YC 683	Philippines	1942
YC 685	Guam	1942
YC 693	Alaska	Feb 1945
YC 714	Philippines	1942
YC 715	Philippines	1942
YC 716	Philippines	1942
YC 717	Guam	1942
YC 718	Guam	1942
YC 857	Cape Cod	12 Nov 1943
YC 869	California	23 Mar 1943
YC 886	Guantanamo	3 Feb 1943
YC 887	Guantanamo	3 Feb 1943
YC 891	Key West	18 Apr 1943
YC 898	Key West	29 Sep 1942
YC 899	Key West	29 Sep 1942
YC 912	North Pacific	13 Jan 1945
YC 961	Biorka Island	May 1945
YC 970	Puget Sound	14 Aug 1943
YC 1272	San Pedro	Jun 1945
YC 1278	Atlantic Coast	10 Mar 1943
YCF 23	Eniwetok	Mar 1945
YCF 29	Eniwetok	Mar 1945
YCF 36	Eniwetok	Mar 1945
YCF 37	Eniwetok	Mar 1945
YCF 42	34° 47″ N, 75° 5″ W	Dec 1944
YCF 59	Delaware	Jan 1945
YCK 1	Wake Island	1942
YCK 2	45° 57″ N, 58° 57″ W	5 Nov 1943
YCK 8	Key West	13 Dec 1943
YD 19	Philippines	1942
YD 47	Philippines	1942
YD 56	Philippines	1942
YD 60	Philippines	1942

Name of Ship	Location	Date
YDG 4	New Caledonia	1 Oct 1943
YF 86	Philippines	1942
YF 177	Philippines	1942
YF 178	Philippines	1942
YF 179	Philippines	1942
YF 180	Philippines	1942
YF 181	Philippines	1942
YF 212	Philippines	1942
YF 223	Philippines	1942
YF 224	Philippines	1942
YF 230	Philippines	1942
YF 317	Philippines	1942
YF 401	35° 7″ N, 69° W	20 Jun 1943
YF 415	42° 24″ N, 70° 36″ W	11 May 1944
YF 487	Caribbean	18 Jul 1943
YF 575	Atlantic City	6 May 1943
YF 579	San Francisco	20 Sep 1943
YF 724	Farallones	22 Mar 1945
YF 725	Farallones	22 Mar 1945
YF 926	Pearl Harbor	8 March 1945
San Felipe	Philippines	1942
Santa Rita	Philippines	1942
Rosal	Philippines	1942
Camia	Philippines	1942
Dapdap	Philippines	1942
Rivera	Philippines	1942
Magdalena	Philippines	1942
Yacal	Philippines	1942
Dewey Drydock	Bataan	10 Apr 1942
YFD 20	California	31 Jan 1943
YG 39	10° 10″ N, 79° 51″ W	27 Sep 1944
YM 4	Philippines	1942
YM 13	Guam	1942
YMS 14	Boston Harbor	11 Jan 1945
YMS 19	Palau	24 Sep 1944
YMS 21	43° 6″ N, 5° 54″ E	1 Sep 1944
YMS 24	43° 23″ N, 6° 43″ E	16 Aug 1944
YMS 30	41° 23″ N, 12° 45″ E	25 Jan 1944
YMS 39	1° 19″ S, 116° 49″ E	26 Jun 1945
YMS 48	14° 25″ N, 120° 34″ E	14 Feb 1945

Name of Ship	Location	Date
YMS 50	1° 18" S, 116° 49" E	18 Jun 1945
YMS 70	Leyte	17 Oct 1944
YMS 71	4° 58" N, 119° 47" E	3 Apr 1945
YMS 84	Java	9 Jul 1945
YMS 103	26° 13" N, 127° 54" E	8 Apr 1945
YMS 127	Seattle	May 1944
YMS 133	Oregon	20 Feb 1943
YMS 304	France	30 Jul 1944
YMS 350	Cherbourg	2 Jul 1944
YMS 365	1° 18" S, 116° 50" E	26 Jun 1945
YMS 378	49° 33" N, 1° 13" W	1944
YMS 385	Ulithi	1 Oct 1944
YMS 409	Atlantic Coast	14 Sep 1944
YMS 481	Tarakan, Borneo	2 May 1945
YO 41	Philippines	1942
YO 42	Philippines	1942
YO 64	Philippines	Jan 1942
YO 156	Sitka, Alaska	May 1945
YO 157	Sitka, Alaska	May 1945
YO 159	New Hebrides	14 Jan 1944
YPD 22	Philippines	1942
YPK 6	Philippines	1942
YPK 7	Philippines	1942
YR 43	Alaska	28 Mar 1945
YRC 4	Philippines	1942
YSP 41	Philippines	1942
YSP 42	Philippines	1942
YSP 43	Philippines	1942
YSP 44	Philippines	1942
YSP 45	Philippines	1942
YSP 46	Philippines	1942
YSP 47	Philippines	1942
YSP 48	Philippines	1942
YSP 49	Philippines	1942
YSP 50	Philippines	1942
YSR 2	Philippines	1942
Banaag	Philippines	1942
Iona	Philippines	1942
Mercedes	Philippines	1942
Vaga	Corregidor	5 May 1942

Name of Ship	Location	Date
Mazapeta	California	14 Oct 1943
YT 198	Anzio	18 Feb 1944
YT 247	14° 14″ N, 158° 59″ W	5 Apr 1944
Shahaka	27° 21″ N, 136° 29″ W	9 May 1944
YTM 467	Marshalls or Gilberts	Mar 1944
YW 50	Guam	1942
YW 54	Philippines	1942
YW 55	Guam	1942
YW 58	Guam	1942

Cargo Vessels

Aludra	Solomons	23 Jun 1943
Deimos	Solomons	23 Jun 1943
Pollux	Newfoundland	18 Feb 1942
Serpens	Guadalcanal	29 Jan 1945

Miscellaneous Auxiliaries

Ailanthus	Aleutians	26 Feb 1944
Asphalt	Saipan	6 Oct 1944
Canopus	Bataan	10 Apr 1942
Cythera	Atlantic Coast	May 1942
Extractor	Marianas	1 Jan 1945
Macaw	Midway Channel	12 Feb 1944
Moonstone	Delaware Capes	16 Oct 1943
Mount Hood	Admiralty Islands	10 Nov 1944
Muskeget	Atlantic	10 Oct 1942
Niagara	Solomons	23 May 1943
Pigeon	Corregidor	3 May 1942
Pontiac	Halifax	30 Jan 1945
Porcupine	Philippines	28 Dec 1944
Redwing	Mediterranean	28 Jun 1943
Rescuer	Aleutians	1 Jan 1943
Robert Barnes	Guam	Dec 1941
Ronaki	Australia	18 Jun 1943
Utah	Pearl Harbor	7 Dec 1941
ex Fisheries	Corregidor	5 May 1942
ex Mary Ann	Corregidor	5 May 1942
ex Perry	Corregidor	5 May 1942
DCH 1	Pearl Harbor	28 Dec 1941

NAVAL OPERATIONS IN NORTH AFRICAN, MEDITERRANEAN AND EUROPEAN THEATERS

1942

November 8-11, The North African Landings.
> US naval forces guarding Casablanca engage French cruiser and destroyers supporting Fedala landings. Support is provided for landing at Port Lyautey. The harbor of Arzew is taken by a US landing party during the Oran landings.

1943

July 10-August 17, The Sicilian Landings.
> US naval forces support landings at Gela, Scoglitti and Licata. Cruisers and destroyers bombard Porto Empedocle and Agrigento and support land forces in movement on Messina.

1944

January 22, Anzio Beach Landing.
June 1, D-day, Normandy.
June 17, Assault on Elba, Mediterranean.
June 25, Bombardment of Cherbourg.
August 18, Invasion of Southern France

1945

April, Final German Submarine Campaign.
May 9, Germany Surrenders.

THE TIDES OF WAR IN THE PACIFIC

1941

December 7, *Japanese Attack Pearl Harbor*
December 8, *First Jap Attack on Philippines*

1942

January 24, *Java Sea Action; Battle of Makassar Strait,* Japanese forces
  moving southward are attacked by US destroyers.
February 1, *Raid on the Marshalls and Gilberts*
  US carriers and cruisers attack enemy bases.
February 20, *Action off Rabaul*
  Aerial engagement near the enemy's major base in New Britain.
February 24, *Raid on Wake Island*
  A US Task Force bombards a former American outpost.
February 27, *Java Sea Action*
  Combined forces attempt to intercept Japanese convoys. The
  end of organized Allied naval resistance in this phase of the war.
March 4, *US Raid on Marcus Island*
March 10, *Raid on Salamaua and Lae*
April 9, *Bataan Surrenders*
April 18, *Doolittle fliers bomb Tokyo*
May 4, *Raid on Tulagi*
May 6, *Corregidor Surrenders*
May 7-8, *Battle of the Coral Sea*
  Carriers exchange blows. Severe damage inflicted on the Japa-
  nese carrier force. *Lexington* is lost, but the Japanese advance
  is checked.
June 3-6, *Battle of Midway*
June, *Attu and Kiska occupied by Japanese*
August 7, *US Landing*
  US Marines establish foothold on Guadalcanal and Tulagi in
  the first Allied offensive of the Pacific war.
August 9, *Battle of Savo Island*
  Japanese night attack on naval forces protecting landing. One
  Australian and three US heavy cruisers lost, other units
  damaged.
August 23-25, Powerful Japanese naval force is intercepted by US
  carrier borne aircraft. Enemy breaks off action after loss of
  carrier support.

October 11-12, *Battle of Cape Esperance*
> US cruisers and destroyers in a surprise night attack engage a sizable enemy force near Guadalcanal.

October 26, *Battle of Santa Cruz Islands*
> Blows are exchanged by US carriers and Japanese carriers operating with a powerful enemy force moving to support land operations at Guadalcanal. Two enemy carriers put out of action and four enemy air groups decimated.

November 13-14-15, *Battle of Guadalcanal*
> Enemy concentrates invasion force at Rabaul. US naval forces covering reinforcements for troops on Guadalcanal meet and decisively defeat this force in a series of violent engagements in which heavy losses are sustained by both sides.

November 30, *Battle of Tassafaronga*
> A Japanese attempt to reinforce is defeated at heavy cost. *Northampton* lost, three US heavy cruisers severely damaged.

1943

February 21, *Russell Island landings*

February 7-8, *Japanese complete Guadalcanal withdrawal*

March 26, *North Pacific*
> Engagement off Komandorski Island.

May 11-31, *Attu retaken by US*

June 30, *Landings on Woodlark and Trobriand Island groups and on New Guinea*

July 2-3, *Landings on New Georgia and Vanganu*

July 4, *Kolombangara and New Georgia bombardment*

July 6, *First Battle of Kula Gulf*
> US cruisers and destroyers intercept the "Tokyo Express." (*Helena* lost.)

July 13, *Second Battle of Kula Gulf*
> The circumstances of the engagement of July 6 are repeated. Three Allied cruisers severely damaged by torpedoes.

August 6, *Battle of Vella Gulf*
> Japanese destroyers escorting reinforcements are intercepted by our forces. Several enemy destroyers sunk.

August 15, *Vella Lavella landings*

August 15, *North Pacific*
> Kiska reoccupied by US.

August 17-18, *US destroyers sink Jap barges and destroyers north of Kula Gulf*

October 6, *Destroyers Chevalier, Selfridge, O'Bannon defeat Jap group south of Choiseul*

October 26-37, *Landings on Choiseul*

November 1, *Landings on Bougainville*

November 5, *Attack on Rabaul*

November 11, *Second attack on Rabaul*

November 19, *Attacks on Gilberts, capture of Makin, Tarawa*

December 25, *Attack on Kavieng*

1944

January 31-February 1, *Operations on the Marshalls*
Landings on Majuro, Roi, Namur, Kwajalein.

February 4, *Bombardment of Paramushiru*

February 17, 18, *Raid on Truk*

February 23, *Raids on Saipan, Tinian, Guam*

March 20, *Landings on Emirau Island, St. Matthias Group, northeast of New Guinea. Bombardment of Kavieng, New Ireland.*

March 30, *Carrier Task Force attacks on Western Carolines*

April 22, *Landings in Hollandia Area, New Guinea*

April 29-May 1, *Carrier Task Force attacks on Marcus Island*

May 23, *Carrier Task Force attack on Wake Island*

May 27, *Landings on Biak Island, Dutch New Guinea*

June 11-14, *Preliminary Carrier Task Force attacks on Marianas Islands*

June 13, *Bombardment of Matsuwa Island, Kurile Islands*

June 15, *Landings on Saipan, Marianas Islands*

June 15-16, *Carrier Task Force attacks on Iwo Jima and Chichi Jima, Volcano and Bonin Islands*

June 19-20, *Battle of the Philippine Sea*

June 23-24, *Carrier Task Force attacks on Pagan Island, Marianas Islands*

June 24, *Carrier Task Force attack on Iwo Jima, Volcano Islands*

June 26, *Bombardment of Kurabu Zaki, Paramushiro, Kurile Islands*

July 2, *Landings on Noemfoor Island, Dutch New Guinea*

July 4, *Carrier Task Force attacks on Iwo Jima, Chichi Jima and Haha Jima, Volcano and Bonin Islands*

July 21, *Landings on Guam, Marianas Islands*

July 24, *Landings on Tinian, Marianas Islands*

July 30, *Landings in Cape Sansapor Area, Dutch New Guinea*

August 4-5, *Carrier Task Force attacks on Iwo Jima and Chichi Jima, Volcano and Bonin Islands*

August 31, *Carrier Task Force attacks on Iwo Jima, Chichi Jima and Haha Jima, Volcano and Bonin Islands*

September 6-14, *Preliminary carrier task force attacks on Palau Islands*

September 7-8, *Carrier Task Force attacks on Yap*

September 9-10, *Carrier Task Force attacks on Mindanao, Philippine Islands*

September 12-14, *Carrier Task Force attacks on the Visayas, Philippine Islands*

September 15, *Landings on Peleliu, Palau Islands, Landings on Morotai*

September 17, *Landings on Angaur, Palau Islands*

September 21-22, *Carrier Task Force attacks on Manila, Philippine Islands*

September 23, *Landings on Ulithi*

September 24, *Carrier Task Force attacks on the Visayas, Philippine Islands*

September 28, *Landings on Ngesebus, Palau Islands*

October 9, *Bombardment of Marcus Island*

October 10, *Carrier Task Force attack on Okinawa Island, Nansei Shoto*

October 11, *Carrier Task Force attack on Aparri, Luzon, Philippine Islands*

October 12-15, *Carrier Task Force attacks on Formosa and Luzon*

October 18-19, *Carrier Task Force attacks on Northern and Central Philippines*

October 20, *Landings on Leyte, Philippine Islands*

October 21, *Carrier Task Force attacks on Luzon and the Visayas, Philippine Islands*

October 23-26, *Battle for Leyte Gulf*

November 5, 6, 13, 14, 19, 25, *Carrier Task Force attacks on Luzon, Philippine Islands*

November 11, *Carrier Task Force attack on Ormoc Bay, Leyte, Philippine Islands*

November 11-12, *Bombardment of Iwo Jima, Volcano Islands*

November 21, *Bombardment of Matsuwa Island, Kurile Islands*

December 7, *Landings at Ormoc Bay, Philippine Islands*

December 8, 24, 27, *Air-surface attacks on Iwo Jima, Volcano Islands*

December 14, 15, 16, *Carrier Task Force attacks on Luzon, Philippine Islands*

December 15, *Landings on Mindoro, Philippine Islands*

1945

January 3-4, *Carrier Task Force attacks on Formosa*

January 5, *Bombardment of Suribachi Wan, off Paramushiro, Kurile Islands*
Air-surface attack on Iwo Jima, Chichi Jima and Haha Jima, Volcano and Bonin Islands

January 6-7, *Carrier Task Force attacks on Luzon, Philippine Islands*

January 9, *Landings at Lingayen Gulf, Luzon, Philippine Islands*

January 12, *Carrier Task Force attack on French Indo-China Coast*

January 15, *Carrier Task Force attack on Formosa*

January 16, *Carrier Task Force attack on Hong Kong, Canton and Hainan, China*

January 21-22, *Carrier Task Force attack on Formosa and Nansei Shoto*

January 24, *Air-surface attack on Iwo Jima, Volcano Islands*

January 29-30, *Landings in Subic Bay Area, Luzon, Philippine Islands*

January 31, *Landings at Nasugbu, Luzon, Philippine Islands*

February 13-15, *Bombardment of Manila Bay Defenses, Philippine Islands*

February 14, *Landings at Mariveles, Luzon, Philippine Islands*

February 16, *Landings on Corregidor Island, Philippine Islands*

February 16-17, *Carrier Task Force attack on Tokyo*

February 19, *Landings on Iwo Jima, Volcano Islands*
Bombardment of Kurabu Zaki, Paramushiro, Kurile Islands

February 25-26, *Carrier Task Force attack on Tokyo and Hachijo Jima*

February 28, *Landings on Palawan, Philippine Islands*

March 2, *Okinawa, Daito Shima bombardments*

March 4, *Landings on Lubang, Burias and Ticao Islands in Philippines*

March 10, *Landings on Mindanao*

March 16, *Landings on Basilan Island, Philippines*
Jap resistance on Iwo Jima declared ended

March 18, *Landings on Iloilu*

March 24, *Operations off Okinawa begin*

March 26, *Landings on Cebu*

April 1, *Landings at Legaspi, Sanga Sanga, Jolo, Masbate, Busuanga and Bohol*

April 27, *Shelling of Tarakan*

May 1-9, *Landings on Borneo*

May 24, *Carrier sweeps at Kyushu*

June 4, *Typhoon off Okinawa*

June 8-9, *Raid on Kyushu, bombardment of Okino Daito, Minami Daito*
June 10, *Landings at Brunei Bay, Borneo*
June 24, *Pre-invasion bombardment of Balikpapan*
July 1, *Landings at Balikpapan*
July 10, *Third Fleet attacks on Tokyo*
July 19-30, *Attacks on Honshu, Hokkaido, Kamaishi, Muroran, Yokosuka, Kure, Tokyo, Hamamatsu*
August 9-10, *Strikes at Honshu, Kamaishi, Tokyo*
August 11-12, *Bombardments of Kuriles*
August 14, *Japan Surrenders*
September 2, *Surrender Signed aboard Missouri*

Rockets away! A rocket-firing landing craft looses a barrage at an enemy island target.

The USS Tolman, one of the latest type destroyers in the Fleet, cuts through heavy seas. These DDs, dubbed "cans" by our sailors, bore some of the main burden of the fighting in the Pacific.

"The Fleet That Came to Stay" was able to stay only because the ships of the service squadrons—part of the Fleet Train—refueled and resupplied the fighting ships just off the edge of the battle areas. Service squadrons consist of tankers, ammunition ships, escort carriers, tugs, storeships, and other auxiliaries which service combat ships near the fighting zones and thus save long trips back to bases of supply. Here a provision ship (center) transfers supplies to two destroyers under way in the Pacific.

A PT (patrol torpedo) boat under way. These speedy, scrappy craft helped cut the Japanese Navy down to size, played a big part in the defense of the Philippines early in the war.

A U.S. Coast Guard cutter, a ship somewhat smaller than a destroyer escort vessel, receives a line fired by a destroyer. After the line is made fast, mail, supplies, or passengers can be transferred by means of block and tackle. The cutter and the DD are here escorting a United Nations convoy in the North Atlantic which is carrying supplies to Europe.

The Saratoga (top) and the Lexington, two of the Navy's earliest aircraft carriers, anchored off Diamond Head, Hawaii, before the war. The Saratoga come through the entire conflict with one of the most heroic records of any ship. The Lexington, which helped spearhead the task force fighting in the lean days following Pearl Harbor, was lost in the Battle of the Coral Sea in May 1942.

End of the war for the cruiser Portland, in action in twenty major Pacific operations from the Coral Sea to the bombardment of Corregidor. Here she is on March 1, 1945, steaming for a Stateside Navy yard for refitting and overhaul. The war ended before she could get back into combat.

A Navy hit-and-run play to win a beachhead. A giant battleship belches smoke, flame and hot steel at Jap defenses on Okinawa while amphtracs (amphibious tractors) in the foreground race for the shore on D-day, April 1, 1945.

A Navy floating drydock large enough to accommodate the biggest battle-wagon in the fleet. These ABSDs (Advance Base Sectional Docks) are moved close to the combat zone, there repair and refit battle-damaged vessels. Here two ships are being worked on in this ABSD in the Pacific.

A German submarine, the U-505, is captured by an Atlantic Fleet hunter-killer task group off West Africa on June 4, 1944. The USS Guadalcanal, an escort aircraft carrier and main unit of the task group, approaches the U-boat to take aboard the tow line. In the foreground are members of the Guadalcanal's boarding party.

A submarine tender and her brood. Three Navy subs alongside their tender in the Pacific to receive supplies and repairs, while the men aboard the subs enjoy a brief rest.

Navy sub rescues aviators. Airmen in raft, thrown into the East China Sea when their Fleet Air Wing One plane went down, are about to be picked up by a Pacific Fleet submarine. Besides sending to the bottom millions of tons of enemy shipping. U. S. subs did valuable scouting and rescue work.

Navy salvage and rescue tugs in Naha Harbor, Okinawa.

Soldiers disembark from an LCI (Landing Craft, Infantry) to storm ashore on Leyte in the Central Philippines. This was part of the largest naval attack force ever assembled for a single strike against the Japanese in the Southwest Pacific. For three days prior to this assault on October 20, 1944, battleships and cruisers blasted enemy installations, and mine sweepers cleared the 300-mile coast. Men and machines went ashore protected by waves of carrier-based planes. Here the beach still smoulders from the fire of battleships, cruisers, rocket ships, and destroyers.

This plane-guard destroyer is bearing down to rescue the pilot and gunner of a scout bomber which crashed just astern of its carrier after a long scouting flight in the Pacific.

The invasion of Saipan. American ships and landing craft, loaded with Marines, move toward Saipan on D-day. This invasion was one of the most important Navy and Marine Corps operations in the Pacific.

INDEX